# HUMAN TRAFFICKING
## BIGGEST SOCIAL CRIME

# HUMAN TRAFFICKING
## Biggest Social Crime

S K Bhagat

MD Publications Pvt Ltd
New Delhi
www.mdppl.com

*Published by* :

**MD Publications Pvt Ltd**
"MD House", 11, Darya Ganj,
New Delhi - 110 002
Phone : +91-11-41563325 (Customer Service)
+91-11-41562846 (Editorial)
E-mail (orders): order@mdppl.com
Website: www.mdppl.com

**ISBN:** 978-81-7533-213-3

Published and Printed by Mr. Pranav Gupta on behalf of **MD Publications Pvt Ltd** at Mohit Enterprises, Delhi.

# PREFACE

Human trafficking is the recruitment, transportation, harbouring, or receipt of people for the purposes of slavery, forced labour (including bonded labour or debt bondage) and servitude. Exploitation includes forcing people into prostitution or other forms of sexual exploitation, forced labour or services, slavery or practices similar to slavery and servitude. For children, exploitation may also include forced prostitution, illicit international adoption, trafficking for early marriage, or recruitment as child soldiers, beggars, for sports (such as child camel jockeys or football players) or for religious cults.

Human trafficking is not a stand alone issue. It is closely related other issues that threaten security well being of the victims. Victims are exposed to continuous threats of physical violence by traffickers to ensure compliance. Many are held in bondage and beaten to suppress resistance. Other threats include absolute poverty due to wage deprivation. They are unprotected by labour laws, long working hours and lack of holiday is common. For example, 15 is the standard working hours per day among Chinese victims in France. In Japan, Thai trafficking victims also complained of breach of work contracts, non-payment of wages, mandatory night work and poor accommodation.

The subject of human trafficking, or the use of force, fraud or coercion to transport persons across international borders or within countries to exploit them for labour or sex, has received renewed attention within the last two decades. While the majority of experts on human trafficking assert that the greatest number of victims of trafficking are women and children; there is little systematic and reliable data on the scale of the phenomenon; limited understanding of the characteristics of victims their life experiences, and their trafficking trajectories; poor. With human trafficking being listed as the second biggest crime after arms and drugs trafficking, experts have called for a holistic legislation to deal with the increasing incidence of the trade in the country. Human trafficking is a kind of International Terrorism. It is the second largest crime after the drugs and arms trafficking in the world. According to UNODC (United Nations Office on Drugs and Crime), approximately 150,000 people are trafficked within South Asia annually making the region the second only to South East Asia in prevalence of human trafficking. And India is an origin, transit and destination country for trafficking in persons. It is the fastest growing criminal industry in the world, with the total annual revenue for trafficking in persons estimated to be between $5 billion and $9 billion.

I am very grateful to Mr. Pranav Gupta, Director of MD Publications Pvt Ltd, New Delhi, for his cooperation and support for this book.

**S K Bhagat**

# CONTENTS

# 1

# Human Trafficking
## An Introduction

Human Trafficking is a crime against humanity. It involves an act of recruiting, transporting, transferring, harboring or receiving a person through a use of force, coercion or other means, for the purpose of exploiting them. Every year, thousands of men, women and children fall into the hands of traffickers, in their own countries and abroad. Every country in the world is affected by trafficking, whether as a country of origin, transit or destination for victims. UNODC, as guardian of the United Nations Convention against Transnational Organized Crime (UNTOC) and the Protocols thereto, assists States in their efforts to implement the Protocol to Prevent, Suppress and Punish Trafficking in Persons.

Article 3, paragraph (a) of the Protocol to Prevent, Suppress and Punish Trafficking in Persons defines Trafficking in Persons as the recruitment, transportation, transfer, harbouring or receipt of persons, by means of the threat or use of force or other forms of coercion, of abduction, of fraud, of deception, of the abuse of power or of a position of vulnerability or of the giving or receiving of payments or benefits to achieve the consent of a person having control over another person, for the purpose of exploitation. Exploitation shall include, at a minimum, the exploitation of the prostitution of others or other forms of sexual exploitation, forced labour or services, slavery or practices similar to slavery, servitude or the removal of organs.

## ELEMENTS OF HUMAN TRAFFICKING

On the basis of the definition given in the Trafficking in Persons Protocol, it is evident that trafficking in persons has three constituent elements:

- The Act

Recruitment, transportation, transfer, harbouring or receipt of persons.

- The Means

Threat or use of force, coercion, abduction, fraud, deception, abuse of power or vulnerability, or giving payments or benefits to a person in control of the victim.

- The Purpose

For the purpose of exploitation, which includes exploiting the prostitution of others, sexual exploitation, forced labour, slavery or similar practices and the removal of organs? To ascertain whether a particular circumstance constitutes trafficking in persons, consider the definition of trafficking in the Trafficking in Persons Protocol and the constituent elements of the offense, as defined by relevant domestic legislation.

## CRIMINALIZATION OF HUMAN TRAFFICKING

The definition contained in Article 3 of the Trafficking in Persons Protocol is meant to provide consistency and consensus around the world on the phenomenon of trafficking in persons. Article 5 therefore requires that the conduct set out in article 3 be criminalized in domestic legislation. Domestic legislation does not need to follow the language of the Trafficking in Persons Protocol precisely, but should be adapted in accordance with domestic legal systems to give effect to the concepts contained in the Protocol.

In addition to the criminalization of trafficking, the Trafficking in Persons Protocol requires criminalization also of:

- Attempts to commit a trafficking offence.
- Participation as an accomplice in such an offence.

- Organizing or directing others to commit trafficking.

National legislation should adopt the broad definition of trafficking prescribed in the Protocol. The legislative definition should be dynamic and flexible so as to empower the legislative framework to respond effectively to trafficking which:

- Occurs both across borders and within a country (not just cross-border);
- Is for a range of exploitative purposes (not just sexual exploitation);
- Victimizes children, women and men (Not just women, or adults, but also men and children);
- Takes place with or without the involvement of organized crime groups.

## RESPONSE TO HUMAN TRAFFICKING

UNODC offers practical help to States, not only helping to draft laws and create comprehensive national anti-trafficking strategies but also assisting with resources to implement them. States receive specialized assistance including the development of local capacity and expertise, as well as practical tools to encourage cross-border cooperation in investigations and prosecutions. The adoption in 2000 by the United Nations General Assembly of the *Protocol to Prevent, Suppress and Punish Trafficking In Persons, Especially Women and Children* marked a significant milestone in international efforts to stop the trade in people. As the custodian of the Protocol, UNODC addresses human trafficking issues through its Global Programmed against Trafficking in Human Beings. To date, more than 110 States have signed and ratified the Protocol. But translating it into reality remains problematic. Very few criminals are convicted and most victims are probably never identified or assisted.

## PREVENTION OF TRAFFICKING IN PERSONS

People like Boy Ngoc and Brim are seeking better lives and are therefore vulnerable to fall into the hands of migrant smugglers and human traffickers. Irregular migrants are increasingly resorting to services offered by migrant smugglers. Their modus operandi ranges from simple provision of falsified or counterfeit documents, but also extends to arranging journeys which cost thousands of lives every year. Nod's research shows that victims of trafficking are often duped by a recruiter who is a relative, a supposed friend or seems like someone they can trust. Traffickers and victims often share the same nationality. In some parts of the world, female traffickers are selected to recruit women.

UNODC helps to make people like Boy Ngoc and Brim aware of these risks by making video and radio spots (public service announcements), which are broadcast in numerous languages throughout the world. UNODC also runs campaigns with NGOs, distributing written information and contacting actual and potential victims of trafficking. In December 2006, UNODC Colombia received a UN21 Commendation award for its anti-human trafficking activities, which included helping Colombian television to produce a prime-time television soap opera about human trafficking. Aired nightly to millions of viewers, the series exposed common traffickers' ruses, such as Internet scams and explained where victims could seek help.

## Vulnerable Communities

Community-led activities are an important prevention tool. The porous border between India and Nepal, for example, is an area of heavy cross-border human trafficking. In 2006-07, UNODC supported NGO initiatives such as the Community Vigilance project, led by local leaders and women's groups, which has mobilized thousands of villagers to detect and prevent trafficking.

In 2006-07, UNODC provided funding for NGOs in Croatia and Bosnia and Herzegovina to run trafficking prevention campaigns among asylum-seekers, a particularly vulnerable group. Counseling was provided to young people like Brim to make them aware of the risks and where they can seek help.

## Conflict Zones

Sometimes the need to move and the threat of trafficking can emerge very suddenly. In mid-2006, during the armed conflict in Lebanon, UNODC became aware that traffickers were targeting some of the 300,000 domestic workers from Sri Lanka, Ethiopia and the Philippines who were left behind when their foreign employers were evacuated. Having abruptly lost their livelihoods and official resident status, the workers quickly became vulnerable. As embassies struggled to assist their nationals, trafficking gangs offered alternative options. UNODC put an emergency information campaign in place within days: it produced 12,000 pages of information in various languages, including the number of a telephone hotline run by the NGO Caritas Migrant for assistance and support. The materials were distributed in shelters, embassies, churches, shops and markets.

## Research

Nod's prevention work includes raising awareness among policy-makers, law enforcement bodies and civil society. In April 2006, UNODC published the report Trafficking in Persons: Global Patterns identifying 127 countries of origin, 98 transit countries and 137 destination countries. The sensitive nature of the issue and the lack of systematic action on trafficking worldwide make information collection a challenge, reflecting the unwillingness of some countries to acknowledge that the problem affected them. The absence of reliable global data, in turn, makes it more difficult for governments and international organizations to fight trafficking effectively.

This UNODC report was a first attempt to get a clearer picture of the problem. It highlighted the complex nature of trafficking, such as women committing trafficking atrocities against other women, and identified national and regional characteristics of offenders, victims and exploitation.

The Report listed states on a scale from "very low" to "very high" as countries of origin, transit and destination. The report continues to have key relevance in initiating and informing discussions on trafficking in persons. In 2007, to date, the report has been downloaded 260,000 times; making it the most frequently used UNODC report after the World Drug Report.

### Tools

UNODC is developing training materials for law enforcers working to prevent human trafficking and smuggling across borders. Such materials place an emphasis on international cooperation and holistic approaches so as to ensure that responses to trafficking and smuggling do not merely result in new routes employed by the criminals behind these crimes.

## PROTECTING VICTIMS OF HUMAN TRAFFICKING

Police and criminal justice staff need standard working procedures to guarantee the physical safety of victims, protect their privacy and make it safe for them to testify against their abusers. These issues are part of Nod's human trafficking training for police, prosecutors and judges.

### Toolkit

In October 2008, UNODC launched its second edition of the Toolkit to Combat Trafficking in Persons. The Toolkit provides practical help to governments, policy-makers, police, NGOs and others to enable them to tackle human trafficking more effectively. The Toolkit includes checklists to help identify trafficking victims as well as guidance on interviewing victims and victim protection.

### Identification

In many countries there is a lack of awareness of the fact that someone like Alexandra could be a victim and not an offender. Trafficking victims also commonly blame themselves for what has happened to them, which can stop them from seeking help. Without identification and recognition as victims of crime, they can unjustly suffer prosecution because of their irregular status.

## Referral

A "rescuer" must know how to refer victims to experts whether in official bodies or NGOs- for appropriate support. In 2003, UNODC helped to set up one of the first victim referral mechanisms in the Czech Republic, which led to a national strategy for combating trafficking in persons in that country. UNODC has helped to introduce such systems in Poland and the Philippines. In late 2006, work started on similar services in Moldova and the Slovak Republic. The purpose of such systems is to ensure that a trafficking victim, like Alexandra, is identified as such, that support is available to them and that those who come into contact with the victim act in an appropriate way.

## Partnerships

Under a major global project largely completed in 2006, UNODC funded support projects for victims of trafficking run by 19 NGOs in India, Mexico, South Africa, Uganda, Ukraine, Moldova, Pakistan, Indonesia and Thailand. The programme offered emotional and practical support, including health care, legal aid, psychological assistance and referrals. More than 280 victims have been repatriated from India to Nepal alone.

## Reintegration

Victims need assistance that extends beyond the end of their exploitation and any criminal prosecution. Vocational training can reduce the risk of them being sucked into exploitative situations again. In 2006, companies in the Philippines joined the fight against re-victimization by participating in the Corporate Apprenticeship programme, a joint initiative between UNODC and the Department for Social Welfare and Development. Trafficking victims are accepted as apprentices for periods of six months to a year to gain on-the-job training in factory work, hospitality and other businesses.

## PROSECUTING HUMAN TRAFFICKERS

Much of Nod's work centres on strengthening national criminal justice systems. Nod's goal is to see a greater number of convictions achieved globally. This means not only that human trafficking must be a criminal offence in the country where an act of trafficking is detected, but also that the law must be enforced. As in the case of Kashmir, successful convictions depend on the police and others making the right decisions.

This can only happen if they have the knowledge and capacity to respond to human trafficking. Things can also go wrong: in some countries, for example, prosecutions are brought but the police fail to protect the identity of witnesses or prevent intimidation of victims and court officials by defendants. To try to prevent this happening, UNODC helps countries to develop effective law enforcement and criminal justice institutions.

UNODC has helped to develop legislation in many countries. Many human trafficking laws are limited in their application to the sexual exploitation of women and girls. That means they provide no assistance to people like Kashmir or, for example, to women trafficked to work in domestic servitude or sweatshops. Without specialized human trafficking laws, victims are subjected to greater uncertainties while traffickers face reduced risks and penalties.

In 2006, UNODC offered Armenia, Lebanon and South Africa assistance in drafting anti-human trafficking legislation. Criminal justice officials from Burkina Faso, Ghana, Nigeria, Togo, Ukraine and South Africa received specialized training. UNODC assisted NATO in training its senior officials to combat trafficking in persons. Three computer-based training modules to combat trafficking in persons were finalized in Thailand. The Training Manuals Assistance for the Implementation of the ECOWAS Plan of Action against Trafficking in Persons, containing an action plan for West and Central African countries, was launched in 2006.

In 2006-07, UNODC also trained police, border guards, prosecutors, judges and NGO staff in many countries, including Afghanistan, Burkina Faso, Finland, Ghana, Laos, Moldova, Nigeria, South Africa, Ukraine and Vietnam. Vietnam has one of the highest conviction rates for traffickers in the world, thanks in large part to training by UNODC. More than 110 people have been convicted of human trafficking offences. Following a UNODC cross-border cooperation workshop, the police of China and Vietnam rescued dozens of female victims trafficked for forced marriage. More than 50 trafficking rings were disrupted by late 2006.

## MODERN FORM OF SLAVERY

Based on data gathered from 155 countries, it offers the first global assessment of the scope of human trafficking and what is being done to fight it. It includes an overview of trafficking patterns; legal steps taken in response; and country-specific information on reported cases of trafficking in persons, victims, and prosecutions. At the launch of the Report in New York, the Executive Director of UNODC, Antonio Maria Costa said that "many governments are still in denial. There is even neglect when it comes to either reporting on or prosecuting cases of human trafficking". He pointed to the fact that while the number of convictions for human trafficking is increasing, two out of every five countries covered by the UNODC Report had not recorded a single conviction.

According to the Report, the most common form of human trafficking (79%) is sexual exploitation. The victims of sexual exploitation are predominantly women and girls. Surprisingly, in 30% of the countries which provided information on the gender of traffickers, women make up the largest proportion of traffickers.

In some parts of the world, women trafficking women is the norm. The second most common form of human trafficking is forced labour (18%), although this may be a misrepresentation because forced labour is less frequently detected and reported than trafficking for sexual exploitation. Worldwide, almost 20% of all trafficking victims are children. However, in some parts of Africa and the Mekong region, children are the majority (up to 100% in parts of West Africa).

Although trafficking seems to imply people moving across continents, most exploitation takes place close to home. Data show intra-regional and domestic trafficking are the major forms of trafficking in persons. The United Nations Protocol against Trafficking in Persons the foremost international agreement in this area entered into force in 2003. The Report shows that in the past few years the number of Member States seriously implementing the Protocol has more than doubled (from 54 to 125 out of the 155 States covered). However, there are still many countries that lack the necessary legal instruments or political will.

"This Report increases our understanding of modern slave markets, yet it also exposes our ignorance", said Mr. Costa. "We have a big picture, but it is impressionistic and lacks depth. We fear the problem is getting worse, but we can not prove it for lack of data, and many governments are obstructing", he admitted. The head of UNODC therefore called on governments and social scientists to improve information-gathering and -sharing on human trafficking. "If we do not overcome this knowledge crisis we will be fighting the problem blindfolded", he warned.

In a Panel Discussion on "Exposing Denial and Benign Neglect", Mr. Costa called on governments, the private sector, and the public at large to step up the fight against trafficking in persons. "More must be done to reduce the vulnerability of victims, increase the risks to traffickers, and lower demand for the goods and services of modern-day slaves", he said. To increase public awareness of human trafficking and rally the world to fight it, Mr. Costa appointed Academy Award-winning actress Mira Sorvino as a Goodwill Ambassador to Combat Human Trafficking. "We know that Mira's commitment to the plight of trafficking victims will move people to take action against modern-day slavery", said the Executive Director of UNODC.

## PROSTITUTION AND HUMAN TRAFFICKING

The countries making up the South Asia region support about one-quarter of the planet's population, with a large number of people unemployed and living below the poverty line. This socioeconomic situation has helped increase social crimes especially like human trafficking, especially of women and children. Prostitution, which is also included in human trafficking, is an intolerant social crime and a major issue in these countries. The ratio of human trafficking is high in this region, with girls kidnapped from Pakistan, Nepal, Bangladesh, Sri Lanka and Maldives and trafficked to mostly Gulf States, where there is a bevy of rich clientele.

Some studies estimate that more than 6,000 girls are being sold to India each year, which adds to the huge number of 172, 0000 girls, mostly from Nepal, working as prostitutes in India. India has around 2.3 million prostitutes working in the region. Most of the girls are driven to this "profession" due to poverty, marriage or adoption. In some regions, prostitution isn't frowned upon. In fact, it is a prestigious religious duty and women involved in this are revered by society. These women are called *devdasi*, where "dev" means "god" and "*dasi*" means "maid" therefore "maid of god" Actually these *devdasis* were "temple prostitutes" This ancient tradition was based on chosen females dedicating their whole lives to a deity and living their lives in temples.

Choosing the *devdasi* was the duty of the temple priests and the social elite, and these women was chosen to look after the deities. The *devdasi* also catered to the sexual needs of the priests and rich patrons of the temple (the latter usually chosen by her mother and the temple) who took responsibility for her social welfare. These women were free to have or refuse sex at their will. However, they were not allowed to the common man. Being so important in the temple hierarchy, they were invited as revered guests to social functions in surrounding villages to dance and sing. These women were considered holy and were not allowed to mix with the common folk.

This tradition saw its downfall when a century ago, the *devdasi* were considered immoral and were no longer held in reverence by society. They were reduced to mere prostitutes, social outcasts. However, it is still practiced in Saundatti, a small village located in the south of India. Then in the 1980s, the Indian government totally banned the tradition and tried to rehabilitate the *devdasi* and give them a better life. The ban did not deter those for whom this tradition is a revered custom, and those who held it dear, especially in South India, continued the practice. Today hundreds of girls are covertly dedicated to temples to don the role of *devdasi* in defiance of the ban.

"It is a revered tradition that has been part of the culture for centuries. If it is part of one's culture and religion, how can we forgo this tradition just because some people think it is not right and immoral? How can serving a temple and dedication to a deity and other duties is immoral when it is in the name of a revered cause?" asks sociologist Shurti Shunkar.

Says historian Guldeep Mehra: "We cannot uproot an ancient tradition just like that. There is a lot of history behind such customs. If we want them to change, we could be hurting someone's feelings. As a historian I would not support it."

Prostitution has become a taboo in the conservative mindset of South Asia, but it remains part of every society and culture. It also serves to constrict certain carnal crimes from growing, even though in most conservative societies crimes against women and children are on the rise. And although conservatives may decry such degradation, the most hypocritical condone the killing of their own women under various other customs and laws, like horrendous honor killings of innocent females at the hands of their male kin, or the selling off (usually after a small ceremony disguised as a wedding to appease the conscience of parents or guardians) of young girls to older men for money.

Sameena, a resident of Hyderabad Deccan, India, hails from a high-caste, poor Muslim family a Syed family, direct descendents of the Prophet Mohammad who hold a revered position in Islamic society. Her father is a low-earning rickshaw driver. Her mother is a housewife, tending to her brood of six daughters and five sons all living in a hovel. Sameena was "married off" at the age of 16 to a wealthy man from an Arab country. Only too happy to get Sameena off their hands, her parents didn't even consider that their new "son-in-law" was double their daughter's age. They were happy that they were getting a daughter married and that this marriage didn't cost them a penny. On the contrary, the groom, who already had several wives, paid them handsomely for their daughter.

The groom and the new addition to his household flew off to Dehli where they spent a couple of days together before he left her in the hotel with divorce papers. Sameena was handsomely rewarded by her husband with jewelry and cash, which her parents laid claim to. The teenager was devastated. She actually believed that she had at last found happiness, if not marital then at least financial. She thought she had been saved from the daily pangs of starvation her family faced and that she would be able to help her brothers and sisters.

Upon coming home, she realized her parents had known all along that her groom would run out on her. And now they were preparing for her younger sister's "wedding," also to a wealthy man from abroad. Sameena's parents silenced her protests and she found nobody else willing to help. The poor selling off their daughters to rich men puts food on the table. Sameena was "married" twice more before her younger sisters took her place. Those around her seemed to accept these marriages as legal in every way.

This is a softer side of prostitution that is accepted and used as a means of living by the poor. It has become acceptable as a means to an end only due to economic impediments, and therefore is not considered a social taboo. Pakistan, as a predominately Islamic country, frowns on this trade, but cannot stop it. The metropolis of Karachi is notorious for receiving a million Bangladeshi and more than 200,000 Burmese women, according to Indrani Sinha of SANLAAP India. Sanlaap is a non governmental organization engaged in improving the life of women, children and adolescents in the red-light areas.

These women are sold in Pakistan for about $1,500 - $2,500 with a 15 percent to 20 percent commission for the police, depending on their "looks, age, docility and virginity" The larger part of the clientele for these "goods" is rich visiting Arabs, the rich locals and rural farmers. The Arabs take "temporary wives" abandoning them and any children afterwards, with or without any benefits, a practice prevalent in India as well.

In Pakistan, the trafficked women are victimized by the authorities and are booked under the Zina Ordinance, part and parcel of the dangerous and controversial Hudood Ordinances, which state that adultery or sex outside marriage is a crime against the state and punishable by death by stoning. Usually these women and girls are often charged under Zina (adultery), if they are caught as prostitutes and maybe imprisoned and punishing them for crimes they were forced to commit.

During the 1980s, President Zia-ul-Haq dispersed prostitutes from their specified localities in red light areas and forced them to seek refugee in residential areas. This gave their profession finesse by providing them strategic places to hunt for respectable rich clients. And this allowed them to camouflage and mingle freely with the public. This shift only allowed their profession to prosper, avoid police raids and commissions and carry on their businesses in private within their premises.

Another major factor adding to prostitution in Pakistan is the slum dwellers. These people live in illegal premises in shanty huts and are continually harassed and abused by the police. Every night, policemen come along and pick out girls for prostitution. Protests are met with dire consequences, which could range from dislocation from the illegal premises, to death, or even the rape of the victim's mother or younger sisters. The hapless concede to these demands, aware that despite the authorities' knowledge of this problem, nothing will be done to change their plight.

Sajida grew up in a slum area of Karachi. Her father is a labourer and her mother works as a maid. She herself is prostituted by policemen, who either take her for themselves or sell her off to clients. There is no monetary remuneration for her services the cops' pimps her out take it all. Instead, Sajida earns only a slim sense of security for the other girls in her family and having a place to live. She sees no future for herself, and says she can't even commit suicide her death would give way for these animals to victimize the ones she has been trying to protect. "No one can help us! Only death will deliver us!" she says.

Bangladesh is one of the major providers of females for trafficking due to extreme poverty and social tolerance. It is one of the countries where many females are sold due to lack of dowry. Parents prefer to sell their daughters and sisters for money, instead of harrowing under the economic grunge. Two judges of the Bangladeshi High Court have ruled that prostitution as a livelihood is not illegal, in a case where two girls were evicted from their home when the landlord discovered they were running a brothel.

Although frowned upon in this Islamic country, prostitution is thus allowed if the trade workers have a license. However, such a license can only be issued if the authorities are convinced that the holders have no other means of income. Legal experts hold that this is an unusual judgment, but it nevertheless validates prostitution as a legal form of livelihood.

Interestingly, the Bangladeshi Constitution states that "gambling and prostitution should not be encouraged" but the largest number of trafficked women is generated in Bangladesh, due mainly to the weak economy and lack of employment. The primary reasons behind such widespread prostitution in most Asian countries seem to stem from widespread poverty. This argument does not hold true in countries with thriving economies, where all too often a blind eye is turned to lucrative immorality.

has been trying to protect. "No one can help us! Only death will deliver us!" she says.

Bangladesh is one of the major providers of females for trafficking due to extreme poverty and social tolerance. It is one of the countries where many females are sold due to lack of dowry. Parents prefer to sell their daughters and sisters for money instead of borrowing under the corrupt [illegible] group. Two judges of the Bangladesh High Court have ruled that prostitution as a livelihood is not illegal, in a case where two girls were evicted from their home when the landlord discovered they were running a brothel.

Although frowned upon in this Islamic country, prostitution is thus allowed if the trade workers have a license. However, such a license can only be issued if the authorities are convinced that the workers have no other means of income. Legal experts hold that this is an unusual judgement, but it nevertheless validates prostitution as a legal form of livelihood.

Interestingly, the Bangladesh Constitution states that gambling and prostitution should not be encouraged. But the largest number of trafficked women is generated in Bangladesh, due mainly to the weak economy and lack of employment. The primary reason behind such widespread prostitution in most Asian countries seems to stem from widespread poverty. This argument does not hold true in countries with thriving economies, where all too often a blind eye is turned to [illegible].

- Previous criminal record.
- Medico-legal report/ Hospital [illegible] STDs.
- Examination of clothes for stains/ Collection of clothes.
- Motive.
- Vehicle used.
- Other accomplices the role and status of trafficked victim.

There is a clear conflict for law enforcers between the fact that many trafficked women will have broken certain laws- in terms of sex work, immigration- but the fact is that they

# 2

# UN Perspective on Crime Prevention and Human Security

The United Nations Crime Prevention and Criminal Justice Programme are among the oldest of the United Nations programmes. Its foundations were laid in the fifties of the 20th century. From the outset the programme has sought to replace retributive criminal justice by policies which are both more effective and more humane. Experts working with the programme in the fifties and sixties typically belonged to the New Movement of Social Defence, advocating sentencing aimed at reintegration of the offender. Respect for human rights of offenders and prisoners were a key consideration behind the standards and norms for crime prevention and criminal justice elaborated in those years. In the eighties, the Crime Commission widened its focus to include a better treatment of victims of domestic violence and of crime in general a Declaration on Victims' Rights was adopted in 1985 by the General Assembly.

And, finally, after almost ten years of debate, the Crime Commission and subsequently ECOSOC, adopted in 2002 the United Nations Guidelines on the Prevention of Crime. The overarching normative aim of the Prevention Guidelines is expressed in its first article: *"Crime prevention offers opportunities for a humane and more cost-effective approach to the problems of crime"*. The United Nations Guidelines for the

Prevention of Crime stand in a fifty year old tradition of efforts of the United Nations to rationalize and humanize criminal justice.

At the Millennium Summit of the United Nations, Secretary-General Kofi Annan invited the world to stand up for fundamental human freedoms, including the right to live free of fear and free of want. The concept of *Human Security*, increasingly used in analyses of UN- based action, refers to policies which protect ordinary people from threats to the very cores of their existence. Fundamental realms of human security are economic security, health security and personal security. Personal security in most countries is mainly threatened by crime and interpersonal violence. In 2002 UNDP conducted a survey on human security among the general public in Latvia. Crime, together with the spread of narcotics and HIV/Aids, were listed as the most important threats to human security.

Everywhere in the large cities of the world – and this is where nowadays half of the world population lives- people are fearful of violence and of theft of property. Fear of crime is an overriding, everyday concern of citizens in both developed and developing countries. Ordinary citizens carry the burden of common criminality. Collectively citizens also bear the costs of organized crime and high level corruption. The criminal- political - nexus existing in many countries impoverishes local communities and impedes peace-building, post-conflict reconstruction and sustainable development. It locks many populations in a double bind of poverty and lawlessness. The negative impact of crime on human security can hardly be overestimated.

Policies which effectively reduce the extent of criminal victimization while respecting the rule of law yield direct benefits for the citizens of the world. Against this background, the United Nations Crime Prevention and Criminal Justice Programme represent a vitally important framework for the promotion of human security. This seems especially true for the recently adopted UN standards and actions for the promotion of victim rights and prevention of crime, just mentioned. These documents provide guidance how criminal threats to human security can be tackled with methods yielding maximum impact at minimum human costs.

## THE UN GUIDE

The UN Guidelines on the Prevention of Crime offer, first of all an introduction into the key theoretical concepts of modern crime prevention. Crime prevention is defined as comprising all measures that seek to reduce the risk of crimes occurring by intervening in its multiple causes. Criminal justice type interventions can also perform preventive functions but these fall outside the scope of the Guidelines. To underline this difference the Hungarian National Strategy for Crime Prevention is called a Strategy for Social Crime Prevention.

The document outlining the strategy specifically makes the important point that criminal justice should not be seen as subordinated to social crime prevention. Social crime prevention is supplementary to the administration of criminal justice. The crime reduction impact of criminal justice can be greatly reinforced if adequate crime prevention mechanisms are in place. Crime prevention cannot replace criminal justice.

In the literature several typologies of crime prevention have been proposed. The UN Guidelines distinguish four main categories of crime prevention:

- *Prevention through social development or social crime prevention, including early intervention;*
- *Community-based crime prevention;*
- *Situational and victim-oriented crime prevention;*
- *Reintegration of offenders.*

The Hungarian National Strategy for Social Crime Prevention follows the same conceptual frame with some adjustments. In the UN Guideline as well as in other UN documents community-based crime prevention is distinguished as a special form of crime prevention. The Hungarian authors of the strategy document regard community-based crime prevention as a special way to organize the implementation of crime prevention rather than as a separate substantive category. The Hungarian document furthermore points out that general employment and health policies have important crime preventive side-effects but cannot be regarded as crime prevention. These are social policies in their own right. Three main types of crime prevention, then, remain: early intervention; situational crime prevention, including victim support and reintegration of offenders. Early intervention in the development of socially problematic lifestyles is key to effective crime prevention. Techniques of early intervention resemble those advocated as demand reduction in drug control policies.

Crime prevention as defined in the UN Guidelines seeks, first of all, to reduce known risk factors of criminality and enhance protective factors. International best practice offers several examples of effective, non-discriminatory support programmes for vulnerable families and children. Programmes offering support to single-parent families and other types of targeted intervention promoting the social integration of children at risk have consistently been found to yield the best returns on investment of all known responses to crime. As calculated by American evaluators of such programmes, every dollar spent on support for vulnerable families eventually yields ten dollars in savings by preventing the development of delinquent lifestyles of the children concerned. From the perspective of human security, investments in support for at risk families with small children show highly favorable returns.

The Hungarian strategy pays due attention to early intervention while showing awareness of the need to prevent negative labelling of the target groups. An internationally known saying learns us that opportunity makes the thief. In Spanish the same criminological insight is elegantly formulated: an open door turns even a saint into a thief. A huge body of knowledge has over the years been developed on the effectiveness of various types of situational crime prevention. Special mention should be made in this connection of combining support to crime victims with advice how to prevent repeat victimization. Since recent victims run a much increased risk of being victimized such advice has not only proven to be highly cost-effective but seems also to be a moral duty of the state.

Those who the state has failed to protect against crime should be given all possible assistance to avoid revictimization. Finally, the Guidelines advocate innovative approaches to reintegrate offenders, especially also ex-prisoners. The Hungarian strategy document applies international best practices in crime prevention as codified in the UN Guidelines in all these domains. The implementation of the strategy offers a welcome opportunity to test out these best practices in a country belonging to a regional group of countries where crime prevention is a relatively new concept. We look forward to the results of the Hungarian experiences with early intervention, situational crime prevention, victim support and social reintegration of offenders.

## ORGANIZATIONAL ASPECTS

Equally important as substantive best practices are lessons learned concerning implementation of crime prevention. The international experience of implementing national crime prevention strategies is in many respects a Boulevard of Broken Dreams. Crime prevention in the eighties enjoyed wide political support in several countries. These new policies have resulted in an impressive body of knowledge on what works and what not, based on well designed pilot studies.

However, the full scale implementation of these proven practices has often been much less successful. Institutional structures for crime prevention implementation have tended to be under-funded, in a state of constant flux and incapable of developing and maintaining specialized expertise.

Countries as Hungary which introduce these policies in the current era can avoid the mistakes made elsewhere over the past two decades. They can incorporate in their planning international lessons learned on how to implement crime prevention. It is perhaps in this respect that the Hungarian strategy document merits the highest praise. The UN Guidelines render extensive attention to the organization and planning of crime prevention. The Guidelines do not shy away from addressing the sensitive issue of funding: "*Crime prevention*", reads article ten" *requires adequate resources, including funding for structures and activities*". Noteworthy in this recommendation is the reference to funding for structures.

All too often in the past governments have launched crime prevention strategies without due regard for the need to fund core structures for sustainable implementation. The universally proclaimed need for a multi-agency approach, involving both central and local government as well as civil society and the business sector seems to have generated the mistaken belief that crime prevention can be implemented without clear political leadership and adequate funding for both activities and fully-fledged administrative structures. Past experiences have taught that without such funding crime prevention cannot deliver sustainable results.

The United Kingdom has probably invested more resources in crime prevention than any other country, including in local directors of crime prevention as well as in several specialized NGO's implementing different forms of crime prevention. A recent evaluation report, titled, investing to Deliver (2004), nevertheless critiques the lack of a sufficiently strong, multi-levelled administrative structure ensuring accountable and sustainable implementation. Independent evaluation of crime prevention implementation in other countries would probably arrive at even more negative conclusions.

The UN Guidelines recommend well funded structures for implementation including the establishment of clear responsibility centres for crime prevention within central government. Such centres must be empowered to offer clear guidance to other ministries, local government, civil society and the business sector. For obvious reasons the Guideline does not provide a one- size- fits- all organizational structure for crime prevention. Each country will have to design its own best fit institutional arrangement. In Hungary the existing Crime Prevention Council will be transformed into a Crime Prevention Board, chaired by an independent expert, appointed by the Prime Minister. Both the Ministers of the Interior and of Justice are members of the Board.

The Board will coordinate crime prevention contributions of all other relevant ministries. The secretariat of the Board is integrated in the Ministry of Justice. A Centre of Expertise on Crime Prevention will be established in the Ministry of Interior. The latter Ministry will also be responsible for the funding of specialized NGO's and for liaising with the business sector. An annual budget of 550 million Hungarian florins has been earmarked for the funding of the strategy within the budget of the Ministry of Justice. This institutional arrangement clearly places responsibility for the implementation of crime prevention with relevant authorities at the central level. The Board, chaired by an independent Chair is mandated to assure the involvement of other ministries as well as of local authorities, NGO's and the business sector.

The Hungarian proposals, as adopted by Parliament, seem to reflect international best practice in crime prevention implementation. The organizational set up seems carefully crafted and offers good prospects of success. The appointment of an independent chair by the prime minister may help to control institutional rivalries between Justice and Interior. It may also help to secure the support of some of the other concerned "spending departments" such as education and health. The budget may still fall short of what ideally should be made available for full scale implementation of the strategy, but seems to allow for a serious start. Integration of resources into the annual budget of a ministry is certainly to be preferred to the establishment of an ad hoc fund for experimental projects as has been the model elsewhere. The Hungarian Government can be congratulated with laying the institutional foundations for a successful implementation of its social crime prevention strategy.

## CRIME PREVENTION AT UNODC

The principle of knowledge-based crime prevention/ reduction requires thorough assessments of the crime problems at issue. Traditionally governments rely for such assessments on data concerning police-recorded crimes. Such police figures do not cover crimes which remain hidden from the police: so-called dark numbers. UNODC collects "police figures" through questionnaires which are distributed among member states every four years. Although the questionnaires provide important information on the resources and outputs of criminal justice systems the data cannot be used to compare levels of crime. The now widely used instrument of victimization surveys- surveys among samples of the public asking about recent experiences with victimization by crime- provides better and more complete data on the level and nature of crime.

The importance of such surveys for better information on the true level of crime can be illustrated by comparing the Hungarian police figures with results from the International Crime Victims Survey carried out by the United Nations in Budapest in 2000. According to official crime statistics the level of crime in Hungary is below the average level in the Europe (in Hungary 450 crimes are annually recorded by the police per 10.000 populations, while the average in Western Europe lays around 800). However, a different picture emerges from the results of the ICVS: the percentage of the general public victimised by crime in the course of last year was 30.5% in Budapest against 27% in all industrialised countries taken together. The true level of crime is above the European-North American average.

This finding confirms the general rule that the proportion of hidden crimes is larger in developing countries and countries with economies in transition, due to a variety of reasons including lower rates of reporting by the public and more limited recording practices. In countries where dark numbers are relatively large, the use of victimization surveys for crime problem assessments is even more imperative than elsewhere. Not only the volume but also trends of police-recorded crime will often be strongly influenced by fluctuations in reporting and recording patterns. Police data can be very misleading if used as benchmarks. If crime prevention/reduction policies are successful, confidence in the police will go up and this will result in more crimes recorded, even if the level of crime remains stable or declines.

Reliance on police figures for the evaluation of the impact of newly introduced policies could lead to quite erroneous conclusions about the policy's impact. The United Nations Interregional Criminal Justice Research Institute in Turin, Italy has been involved in the conduct of previous rounds of the International Crime Victims Survey. The ICVS was for example carried out in 16 Central and Eastern European capitals in 2000. For this year UNODC/UNICRI plans a fifth round of the ICVS. Funding for the existing fifteen members of the EU has been secured from the European Commission. Twenty or more other countries have indicated their willingness to participate in the survey on the basis of cost sharing. It would seem important to also repeat the survey in Hungary and in as many other countries in the region as possible.

**Standard Setting**

As mentioned above, the Economic and Social Council of the General Assembly adopted in 2002 the UN Guidelines for the Prevention of Crime, previously called "Elements of Responsible Crime Prevention". In 2003 the Commission on Crime Prevention and Criminal Justice followed up with a resolution requesting the secretariat to develop a practical manual on the use of the Crime Prevention Guidelines. In a joint venture with UN Habitat a first meeting was convened in Durban, South Africa of a group of experts to discuss the outline of the manual. Since several databases with best practices in crime prevention from developed countries are available, the development of a UN manual could lead to a duplication of efforts. More added values would come from collecting experiences with crime prevention from developing countries and countries with economies in transition. UNODC will continue to collaborate with UN Habitat in the development of the manual which will take the form of a web-based resource facility. Possibly the Hungarian Academy of Crime Prevention established in 2003 could also contribute to this effort.

## Technical Assistance and Advice

The integration of the crime and drugs control programmes of UNODC has led to the establishment within the Division for Operations of a Branch responsible for the substantive back-stopping of all projects on crime prevention and drugs control. The Branch has been labelled the Human Security Branch. The Branch will contribute to the design and backstopping of crime prevention projects. The prevention and treatment unit, currently exclusively engaged in drugs-related demand reduction activities, will in the future widen its scope to also cover prevention of delinquency. The criminal justice reform unit will expand its work in the areas of juvenile justice reform, victim support and domestic violence. At this juncture the ongoing UNODC projects in the field of crime prevention can be classified in four main groups:

- Urban security
- Juvenile justice/ early intervention
- Domestic violence
- Victim Support

Under the rubric of urban security, a project is under preparation on Inter-agency partnerships for safer favela's in the city of Rio, Brazil. The Project will strengthen the strategies for actions of the Rio de Janeiro City Hall, involving partnerships with non-governmental organizations and including the systematized collection of data and use of victimization survey methodologies, the launching of awareness raising campaigns and the training of staff involved in community crime prevention interventions. Another, ongoing, project promotes urban crime prevention in the Dakar Region through the establishment of local Houses of Justice and the setting-up of community policing structures in difficult neighbourhoods.

As far as juvenile justice/early prevention is concerned, UNODC implements several projects on Juvenile Justice Reform and Delinquency Prevention in the Middle East Region (Lebanon, Egypt, Jordan) and Afghanistan. Governments in these countries are faced with increasing levels of juvenile delinquency, often related to drug trafficking and consumption, as well as with large numbers of street children. These projects aim to formulate a strategy directed towards the improvement of detention conditions for young offender, the protection directed towards the improvement of detention conditions for young offenders, the protection of young people in difficult circumstances and the prevention of delinquency and recidivism. Juveniles receive educational and vocational training during the time they are in closed institutions as well as after their release, which allows them to develop their skills, mental and physical abilities and which facilitates their social reinsertion.

Based on lessons learned from pilot testing in South Africa, a number of projects are envisaged for Southern African countries to counteract and prevent violence against women. One Stop Centres are created, which provide a range of services to victims of violence, including counselling, support groups, provisional shelter and fast referral for medical and legal assistance. The projects also include prevention and rehabilitation programmes for male perpetrators. The Office is also involved in the promotion of support structures for crime victims in several developing countries. Through the internet NGO's were invited to submit proposals for the establishment of support structures of victims of violent crime, including victims of human trafficking.

The Office received over two hundred well-prepared submissions. In March 2004 the Office will announce which 15 projects have been selected by the international jury to receive grants and become subject of a special monitoring mechanism. Noteworthy is further a new UNODC project, entitled "South-South Cooperation for Determining Good Practices for Crime Prevention in the Developing World", approved by the United Nations General Assembly as part of its programme to strengthen South-South cooperation under the Development Account. The first planning meeting took place in February 2004 in Jamaica. The general objective of the project is to assist in building up a systematic process of information exchange on crime prevention in the developing world.

Specifically, this will be carried out by establishing a network of information exchange between the Caribbean and Southern Africa, two regions in the developing world with high levels of violent crime, caused by similar factors, including high levels of unemployment and income inequality, a significant involvement of juveniles in criminal activity, the proliferation of unlicensed firearms and a critical need for police reform. UNODC's project will assist countries to build up their own capacity to share and implement knowledge and expertise on crime prevention. This should in the longer run, lead to crime prevention activities in the countries of the sub-regions, which are more comprehensive, better adjusted to local needs, more professional and what counts most more effective, in terms of successful crime reduction. These projects are prime examples of the special mission of the Human Security Branch, to promote human security through cost-effective and humane crime prevention and drugs control policies. The Human Security Branch therefore attaches great importance to the successful implementation of these projects.

# 3

# Best Practices to Counter Human Trafficking

Found in nearly all human societies, an age-old practice, the trade in human beings has become widespread and complex, with an increasing order of magnitude since the end of the Cold War. Now officially coined as human trafficking, this trade has become transnational and affects every continent on the globe. Global connectivity has produced diversified patterns of transnational mobility through networks that operate at different degrees of organisation and complexity. This makes the links between migration, trafficking and smuggling very context-bound and poses a considerable challenge to scholarly analysis. Although addressing human trafficking has become a political priority for many governments, many aspects of the phenomenon remain poorly understood. Available information about the magnitude of the problem is limited. Laczko and Gramegna (2003) note the growing consensus on the existing difficulty in measuring and monitoring trafficking given the wide range of actions and outcomes covered by the term (including recruitment, transportation, harbouring, transfer and receipt).

In general, the existing body of knowledge about human trafficking serves to raise public consciousness about the issue, but remains insufficient to lend support to a more comprehensive action programme for addressing different dimensions of the problem. The struggle against human trafficking requires a different approach from that of trafficked goods such as drugs and small arms – despite the similar condition of illicitness. As in the case of the trafficking of goods, the trafficking of human beings involves a number of key aspects, such as:

- Certain degrees of weakness in the state. Besides the transatlantic slave route, many internal forms and trends of trade in humans are also known to have existed in different regions of the world.
- Apparatus of the countries which send, serve as transit, and receive; large tax-free profits; the use of violence and threat to deter denouncement and prosecution. However, unlike illicit goods, human trafficking involves a process of exploitation from debt dependency to enslavement to ensure continued income from the same trafficked persons.

Traffickers objectify persons under their control, place them to work without payment, subject them to repeated sale, and may murder them or force them to take deadly options to destroy evidence. Governments and civil society – seeking to free trafficked persons from enslavement or servitude and to prosecute traffickers must deal with human beings placed in a wide range of difficult situations which may transform their perception and manipulate their coping and surviving in ways that may enhance rather than reduce dependency. Current policy for counteracting human trafficking falls into three categories:

- Prevention and deterrence,
- Law enforcement and prosecution of traffickers,
- Protection of trafficked persons, 'rehabilitation' and assistance in social reintegration. However, these official actions unfortunately face many problems of circumvention such as fragmented evidence, judicial disharmony within and between national legislative systems, weak social institutions with logistic problems and inadequate professional capability to lend support to trafficked persons.

Such circumvention indirectly serves to boost the impunity of perpetuators and maintain the opportunity for re-trafficking. A proliferation of funds and resources now exists for raising public awareness, legal reforms and developing new practices of human rights protection. The diverse manifestation of forms of human trafficking particularly those with transnational links tends to defy the authority of science in migration and affiliated analytical tools. Where theory is in the making rather than ready made, engaged organisations tend to turn to social learning to develop their practices. Throughout this report we refer to those trafficked as 'trafficked persons', 'trafficked children' or 'trafficked women' rather than 'victims' or 'victims of trafficking.' Wood (1985) forcefully argues that the labels used about certain 'categories of persons' reflect the power relations between the namer and the named.

We therefore chose a less disempowering term in this report and avoid use of the term 'victim' even though the majority of the literature still uses the term. It is used in this report only in direct quotes or as official titles and statements. We use the term 'rehabilitation' here to refer to medical and psychological assistance for trafficked persons' recovery from abuse and related illnesses. It does not carry the meaning of moral 'rehabilitation', an issue still subject to inconclusive debates, learning emphasises the merit of hands-on experiments or direct trial-and-error as well as the power of concrete examples of intervention in creating lasting effects on knowing what constitute success or failure.

The preference for immediate action shaped by learning from actions taken in practice is driven by the concern for efficient use of time, money and other resources. The documentation of practices and projects that have been perceived to deliver the desired outcome may be regarded as part of the process of inductive codification of new norms of intervention. Considering the complexity of the problem and the context of our research being without the benefit of field research and observation of practices in action, it is both impossible and unethical to make pronouncements on the impact of a particular practice, let alone to name any of them as 'best practices'. Our emphasis is on an understanding of the cognitive functioning of particular epistemic communities engaged in the struggle against human trafficking in order to appreciate the specific choices made (for action) in their context.

The challenge in the search for technical and analytical tools to make the concept of 'best practice' useful lies in the unpacking of the social and political world in which it is embedded and in so doing to contribute to a resolution of tension and create bridges between different epistemic communities. Given the current status of knowledge on human trafficking and the risk of erroneous claims, our aim is to direct the reader towards the need for public dialogues on diversity to be undertaken in the spirit of epistemic egalitarianism. Epistemic egalitarianism, we suggest, begins with the acknowledgement that each perspective has its own merits. Building and sharing a body of knowledge should be a democratic endeavour, continually generated and regenerated through what Sandra Harding calls 'fruitful coalitions and respectful dialogues' between different perspectives.

In the field of human trafficking, epistemic egalitarianism should foster such dialogues between policy-making bodies, engaged grass-roots organisations and scholars to address the congruence of forces behind the phenomenon in the interest of human rights protection. This means including also 'people living with human trafficking' (as trafficked persons, returnees and their families) to take part as 'knowing subjects' on how best to protect their rights. Such dialogues can be built on experiences of inclusion already taking place in several countries, notably the participation by returnees in the formulation of intervention at micro level. Their narratives and insights should be channelled into the policy field and scholarly interpretative works. This may help to foster a shared understanding of the problem and a collective support that does not take for granted some standardised definition of human trafficking, but is capable of responding to diversity of needs and 'situated' rights of trafficked persons and their families.

## FOCUS ON WOMEN AND CHILDREN

Social structures mediate human mobility. Inevitably, the experience of being trafficked or mobile through exploitative means varies according to the persons' social position and identity as regards class, gender, age, religious affinity and citizenship. Known patterns of illicit human mobility suggest that women and children are most vulnerable to human trafficking, although a large number of trafficked men and boys have been found. From the perspective of gender and age, Radhika Coomaraswamy the United Nations Special Rapporteur on Violence Against Women – notes the following: "...the lack of rights afforded to women serves as the primary causative factor at the root of both women's migration and trafficking in women. The failure of existing economic, political and social structures to provide equal and just opportunities for women to work has contributed to the feminisation of poverty, which in turn has led to the feminisation of migration, as women leave their homes in search of viable economic options. Further, political instability, militarism, civil unrest, internal armed conflict and natural disasters also exacerbate women's vulnerabilities and may result in an increase in trafficking". She adds that the phenomenon of trafficking in children needs child-specific remedies which take into account gender-specific features.

Dottridge (2004:19) endorses this view and further proposes that child-focused action should try to minimise their specific vulnerabilities, enhance their capacity to assess risk and articulate worries, and pay attention to gender and age differentials. Sub-articles (c) 9 and (d) 10 under Article 3 in the United Nations Protocol to Prevent, Suppress and Punish Trafficking in Persons, especially Women and Children, supplementing the Convention against Transnational Organised Crime (also abbreviated as the Trafficking Protocol) gives specific attention to the trafficking of children. The article places special onus on parents not to abuse their position of authority or the vulnerability of children in their care.

## Analysis

Our interest in this research project stems from our long-standing practical and theoretical engagement with issues on the margins that have become a new epicentre of a global social crisis in the last decade. Aware of the complexity of issues underlying the constellation of practices framed as human trafficking, we see the merit in bringing to the fore the significance of appreciating reality from the standpoint of those whose daily lives are most affected by policy choices. We view policy as a deployment of different fields of social energy guided by a variety of knowledge frameworks and interests, capable of cooperation, competition and conflict. Those unrepresented by the guiding frameworks tend to carry the social burdens of errors in decision-making without having an avenue for criticising the beliefs upheld by policy-makers; nor for exacting a response to their requests for change.

Extant avenues to assert alternative beliefs such as the World Bank's 'Voices of the Poor' or the World Social Forum are inaccessible to those stranded in different frameworks of legislation without effective citizenship, as are trafficked persons. We therefore see our task as contributing to an avenue through which the rights and dignity of trafficked persons can be addressed from the standpoint of their location, so as to give socially grounded meanings to human rights protection as a policy objective. We concur with Kardam (2004) that emerging global regimes of rights and social equality need new methods of scrutiny at the point of application of standards and principles. We regard the transformation of policy practices from the control and discipline of the social body to a process of dignity enhancement for those stripped of their rights as a key objective in this scrutiny. Lack of resource deprives us of an opportunity to observe first-hand the application of best practices in the anti-human trafficking campaign in Africa.

We rely on the diversity of routes of knowledge on the Internet and databases of various organisations. Aware of the fact that the diffusion of information also means the spread of misinformation, we supplement the knowledge provided on websites with a thorough review of publications and reports of meetings that offer additional insights on organisations in Africa engaged in the anti-human trafficking campaign. Our research focus has evolved through the data-gathering process. Our attempt to create a framework for the analysis of best practices was vexed with major questions regarding norms and values, leading to the decision to provide an analytical lens through a social learning approach. Analysis of the political, legal, social and cultural aspects of trafficking of women and children in Africa reveals tensions between international regulatory frameworks and the diversity of practices of human mobility.

We note that communities of practitioners in Africa share an awareness about the significance of bridging and synchronizing the three levels of intervention (prevention, prosecution and protection), but this awareness at times remains detached from actual action owing to the lack of resources and institutional capabilities. Rather than treating this as a separate entity, our evolving understanding has shaped our belief that such practice may best be treated as part of a broader process of transformation of a web of social relationships. Depending on the context, some relations are stronger than others in causing human trafficking. BP cannot be adopted as a 'one-size-fit-all' instrument, but requires context-specific knowledge. Society must be able to ensure a minimal level of security for individuals, families and communities to resist human trafficking without fear and anxiety about the consequences of their choices, be they socio-economic, cultural or political. The general enhancement of their capabilities and entitlements and an increasing responsiveness among institutions can contribute to confidence-building among communities at risk. Successful community participation in prevention activities, cooperation in the prosecution of perpetrators, recovery as well as social re- integration of returnees depend on the trust generated between all concerned.

## DIVERSITY IN PRACTICE AND TENSION IN REGULATORY FRAMEWORKS

Like a coin contemporary regulation of human mobility has two faces. The prohibitive face addresses human trafficking, and the enabling face the principle of free movement of people. Both faces are strongly related to issues of identity and citizenship. In the African context control over human mobility through identity control is a fairly recent phenomenon, affiliated with colonialism and the creation of the modern state. In previous times borders such as they existed at all were fluid and permeable. Recent concern about human trafficking in the region and attempts to produce a precise definition of human trafficking as an emerging form of human mobility often labelled as the 'New Slavery' have provoked much controversy owing to the diversity of perspectives through which the subject may be viewed (Save the Children-Sweden, 2003:14). Existing perspectives on human trafficking manifest the tension between two key sets of concerns: the sovereignty and interests of nation-states as discrete units in international relations; and the violations of the human rights of persons in a particular process of migration labelled as 'human trafficking'.

In the absence of adequate explanations for the phenomenon of human trafficking being but one form of human mobility, policy tends to lurch inconsistently in different directions often suppressing the voices of those affected. This chapter illustrates how different concerns and priorities for combating human trafficking in Africa particularly involving women and children have yet to find harmony in several dimensions. Most notable are the specific social and cultural milieus in which human trafficking is embedded and the current tension in the regulatory frameworks concerning human mobility more generally.

The manifestation of human trafficking became visible to policy makers in the 1990s. Its deeper roots are being revealed in the process of intervention to counter the problem. In general, intervention measures share the following objectives:

- To define the different forms of abuse faced by women and children in the process of trafficking for labour exploitation.
- To locate the corresponding perpetrators or complicit agents, Six perspectives on sex trafficking and related actions.
- A moral problem that leads to intervention for the abolition or prohibition of prostitution or commercial sex.
- A problem of organised crime that leads to legislative reforms, policing and penalising criminal networks.
- A migration problem that leads to border controls (passport and identification papers).
- A public order problem that leads to awareness campaigns, publicity about risks, and changing cultural practices.
- A labour problem that leads to intervention such as improving working conditions, abolishing child labour or labour monitoring systems.
- A human rights problem, or a gender issue, that leads to intervention to address violence against women and children.
- To devise specific policy instruments to counteract the problem.
- To establish new forms of cooperation between different agencies involved in this area.

In West and Central Africa the different perceptions of human trafficking combined with different socio-economic and political situations in the various countries have created a mixture of policy responses. Guided by knowledge derived from action-oriented research initiated by a number of international governmental and non-governmental organisations, responses have included a variety of measures. These are directed at: raising awareness among families, communities, local chiefs, government ministers and law enforcers; legislative changes to protect trafficked persons and prosecute traffickers; providing training for border patrol police and social workers, and providing direct support to trafficked persons and their families. Direct support has covered interception, rescue and socio-economic reintegration often using micro-credit as an instrument to alternative livelihood and economic self- sufficiency. In the process of implementing anti-trafficking practices, the significance of the social and cultural milieus conducive to human trafficking and re-trafficking emerged as a new subject requiring analytical attention.

This analysis covers a variety of social structures such as gender, sexuality, age and ethnicity, as well as intra-household dynamics and attitudes of communities. The first wave of trafficking in adult women from West Africa to Western Europe began in the 1980s and continued through the 1990s. This was followed by the trafficking of minors involving both males and females. Where children are concerned, the specificities of their vulnerability deriving from local contexts (such as belonging to marginal ethnic groups, subservient castes, or dysfunctional families affected by war or disaster) have contributed to the creation of child-specific demand for wide-ranging types of work. Children are trafficked into a variety of exploitative situations including commercial sex, domestic service, armed conflict, service industries like bars and restaurants; or into hazardous forms of work in factories, mines, agriculture and fishing, construction; also begging.

Exploitation of trafficked children can be progressive. Those trafficked to work in factories, domestic service or restaurants, may subsequently be forced into prostitution. Those trafficked for prostitution may be subject to re-sale more than once. The vulnerability of women and children to re-trafficking is due to a number of factors such as the forms of intra-household decision-making and tacit 'tolerance' of trafficking mechanisms among the wider public, but also to the mishandling of trafficked persons driven by social and cultural values that carry stigmatising effects. Reports have revealed many cases wherein the children and women who have been intercepted and/or later returned to their communities do not stay in their communities for long, being subject to re-trafficking. ILO-IPEC (2001) offers a detailed picture of the context, patterns and backgrounds of families and communities which have facilitated trafficking in West and Central Africa.

It identifies three key clusters of factors, as follows:

1. Socio-cultural factors such as the social acceptability of putting children to work, traditions of migrations that are centuries old in Africa, illiteracy or low education levels, preparations for marriage (sometimes having to engage in domestic work to pay for dowry).
2. Economic factors such as the imbalance between rural and urban wealth levels and a desire to escape poverty.
3. Juridical and political factors such as absence of legislation and the ignorance of parents and trafficked persons of their rights under the law or mistrust of the law and open borders.

The traditional system of educating children to be independent and to initiate them to the world of work has been a recurring theme addressed by a variety of organisations. The tradition of 'placing', 'placement', 'confiding', or 'socialisation' has been variously portrayed as happening only during school holidays and for a variety of purposes such as to acquire social and life skills, to pay off debts, to prepare for marriage, or to prove that children can live independently. ILO report (2001) also notes that these children nonetheless end up doing household chores, selling in the market, helping in the agricultural farms or in the mines. The social construct of 'placement' of children in the world of work per pro migration, as being a tradition, remains a contested domain. National governments maintain a distinction between child placement and the traditional seasonal migration which has linked West and Central Africa for generations.

Anti-Slavery International (2003:1) notes that this traditional system of educating children by initiating them into work has been distorted into a commercial transaction which in turn has led to the trafficking of children from villages to the urban areas, and between countries within West and Central Africa. Recognising the placing of children to live and work with relatives in better-off households as long-standing practice, some analysts have noted that cross-border trafficking has increased significantly in the 1980's and by the 1990's from impoverished areas to the relatively well-off areas of Gabon, Southwest Nigeria and southern Côte d'Ivoire, where there has been an increased demand for child labour. Dottridge (2002) records some gender-specific patterns of child trafficking with girls being placed in prostitution and other gender-based forms of work such as domestic service and street vending, where only some get paid and most do not.

He also notes some gender-specific traditional practices that contribute to the aggravation of the trafficking situation of young women. For instance norms of kinship instill a custom which requires young women to have a wedding trousseau and to leave their family and community when they get married. Gender-bias in investment in education tends to keep girls at home to help in the household chores, giving preference to the education of boys. Inheritance rules for land tend to exclude women and girls.

Taken together, these gender-specific practices tend to marginalise women and girls in the community and render them vulnerable to risky 'work-placement' abroad. Dottridge (2002) emphasises that in many parents' cognitive frame, 'placing' their children does not constitute the act of 'selling'; it is sending them away in the hope that they will be better off in wealthier cities or countries. In many cases the 'consent' of parents and sometimes of the children, has been obtained before the designated child goes with the trafficker who may be a relative or a person who has gained the 'trust' of the parents and family to take care of the needs of the child.

On some occasions there is no choice other than to 'trust' this person to take care of the child. As regards trafficking routes, Anti-Slavery International's (ASI) 1999 report suggests that the trafficking routes reflect the routes used by the populations themselves. These have formed intricate regional intersections which are flexible, depending on border control activity and labour market demands. The ASI report in 2000 presented findings of another research project based on interviews with 884 people, including children who had been trafficked. They noted that many of the families interviewed had more than one child living abroad and that a significant number of parents acknowledged the reason for being prepared to turn over their children to traffickers was their inability to earn enough to cover the needs of the family. Of the 281 children interviewed in Benin, ASI reports that 75 percent said they would go at their parents' request a significant revelation on parents' influence and truncated cognition about human trafficking as a whole process.

Less information is accessible about the incidence, trends and routes of trafficking of women and children in Southern Africa. Molo Songololo (2000) has produced one of the few in-depth reports on the internal trafficking of children in South Africa for the purposes of commercial sexual exploitation. The findings show that girl children are primary targets and boys secondary. Parents, local gangs, and brothel owners are active in the recruitment of children into the sex work. Molo Songololo (2000) delineates the primary causal factors that give rise to the increase of in-country trafficking. Among these are the poor economic situation among those trafficked, the breakdown in extended and nuclear families - often accompanied by changes in cultural attitudes and practices, and the high demand for sex with children. With regards to cross-border trafficking, two reports prepared by ASI in 1991 and 1992 have documented trafficking from Mozambique to South Africa. An IOM report (2003) has documented the trafficking of refugees from Angola and the Great Lakes region sometimes from further north to South Africa, with some additional references to child trafficking from Lesotho, Mozambique and Malawi to South Africa.

The reports also note incidences of inter-continental trafficking of young women to South Africa from Russia, Eastern Europe, Thailand, China and Taiwan, involving crime syndicates based Mozambique, Eastern Europe and Thailand. The IOM 2003 report specifies that although information is scarce the evidence suggests that trafficking between Europe and Southern Africa documented for at least the past century is persistent and widening. South Africa also emerges from these reports as a source and transit country as well as being a major destination.

## POLITICAL AND LEGAL FRAMEWORK

Since 1996 West and Central African governments, individually and collectively, have made significant efforts to reform the judiciary to address human trafficking. The Libreville Common Platform of Action of the Sub-regional Consultation of the Development of Strategies to Fight Child Trafficking for Exploitative Labour Purposes in West and Central Africa was signed in 2000 by 21 countries in West and Central Africa, supported by UNICEF and ILO with the cooperation of the government of Gabon. This was followed by the Declaration of Action Against Trafficking adopted by the Economic Community of West African States (ECOWAS) and the endorsement of ECOWAS Plan of Action in Dakar in 2001 by 15 member-states. This Common Platform of Action identifies the main characteristics and causes of child trafficking, and specifies government commitment in several areas. These are: advocacy and sensitisation campaigns; setting up appropriate legal and institutional mechanisms to address child trafficking; improving care received by trafficked children; monitoring the incidence of trafficking through collecting data and improved research; improving inter-governmental and inter-ministerial cooperation.

The ECOWAS Plan of Action specified key initial actions to be undertaken by signatory states for the years 2002-2003. The Plan covers several crucial areas:

1. Legislation and ratification of the relevant international and regional covenants;
2. Interstate collaboration in collecting and exchanging information on trafficking incidence and trends, and in training personnel including special police units, border police, judges and other law enforcers;
3. Prevention of future trafficking through intensive awareness campaigns and
4. Monitoring of the implementation of the plan of action.

More recently, in January 2002, high level ministers from West and Central African States met again in Yamoussoukro, Côte d'Ivoire during the 'First Specialised Meeting on Child Trafficking and Exploitation in West and Central Africa' to exchange information and review the national strategies. In March 2002 representatives from West and Central African States met in Libreville, Gabon to discuss the feasibility of adopting a sub-regional convention on trafficking. At this meeting organised by UNICEF and ILO, the representatives mapped out the phases towards the ratification of a sub-regional convention against trafficking including continuing technical cooperation in 2003 and agreed on ratification by the end of 2004.

There are variations in the incorporation of these international and regional agreements into domestic law. Within West Africa, active changes in legislation have been observed in Togo, Mali, Cameroon, Benin (which enacted legislation in 1995 regulating travel of children under the age of 14) and Burkina Faso. In Burkina Faso, for instance, in May 2003 the national assembly adopted a law defining child trafficking and punishing traffickers by imprisonment or a fine.

Togo does not have an anti- trafficking law but uses other parallel laws to prosecute traffickers. Several countries have entered bilateral agreements. In 1996 an agreement was signed between Ghana, Togo, Benin and Nigeria to address trafficking. Mali has established a national commission focussing on child trafficking between Mali and the Côte d'Ivoire. Togo and Benin have signed an agreement for cooperation in the rehabilitation of trafficked children. Encouraging as they are, domestic laws and bilateral agreements remain inadequate to respond to the complexities of trafficking. Lack of coordination, and national and regional budgetary commitments, may well put implementation of these well-intended plans in jeopardy. With the exception of South Africa, there is a noticeable absence of domestic anti-trafficking legislation in Southern Africa countries.

Most countries in Southern Africa use the framework of illegal immigration – which tends to criminalise the trafficked person rather than the trafficker. In South Africa national legislation contains several pieces that may be applied to the prosecution of traffickers, though they are not specific to human trafficking. Examples of these separate pieces of legislation are the Sexual Offences Bill, the Children's Bill, the Child Care Act and certain clauses in the Criminal Act. The prevalent unwillingness to draft legislation that deals specifically with trafficking is slowly changing. A draft of the Human Trafficking Legislation is now on the table and being discussed. South Africa is in the process of reforming national laws to bring the legal system in line the United Nations Convention against Transnational Organised Crime in 2000 and its Protocol to Prevent, Suppress, and Punish Trafficking in Persons, Especially Women and Children.

To recapitulate, current perspectives on the trafficking of women and children in Africa exhibit some tension at various levels. A key tension lies between human rights norms and the definition of 'tradition'. The failure to integrate human rights norms to protect trafficked persons is due to the absence of a definition of human trafficking in judicial systems in many countries combined with structural weakness of the judiciary. This weakness is regarded as an outcome of 'missing ingredients' such as: political will, resources and awareness among law enforcers (border police, magistrates, local chiefs and others).

Notwithstanding the merit of the concern for this failure, it is important to point out that the discussion on 'traditions' has not fully unearthed their dynamic nature. A tradition such as the 'placement' of children can be subject to alteration by exogenous forces which commercialise it and turn it into child trafficking. The issue at stake is not only what kind of legal label should be placed on this practice, but also adequate understanding of exogenous forces that can help neutralise them. Public debates and political contestation about human trafficking should be about ways to connect cultural factors with other structural issues regarding human mobility.

Driven as it is by both supply and demand, human trafficking has gradually acquired a combination of local and global characteristics that resemble commodity chains with different nodal points involving different actors with a varying degree of power and authority. Therefore, the 'realities' that are being shaped and formed need to be subject to cross-cultural and historical comparisons in order to sharpen analytical tools and interpretation.

Too previous a pronouncement of root causes with limited validation can be counter-productive. For example, pronouncements about 'traditions of migration' and 'traditions of placing children' being the causes of greater incidence of trafficking can obliterate labour market dynamics and policy neglect of the social domain in an era of global competition.

Furthermore, a strong focus on traditions as a root cause can lead to the practice of blaming the trafficked person rather than promoting needed structural changes. In addition to the required deep understanding of the social, political, economic and cultural milieu, more questioning is necessary by which to ascertain the source(s) of this understanding and to discover exactly which 'understanding' becomes the 'received' knowledge that influences policy processes.

## THE UNITED NATIONS PROTOCOL TO PREVENT, SUPPRESS AND PUNISH TRAFFICKING

The strong call for the adoption of an internationally recognised definition of human trafficking in the late 1990's sought to consolidate the diverse ways of understanding it. Since the adoption of a definition of trafficking from the United Nations Protocol to Prevent, Suppress and Punish Trafficking in Persons, Especially Women and Children, supplementing the Convention against Transnational Organised Crime in 2000, the discussion on human trafficking has been made easier, but not without controversy. The definition is contained in Article 3 of the Protocol:

- *"Trafficking in persons"* shall mean the recruitment, transportation, transfer, harbouring or receipt of persons, by means of the threat or use of force or other forms of coercion, of abduction, of fraud, of deception, of the abuse of power or of a position of vulnerability or of the giving or receiving of payments or benefits to achieve the consent of a person having control over another person, for the purpose of exploitation. Exploitation shall include, at a minimum, the exploitation of the prostitution of others or other forms of sexual exploitation, forced labour or services, slavery or practices similar to slavery, servitude or the removal of organs;

- The consent of a victim of trafficking in persons to the intended exploitation set forth in subparagraph (a) of this article shall be irrelevant where any of the means set forth in subparagraph (a) have been used;
- The recruitment, transportation, transfer, harbouring or receipt of a child for the purpose of exploitation shall be considered "trafficking in persons" even if this does not involve any of the means set forth in subparagraph (a) of this article and
- "Child" shall mean any person less than eighteen years of age.

The Protocol provides an internationally binding definition. It aims to eliminate differences between national legal systems and to set standards for domestic law to address organised crime. Bound as it is by social and cultural contexts the interpretation of crime and penalty has been subject to many queries.

Particular concern about the interpretation of crime in the context of those who give non-commercial help to would-be migrants crossing national borders for reasons of political safety perhaps destroying ethical norms of human solidarity has led to a differentiation between 'human smuggling' and 'human trafficking'. As Nadig (2002) points out, only human smuggling in the context of offering the service of undocumented or falsely documented entry against payment would be liable to penalty. Practices of human trafficking are embedded in social relations and are therefore diverse. It is difficult to generalise interpretations based on fragmented evidence.

As illustrated earlier, a number of international non-governmental organisations have noted peculiarities of human trafficking in Africa that do not entirely fit the international definition. The definition bases itself on the 'model' of transnational trafficking, often attributed to the presence of large networks of organised crime. Trafficking in Africa is through small, family-related networks and does not always take place across national borders.

Terms such as 'trafficking', 'abduction' and 'sale of children' all have different meanings, depending on the particularity of contexts. Even the term consenting party is controversial as regards the involvement of the parents and sometimes the children in the decision-making process. A criminalisation approach may have to impose penalty on entire communities. A more positive perspective is the broad definition adopted by ILO-IPEC that allows for its application in a wider variety of situations.

In a 2001 report ILO-IPEC states the following: "[i]n some respects, the variations found in the definition of trafficking in international instruments and frameworks are both inevitable and legitimate, and in no way represent confusion or disagreement. Each international instrument relates to the place the organisation of reference occupies in the international multilateral structurebe it a crimefocused or rights- focused body. As a result, what might at first seem an uneven handling of trafficking issues across organisations is actually more a question of approach and context than a difference of intent."

ILO-IPEC sees the merit in maintaining some flexibility in the use of the concept of 'trafficking' to accommodate institutional objectives and contextual requirements. A wide definition permits the practical accommodation of the specific objectives of the different, yet complementary, international instruments.

## OTHER INTERNATIONAL CONVENTIONS

Other international organisations have formed an understanding of 'trafficking' and its related situations by combining the definition in the Trafficking Protocol with other related agreements and conventions. Among these are the UN Convention on the Rights of the Child of 1989 (UN CRC), the ILO Worst Forms of Child Labour Convention of 1999 (No. 182), the ILO Forced Labour Convention of 1930 (No. 29) and the UN Convention on the Elimination of All Forms of Discrimination Against Women (CEDAW) of 1949. Additional international frameworks that can be used to supplement the Trafficking Protocol include the General Agreement on Trade in Services (GATS) and the International Convention on the Protection of the Rights of All Migrant Workers and Members of their Families (also called the UN Migrant Rights Convention). Using ILO Convention 182 as a reference point, Article 3 of the convention clearly indicates the inclusion of trafficking of children in the areas of concern.

"For the purposes of this Convention, the term *the worst forms of child labour* comprises:

- All forms of slavery or practices similar to slavery, such as the sale and trafficking of children, debt bondage and serfdom and forced or compulsory labour, including forced or compulsory recruitment of children for use in armed conflict;
- The use, procuring or offering of a child for prostitution, for the production of pornography or for pornographic performances;
- The use, procuring or offering of a child for illicit activities, in particular for the production and trafficking of drugs as defined in the relevant international treaties and
- Work which, by its nature or the circumstances in which it is carried out, is likely to harm the health, safety or morals of children."

The Convention on the Elimination of All Forms of Discrimination against Women (CEDAW) adopted in 1979 by the UN General Assembly and often described as an international bill of rights for women defines what constitutes discrimination against women and sets up an agenda for national action to end such discrimination. By 20 October 2004, 179 countries had ratified or acceded to the convention (with 98 signatures).

Discrimination against women is defined as: "...any distinction, exclusion or restriction made on the basis of sex which has the effect or purpose of impairing or nullifying the recognition, enjoyment or exercise by women, irrespective of their marital status, on a basis of equality of men and women, of human rights and fundamental freedoms in the political, economic, social, cultural, civil or any other field."

Pertinent to trafficking of women and children the convention calls on states to take appropriate measures against all forms of trafficking in women. It also affirms the reproductive rights of women as well as their rights to acquire and change or retain their nationality and the nationality of their children. The UN Convention on the Right of the Child (UN CRC) is the most universally accepted human rights convention with the most number of ratifications by member states with 192 countries being party to the convention. This convention recognises the human rights of children and the standards to which all governments must aspire in realising these rights.

By ratifying the convention national governments commit themselves to protecting and ensuring children's rights. It elaborates the basic human rights which *all* children *everywhere* are entitled to, which are: the right to survival; to develop to the fullest; to protection from harmful influences, abuse and exploitation; and to full participation in family, cultural and social life. It includes the child's human right not to be trafficked or exploited. There are two Optional Protocols to the convention that have been adopted to strengthen the provisions of the Convention in specific areas, being: the involvement of children in armed conflict and on the sale of children (entered into force in February 2002); child prostitution and child pornography (entered into force in January 2002).

## FRAMEWORKS FOR THE MOVEMENT OF PEOPLE

The International Convention on the Protection of the Rights of All Migrant Workers and Members of their Families and Mode 4 of the General Agreement on Trade in Services are frameworks governing the movement of people. The issues they individually cover, and the relative strength and status they enjoy as international legal instruments, reflect the current patterns of polarisation in international political economy. The International Convention on the Protection of the Rights of All Migrant Workers and Members of their Families manifests the belief in the principle of indivisibility of rights (civil political, socio-economic and cultural). It took more than 12 years for the convention to come into force on July 2003 after reaching the minimum required ratification of 20 countries in addition to the ten countries which had signed the convention. By 5 October 2004 there was a total of 27 ratifications and 15 signatures by UN member states. Of these, 11 ratifications and 7 signatures are from African countries.

The countries ratifying this Convention are low-income countries and home to some 4.5 million migrants (2.6 per cent of the world total migrant population). Major migrant-receiving countries located in wealthy regions such as Western Europe and North America have not ratified the Convention, even though they host the majority of migrant workers (nearly 100 million out of a total of 175). Other important receiving countries India, Japan, Singapore, Malaysia, Australia, the Gulf States have not ratified the Convention either. Irrespective of the form of migration whether 'regular' or 'irregular', the Convention recognises that migrants are entitled to a minimum set of rights which includes humane living and working conditions, education and health services, legal equality including correct procedures and the freedom from sexual abuse. The Convention also specifies that migrants have the right to return to their country of origin and participate in the political procedures of their home country.

The Convention accepts that even undocumented migrants are entitled to basic protection and recognition of their rights as human beings. Although countries that have ratified and signed the Convention are primarily sending countries, some are also transit and receiving countries. Signatories must treat migrants according to the principles of the Convention, irrespective of their documented or undocumented status. Articles 10 and 11 make provision for the prevention of and the imposition of penalties on human trafficking.

As Taran points out (2000: 30) 'the fundamental challenge for the extension of human rights to migrants is the sharpening contention between basing an overall international approach to migration on a framework of control versus establishing a migration management framework in which human rights is a fundamental basis'. As he notes (2000: 36), the tension between global competition and the protection of migrants is tending to shift migration issues into a framework of migration management. States may still use their discrete sovereign power to refuse to extend human rights provisions to undocumented migrants - especially socio-economic rights.

Less *ad hoc* preferences with discriminatory consequences - may be found in the other regulatory framework that touches on the 'free movement of natural persons', notably Mode 4 of the General Agreement on Trade in Services (GATS). Mode 4 defines the supplier in technical terms as a 'natural person' as opposed to a 'juridical person' such as a business firm. In principle, although Mode 4 covers all skill levels, the commitments of labour-importing countries have largely been restricted to the highly skilled corporate sector (intra-corporate transferees, business visitors, consultants, or contract-suppliers).

Mode 4 has raised considerable debate among high-income and lower-income countries about the implications for labour migration, immigration policy and border controls. High-income countries are concerned that full liberalisation of Mode 4 will facilitate permanent migration and unauthorised migration or open the borders to a 'flood' of unskilled and semi-skilled migrants. Lower-income countries are concerned that Mode 4 will facilitate 'brain drain' or, in reverse, a flood of highly paid consultants into their countries. The application of Mode 4 so far fails to address the hierarchy of labour relations in the service sector, leaving migrant workers in the lower skill strata more vulnerable to the risks of irregular forms of mobility where they are subject to the unruly practices of those who organise it.

Judicial reforms in West and Central Africa have produced new legal resources to enhance human rights protection for trafficked persons. The emphasis on problems caused by the supply side appears one-sided. Overemphasis of the supply side can obliterate the dynamics on the demand side that have been brought to light by a number of grass-roots organisations. More generally, the current framing of human trafficking for policy choices has tended to fragment the totality of human mobility as a process. This fragmentation has led to much tension around policy issues of public order, economic competition, efficiency and human vulnerability. Those concerned for public order purport that cross-border human trafficking reflects the weakening of states and local systems of governance.

By contrast, those concerned with human vulnerability see the state as a key actor driven by plural interests and currently being stranded between three poles crime control, human rights protection, and economic efficiency in an era of global competition. To avoid human rights from being overridden by other interests it is important that those three regulatory regimes concerning human mobility are treated as three dimensions of an interconnected whole. A migration management framework is now emerging as a new approach for protecting both the interests of states and the protection of the human rights of the migrants included in the frameworks of policy negotiation. The fate of those excluded from such frameworks remains in the hands of the Palermo Convention and its Trafficking Protocol.

## EPISTEMIC COMMUNITIES AND BEST PRACTICES

Far from being exhaustive in scope and depth, our attempt is but a first step towards locating areas in which a shared understanding of the problem be gradually fostered. Our data consist of ideas expressed in policy documents and information materials from the websites of a number of governmental, inter-governmental and non-governmental organisations active in the global struggle against human trafficking. We begin with a conceptual discussion, emphasising the need to come to terms with the normative assumptions underpinning BP and the socio-political terrain of application. We then contrast a selected number of approaches adopted by a number of epistemic communities and illustrate how similarities and differences are translated in policy agendas. We present some examples of BP to highlight diverse norms of assessment and the need for a more egalitarian approach to knowledge construction and standards of evaluation.

# 4

# The Concept of Best Practice and Social Epistemology

Referring to the UN Centre for Human Settlements (UNCHS) database on Best Practices, Oyen (2002) tells how the concept supplies practical ways of partnership between communities, governments and the private sector to improve governance, eradicate poverty, provide access to shelter, land and basic services, protect the environment and support economic development. Defined by the international development community as an attempt to integrate internationally agreed norms in the discourses and ways of functioning of state and non-state actors, the concept and its introduction as a tool for the design of development intervention signify a shift of emphasis regarding learning from learning being receiving-from- above to a form of horizontal learning: experimenting and accumulating knowledge through engaging with the daily experiences *in situ*. Such a shift carries significant epistemological implications requiring attention. Behind every practice and its dissemination exists a relationship between two or more knowledge systems that may not necessarily share the same beliefs and values.

Attempts to promote a horizontal form of learning need to consider the context of social action and participating individuals or collective entities as 'knowing and practising subjects'. Given that actions are guided by worldviews and values which shape motivation and behaviour, applying what is designated as BP does not occur on a neutral terrain, but on one where different values systems and motivation may blend, compete or clash with one another.

Non-state actors include organisations in civil societies as well as private enterprises. Truong's field work in Tuyen Quang Province in Vietnam in 1999 revealed the problem of non- permeability of agricultural knowledge in extension activities. For some time, ethnic minorities in the highlands continued to plant three corn seeds even though they were using High-Yielding varieties (HYV). In their traditional local knowledge, planting three seeds is a matter of security assuming that at least one of them will grow. Because extension workers believed that household heads the men who received the training would transmit the knowledge on HYV to their wives who planted them, no effort was made to monitor men's practices after they left their training sessions at the research centre. After discovering the problem, extension workers organised training sessions in the field directly with those who farm (including women) to alter their belief on the necessity of this specific security practice when using the HYV seeds. This example shows that knowledge from research centres cannot be applied unless the knowledge behind quotidian practices of local users is also addressed.

A horizontal form of learning therefore requires an extension of the view of epistemology (as the veracity of claimed knowledge) beyond the confines of the academia, laboratories and research centres to accommodate the politics of knowledge in daily life. Institutions and rules governing a particular policy domain and sites of implementation mediate BP. Neither the administrative characteristics nor the internal culture of implementing organisations can be ignored. The negotiation of administrative procedures and the validation of the 'known' as well as the status of the 'knower' in daily functioning play an important role in shaping practices. For example, despite their endorsement of UN CRC, institutions catering to the needs of asylum-seeking minors who migrate independently must administer their activities in ways that abide by governments' principles and regulations.

Research findings show that a criterion for 'return' adopted by some countries in Western Europe has shaped practices which defy the objective of UN CRC. The policy involves the classification of some countries in transition, from a situation of conflict to one of post-conflict, as being 'safe for return' verifiable by the existence of orphanages or relief agencies. Asylum-seeking minors from countries classified as 'safe for return' may apprehend their personal 'safety' differently from the norms of safety recommended by the above administrative criterion, yet cannot be assisted by civic organisations to claim their right to protection by the host state. Minors who are unable to validate their knowledge about their insecure conditions in their country of origin often disappear to unknown destinations, without the knowledge of institutions who act as their guardian. Assessing BP therefore cannot stop at the level of mere techniques and tools shown to perform effectively. Such an exercise should consider the links between techniques of doing things with its implicit worldview (including its inherent norms of validity) as part of the consideration on what may be categorised as 'best'.

BP in international cooperation seeking to enhance the human rights protection of trafficked persons involves several dimensions of contesting knowledge including the administrative dimension of a policy and the means of validating outcomes, the socio- anthropological dimension of social entities designated as target groups and the interpretation of their needs. It is therefore important to find ways to resolve administrative tension as well as to bridge the gaps of knowledge that exist within an epistemic community (child-focussed) and between two or more such communities (crime-focussed or poverty-focussed).

Truong (1999) suggests that if we place knowledge in a matrix of everyday activities, what emerges is a network of different knowledge systems from which people choose (consciously or unconsciously) to guide their action.

The co-existence between western medicine and other ways of curing illness in Asian societies is a case in point. Each way is derived from a particular vision of the body as a body mass or as networks of energy-flow governed by specific nodal meridian points. Each system helps solve a specific range of problems, but neither can solve all problems.

"An epistemic community is a network of professionals with recognized expertise and competence in a particular domain and an authoritative claim to policy-relevant knowledge within that domain or issue-area. Although an epistemic community may consist of professionals from a variety of disciplines and backgrounds, they have

- A shared set of normative and principled beliefs, which provide a value-based rationale for the social action of community members;
- Shared causal beliefs, which are derived from their analysis of practices leading or contributing to a central set of problems in their domain and which then serve as the basis for elucidating the multiple linkages between possible policy actions and desired outcomes;
- Shared notions of validity that is, inter-subjective, internally defined criteria for weighing and validating knowledge in the domain of their expertise; and
- A common policy enterprise that is, a set of common practices associated with a set of problems to which their professional competence is directed, presumably out of the conviction that human welfare can be enhanced as a consequence."

To trace the formation of communities of 'knowers' and their social interaction with policy-making bodies and with each other the concept of epistemic communities appears useful. Haas defines epistemic communities and their role in problem-solving in the context of international cooperation in terms of commonality of beliefs, notions of validity and policy enterprises. They are carriers of scientific knowledge into the policy field: 'channels through which new ideas circulate from societies to governments as well as from country to country'. Because of the knowledge they have, epistemic communities are able to penetrate government departments and make their ideas part of policy. Epistemic communities operate only in fields of policy where science is significant. In the field of human rights, for example, Haas believes that there is no epistemic community.

Haas' perspective is useful for locating and defining the social formation of discourse and practices against human trafficking and the affiliated societal agents, but his usage of the term epistemic community requires some revision for a number of reasons. Both human rights legislation and the study of its implementation constitute a body of scientific knowledge in the humanities and the social science. Amartya Sen suggests that human rights may be seen as 'pronouncements in social ethics, sustainable by open public reasoning. They may or may not be reflected in a legal framework through specific "human rights legislation", but there are also other ways of implementing human rights (including public recognition, agitation and monitoring)'. All these activities are mediated through a variety of forms of local knowledge and institutions. Hence their analysis requires a view on epistemology that can address the politics of everyday knowledge.

Organisations such as Anti-Slavery International, Coalition Against the Trafficking in Women (CATW), Global Alliance Against Trafficking in Women (GAATW), Human Rights Watch (HRW), Amnesty International (AI) and End Child Prostitution, Child Pornography and Trafficking of Children for Sexual Purposes (ECPAT) have been active in laying the ground work for governments' acceptance of human trafficking as a global reality. Although the concern for the protection of the rights of trafficked persons is shared, tension may be noted with regard to the relative emphasis each organisation accords to causal relationship (gender, class or ethnicity) and how they view the process of recovery. Public policy circles tend to view some organisations as more 'politically' correct than others and therefore are more inclined to defer knowledge authority to them. Buchanan (2004) offers the concepts of epistemic deference and risks in moral action. He coins the term 'epistemic deference' to mean the reliance on certain persons and institutions as knowledge authorities.

Epistemic deference is inevitable because individuals and institutions depend on each other for information and knowledge to guide their action. Epistemic deference can be a risky venture, in the sense that all institutions and persons are capable of being a source of error, or of holding partial beliefs while aspiring for holistic representation. Democratizing the claims to know, and ensuring participatory methods in horizontal learning processes, should serve to minimize both the partiality of accounts of reality and the risks of transferring such accounts into action. We cannot ignore the purpose of cautious deference.

## EPISTEMIC COMMUNITIES AND THE HUMAN TRAFFICKING POLICY AGENDA

The United Nations and its specialised agencies have played a leading role in encouraging efforts to foster collabouration between different epistemic communities to implement international conventions protecting the rights of trafficked persons. Bound as they are by their mandates, internal culture, networks of like-minded professionals and partners, UN organisations tend to display policy profiles that manifest differences of emphasis and representation of the social worlds of human trafficking. Within the United Nations system there are differences of perspective, policy agenda and cooperation with the non-state sector. UN specialised agencies are channels through which new ideas circulate from country to country and shape local practices. In this sense, these agencies also act as epistemic communities apart from being policy-making bodies. In this study, we focus our analysis on a couple of agencies, keeping in mind that the groups included in this section are not all inclusive.

The following section illustrates how the International Labour Organisation (ILO) and the United Nations Children's Fund (UNICEF) address the human rights of trafficked persons including children. We contrast different approaches to migration adopted by the ILO, the International Organisation for Migration (IOM) and the United Nations Educational, Scientific and Cultural Organisation (UNESCO) to highlight key areas of policy tension in need of resolution. An observation on crime control at international level engineered by the Department of United States of America (US State Department) on the one hand and the United Nations Office on Drugs and Crime (UNODC) on the other hand is also included.

## HUMAN RIGHTS

The human rights theme is the central concern of all epistemic communities working on human trafficking. Two frames for human rights issues can be discerned. One uses the definition of human trafficking by the Trafficking Protocol for trafficked persons, and the other follows the lines of socio-economic rights taking the identification of poverty, gender, vulnerability and ethnic identity as causal factors. The International Labour Organization (ILO) whose original mandate is to protect the rights of organised labour, has extended this mandate in the last decade to cover the rights of women, children and indigenous labourers in the informal sector. Its mandate is to 'promote social justice as the foundation of international peace, specifically by articulating and supervising fundamental human rights in the world of work'. Throughout its standards-related work, the ILO has dealt with the issue of human trafficking in relation to forced labour, to the abuse of migrant workers - particularly where certain sections of society such as women or indigenous peoples are affected and to its being one of the worst forms of child labour.

The ILO International Programme on the Elimination of Child Labour (ILO- IPEC) was created in 1992 to address specifically issues of child labour and child trafficking. ILO-IPEC conducts action-research on child trafficking. The knowledge is used to support the efforts of governments, workers' and employers' organisations and civil society in the prevention of trafficking, in the rescue, repatriation and restoration of the rights of trafficked persons. Prior to the entry into force of the ILO Convention 182 in 1999 on the Worst Forms of Child Labour, ILO had been addressing child trafficking in the context of migrant workers in the framework of the ILO Convention 29 on Forced Labour. ILO Convention

182 views child trafficking as a practice similar to slavery, subject to elimination. Today there are 150 ratifications for this convention, 47 of which are from Africa the fastest pace of ratification since ILO was founded in 1919. The UN Convention of the Rights of the Child (UNCRC) also guides ILO work. ILO-IPEC's mandate intersects with that of the United Nations Children's Fund (UNICEF) whose approach to children's rights extends beyond the world of work to cover the entire social universe of childhood.

Recent reports by the UNICEF Innocenti Centre cover trafficking of women and children in over fifty African countries. The Centre hosts a child trafficking research hub, dedicated to data collection, knowledge transfer and the development of methodologies related to research on child trafficking. UNICEF recognises child trafficking as a global problem and draws its standpoint from the UNCRC. It views trafficking of children as a fundamental violation of children's rights. It recognises the links between child trafficking with a wide range of problems such as criminal activity and corruption, birth registration, child labour, discrimination, armed conflict, juvenile justice and gender-based practices such as early marriage. Thus, UNICEF accords greater emphasis on the link between children's rights, the social worlds of childhood and development.

Both organisations accept poverty and human vulnerability as root causes of trafficking. They also share a particular attention to poverty reduction and children education. Whereas UNICEF emphasises education as training for children's life skills, and monitoring of the rates of school dropout and abuses at the local level, ILO-IPEC emphasises the provision of quality education, skills training and job creation, being more concerned as it is with issues of the labour market than issues of childhood in school systems. UNICEF lobbies for child-focussed poverty reduction interventions and governments' commitment to education. All UN agencies cooperate in lobbying for the strengthening of legislation and law enforcement to protect the rights of trafficked persons.

UNICEF appears more concerned with 'the recovery and reintegration of trafficked persons', whereas ILO- IPEC exhibit a more pronounced profile on the rescue, repatriation, and restoration of the rights, of trafficked persons, the prosecution of offenders through the strengthening of the judiciary and police.

Action at the sub regional level reinforces its in-country programmes, as the organisation believes that concerted action is needed in both sending and receiving countries to stop child trafficking that occurs across borders. In comparison it is fair to say that both UNICEF and ILO have extended or adjusted their mandates to address human trafficking as a sociological problem in order to enhance the protection of the rights of trafficked persons through legal measures. Adhering to its original mandate, ILO derives its approach to human trafficking from the norms, values and standards of the world of work, now extended to cover the rights of vulnerable groups in exploitative work conditions including women and children. Similarly, UNICEF derives its child trafficking approach from the sociology of childhood and the conditions for its development and therefore appears to have given emphasis to the Convention on the Rights of the Child more holistically.

The world of childhood in the purview of UNICEF covers an array of cultural practices and a variety of institutions such as family, school, places of incarceration and militia. Diverse sites of social power undermining children's rights other than the workplace constitute its key areas of concern. Consequently, at the risk of over simplification, we may observe that UNICEF is more embedded in the cultural rights of children as a social group, whereas ILO maintains its focus on socio-economic rights of children as a vulnerable group. Migration From the standpoint of the world of work the ILO posits the belief that 'legal labour migration channels contribute to both reducing trafficking in children and women and the smuggling of migrants'. A combination of migration policy with the labour market framework supported by standards-based labour and human rights constitutes the core of its activities on undocumented migrant workers.

Its 'Special Action Programme to Combat Forced Labour' addresses issues of forced labour (in relation to irregular migration and human trafficking) in consultation with representatives of workers' organisations and academic resource persons. ILO considers a global strategy for the protection of migrant workers led by trade unions as an important goal. It promotes the ratification of Conventions 97 and 143 on migrant workers, as well as the International Convention on the Protection of the Rights of All Migrant Workers and Members of their Families. In a number of industrialised countries ILO cooperates with unions which have opened their membership to undocumented migrant workers, and with those who work closely with the '*sans papiers*' movement to provide assistance to undocumented workers to achieve a legal status. By contrast, the International Organization for Migration (IOM) is required *per pro* its mandate to protect 'humane and orderly migration from the perspective of 'migration management'.

The organisation has played a leading role of intellectual leadership on migration studies. Based on the explicit definition of various terms such as recruitment and deception and in line with the Trafficking Protocol, IOM identifies the technical differences between trafficking and smuggling. Owing to the complexity of human trafficking requiring concerted action by different organisations, IOM specifies the existence of 'a variety of bodies that seek to address it, including governments, NGOs, police and migration authorities. Each will define the problem from the perspective of its own mandate'. IOM has integrated concerns for the protection of migrants through its efforts to address trafficking (research and direct assistance) and to conduct information campaigns about the risks of unauthorised migration. The IOM webpage maps out its policies and specifies the different ways of understanding migration and human trafficking.

Human trafficking is framed as an issue of concern since 'it poses a migration management problem to governments of sending countries as well as transit and receiving countries, because orderly migration and several types of national legislation, including migration legislation, are violated' This approach to human trafficking hinges on the concept of public order and lack thereof. The organisation policy objectives inevitably bear conflicting interests. On the one hand it seeks to protect trafficked migrants and would-be trafficked migrants from abuse. On the other hand, it also considers human trafficking a violation of the principle of sovereignty, hence is ready to consider the state as a victim of unruly practices of migrants. Tension emerging from application of policy principles reflects the practical difficulty of applying norms used to categorise migrants, and raises doubt about the possibility of migration management in a situation of shifting international norms. Human rights organisations such as Human Rights Watch and Amnesty International and others have criticised IOM for its greater focus on 'orderly migration' and 'voluntary return' of trafficked people, asylum seekers, and refugees rather than protecting the human rights of trafficked persons, refugees and displaced people.

The International Migration Programme of the United Nations Educational, Scientific and Cultural Organisation (UNESCO) has the central objective to promote the respect for the human rights of migrants, and to contribute to peaceful integration of migrants in society. To fulfil this general goal the programme seeks to achieve five objectives, as follows: (1) increase the protection of human rights of migrants, (2) improve national policies to handle the impact of migration on society, (3) promote the value and respect of cultural diversity in multicultural societies, (4) contribute to the global fight against human trafficking and (5) strengthen the capacity, sustainability and effectiveness of Diaspora networks. UNESCO activities also include promoting the ratification of the UN Convention on the Rights of Migrant Workers and Members of their Families. Since 1996, UNESCO has been engaged in the fight against human trafficking, first in South-East Asia and more recently in Africa in its field of competence, namely education, science and culture.

UNESCO also focus on strengthening research capacities by developing mapping and databases on trafficking numbers

(UNESCO Trafficking Statistics Project), leading research and commissioning studies on structural vulnerability factors leading to human trafficking in pilot countries.

It also promotes culturally appropriate awareness-raising among local communities and develops training of policy-makers, community leaders and the media to better fight the phenomenon. UNESCO collects Best Practices in addressing human trafficking based on the view that 'carefully documented case histories can be a source of information and inspiration to policy makers on how to design creative, successful sustainable solutions to the management of migration'. UNESCO shares with others the recognition of the destructive role of global human trafficking, but does not conflate migration with crime.

It endorses an enabling approach to migration management and views issues of international migration from the perspective of cultural diversity; thereby enabling migrants to exercise their rights and enabling governments to design creative solutions. A positive role is attached to Diaspora networks in fostering pluralism, and a cooperative role to the state. Implicitly the state is viewed as a flexible and permeable entity, and migrants as cultural assets rather than economic burdens.

Crime approaching human trafficking as a crime is most strongly manifested in the activities of the United Nations Office on Drugs and Crime (UNODC). UNODC sees its mission to 'bring to the foreground the involvement of organised criminal groups in human trafficking and to promote the development of effective criminal justice-related responses'. UNODC specifically looks at smuggling routes, methods of trafficking, and other mechanisms of exploitation and abuse. Its programmes have the dual perspective of victim and law-enforcement but are not gender or age-specific. UNODC identifies its comparative advantages as:

1. Being the key actor behind the formulation of the Trafficking Protocol in the context of transnational organised crime.

2. Providing a criminal-justice perspective which recognises that in most cases organised crime is active in the recruitment, transfer and exploitation of persons.
3. Taking a global or transnational perspective in investigating the criminal components of trafficking. In a similar vein, the government of the United States of America passed the 'Victims of Trafficking and Violence Protection Act' in 2000.

The US State Department views this piece of legislation as 'an act to combat trafficking in persons, especially into the sex trade, slavery, and involuntary servitude, to reauthorize certain Federal programs to prevent violence against women, and for other purposes'. A key rider to the act is a three-tiered ranking system adopted in the annual report produced since 2001, as an attempt to 'encourage' governments around the world to fall in line. This system reviews governments' compliance with a set of minimum criteria set by the US State Department for the application of the Victims of Trafficking and Violence Protection Act on a global scale. Tier 1 means full compliance; Tiers 2 and 3 infer different degrees of 'deviancy'. As pointed out by Chapkis (2003:934) only one person a four-year old boy had qualified for a T-visa (granted to victims and witnesses by the Act) during the first two years after its introduction.

Since 2004 the Tier placements have been linked to penalties and sanctions that the United States can declare. Countries in Tier 3 risk facing US opposition to assistance (except for humanitarian, trade-related and certain development-related assistance) from international financial institutions, specifically the International Monetary Fund and multilateral development banks such as the World Bank; but the Act specifies that 'all or part of the Act's sanctions can be waived upon a determination by the President that the provision of such assistance to the government would promote the purposes of the Act or is otherwise in the national interest of the United States. The Act also states that its sanctions shall be waived when necessary to avoid significant adverse effects on vulnerable populations, including women and children'.

## PLURAL NOTIONS OF 'BEST PRACTICES'

The rapid increase in the number of actors involved in child trafficking and their contrasting approaches only add to the complexity of evaluating actions and their outcomes. It is impossible to find a common parameter to assign the status 'best' to a practice: parameters appear to be context-based and organisation- dependent. For instance, Anti-Slavery International 67 looks at what is 'best' in terms of effective protection of the human rights of trafficked persons from the point of view of administration of justice and enforcement of the law. It puts forward a set of recommendations for the protection of trafficked persons' rights based on a comparison of practices in ten countries. Save the Children-Sweden (2003:14) looks at human trafficking as a problem with two kinds of tension. One is between governments' obligations to protect and promote human rights and their desire to restrict irregular forms of migration (often regarded as a matter of state sovereignty).

The other stems from the conflation of trafficking and prostitution, which often leads to an exclusive focus on sex trafficking. On sex trafficking, Save the Children-Sweden chooses the perspective of a demand-led problem, and therefore would support the view that the best practice to curtail demand is the imposition of penalty on the clients, as well as the procurer and the employer as in Swedish prostitution law. UNDP has an anti-trafficking manual funded by United States Agency for International Development (USAID) covering thirteen countries in South-eastern Europe entitled 'Best Practice: Law Enforcement Manual for Fighting Against Trafficking in Human Beings'. Launched in Vienna in December 2003, as part of its Comprehensive Anti-Trafficking Training Strategy for South Eastern Europe 68 and bearing a distinct 'deterrence' perspective, the manual is primarily for law enforcers responsible for the investigation of 'criminal' elements of trafficking police, border officials, immigration officers. The section on best practices includes specialist guidance on the treatment of trafficked persons, intelligence gathering, international judicial cooperation, joint pro-active operations and specialist pro-active investigative techniques.

The manual seems far removed from the world of community organisers and grassroots workers engaged with 'persons living with human trafficking'. A major part of the US State Department annual report on human trafficking also singles out a few practices as best. Its descriptions of effective low-cost sustainable BP around the world are of mixed practices with different objectives.

For example, campaigns which address child labour such as 'Red Card against Child Labour' in Africa are bracketed with those addressing the worst forms of child labour (child prostitution) such as 'Discouraging Sex Tourism' in Brazil and 'Public Awareness Campaign' in Mozambique. And actions which address prostitution and children affected by war and conflict situations such as the 'Listening to Exploited Children' radio programme in Sierra Leone are also categorised as ones which address child trafficking.

The criteria for judging a practice as 'best' are far from clear, aside from the initial suggestion that they are low-cost and sustainable. For instance, one practice of interception in Colombia, cited as best entails immigration and police officers in civilian clothes approaching 'potential' subjects of trafficking or people who look like they might be trafficked and asking them questions, giving advice and recommending that they do not travel. The object of control appears to have shifted here from controlling traffickers to curtailing people's civil liberty.

An innovative but costly practice, which effectively identifies and rescues the children trafficked from South Asia to serve as camel jockeys on the racetracks in the United Arab Emirates (UAE), involves a random DNA testing of alleged parents and children whose 'looks' are questionable. Most of these children are trafficked through the use of false documents from their home countries attesting to higher ages, and false parents who accompany the children to UAE. Since January 2003 authorities in UAE have DNA-tested 446 children and exposed 65 false claims of parenthood by traffickers bringing these children into the country.

During 2003 the practice succeeded in identifying over 250 children from Bangladesh and Pakistan (who were returned to their countries) and arresting many of their traffickers for prosecution. Other countries in the Gulf are adopting the DNA testing of child camel jockeys and their purported parents. The Centre for Crime Prevention under the UNODC is also preparing a manual or a Toolkit on promising practices by government agencies, international organisations and NGOs, focussing on four sectors: legislative reform, strengthening criminal justice responses, trafficked persons' protection and support and international cooperation. It closely associates trafficking with illegal migration and prostitution or commercial sexual exploitation.

Practices based on the principle of crime control generally exhibit more state intrusion in civil society and direct control of the social body. Pre-emptive actions to protect the integrity of national borders are also prominent. Although preventive measures that address poverty as a root cause appear as a major concern in the policy agenda, actual commitment reveals the wide discrepancy between words and deeds, as also transpired through voices from the field. Our review of the profile of epistemic communities active in the global struggle against human trafficking reveals a way of functioning which does not entirely fit the original meaning of the concept. In its original meaning an epistemic community carries scientific knowledge into policy making, and hence seeks to affect outcomes. In human trafficking such communities appear more bound or obstructed by the 'realist' politics of sovereignty and interests of nation-states.

The knowledge generated by the humanities and social sciences does not yet seem to have made major impacts on policy decisions. Evidence produced on human trafficking is now subject to query from a methodological point of view. Processes of epistemic deference in policy choices are not transparent at many levels, and therefore the risks of making inappropriate judgement cannot be overstated. Socially meaningful ends such as human rights protection are currently being pulled in different directions by the disparate interpretations depending on which humans, which location and which interest.

Contending epistemological dispositions on human trafficking are closely linked with how international migration is explained in the contemporary context of organizations. Despite the shared position that accepts human trafficking as an assault on human dignity and endorses the protection of the human rights of those trafficked, substantive differences regarding practical approaches are prevalent. There is no consensus on the objectives of BP nor is there a common understanding of causation. What is 'best', for whom, and under what specified conditions remains contested. The choice of a particular BP cannot be isolated from the shared causal beliefs, policy agenda, and notions of validity of a particular epistemic community choosing it. The concept of BP may merely serve as a heuristic device to raise questions about the relationship between different forms of social knowledge, power and policy. It is important for organizations to clarify for themselves the epistemic dispositions they adopt in order to shed light on differences with others so as to set transparent parameters for negotiation of interests in ways which contribute to an enhancement of rights of trafficked persons.

Without such a clarification, evaluative norms guiding the search for best practices cannot be freed from vested interests. Professional evaluators for instance might look for sustainability, reliability, and cost- effectiveness in a practice. Law enforcers will mainly consider how much a practice helps reduce crime. Immigration officials will likely pick out practices which enforce border rules. Trafficked persons in search of a secure life space might see a BP as one which safely allows for migration free from abuse, which upholds norms of human dignity and which promotes equal treatment under the law. Citizens of low-income countries in search of work opportunities organization as unskilled and informal work who are much in demand in higher-income countries but generally barred from entry might see as 'best' those which allow them the same rights for mobility as the ones applicable to other categories of labour.

## RESPONSES FROM THE FIELD

The first questionnaire, structured along standard guidelines for best practices, was sent to more than 200 email addresses of organizations in Western and Southern Africa to gather information on the technical and organizations aspects. Several databases on BP in different contexts were reviewed to draw useful insights for comparison with the relevant literature on BP when applied to the anti-trafficking campaign in West and Central Africa. A second questionnaire was sent to those organizations which agreed to share their experiences, asking fewer but qualitative questions organisation on the organisations' understanding of the context and of possible solutions. The responses from the field show that some organisations did not isolate a particular practice or a particular project from the sum total of activities and strategies of the organisation as a whole. Other organisations were able to describe a particular practice or project and isolate its effects. Our discussion therefore seeks to accentuate how perspectives and practices are interwoven with an organisation's activities.

The responses also show a keen awareness of the significance of evidence-based intervention, of the maintenance of a database and of a participatory approach which involves children, youth, their families and the communities. Poverty, fractured communities and hegemonic masculinity are regarded as key causative aspects regarding the trafficking of women and children. Causative aspects on the supply side are noted and monitored but not analysed. Organisations also convey a sense of despair regarding their ability to redress poverty, and a certain degree of scepticism concerning the political will and ability of national governments so to do. In the following sections we introduce the participating organisations and their activities; then we proceed to discussing their expressed need to bridge existing gaps and to find common points.

## ORGANIZATIONS AND THEIR ACTIVITIES

ONG-ESAM operates in Benin and aims to eradicate child abuse and transborder recruitment of children as domestic workers. Its target groups are: children in domestic work communities at risk and/or affected by trafficking, trafficked persons and their parents. Most efforts are concentrated on advocating the adoption of a code of conduct among employers on the treatment of child domestic workers. It also involves the media and other NGOs. The organisation provides capacity-building for NGOs and conducts research on child trafficking. The organisation's activities and strategies include the withdrawal of children from abusive situations, their reintegration into school or professional training, sensitisation of households and communities, and data-collection by which to identify the best ways to redress trafficking. In addition the organisation provides alternative sources of income for those engaged in trafficking, and facilitates meetings between employers and children which focus on the promotion of a code of conduct for employers of child domestic workers.

The strengths of the practice include the use of computers to maintain a database on children in domestic work and the participation of children in the programmes. There is also strong networking with sub-regional, regional and global groups. Given that the demand for action increases, the organisation finds itself unable to fully respond owing to high communication costs and limited resources. There are blurred lines between the two categories of children: those in domestic work and those trafficked. The potential for replicating this practice is high; sharing experiences with the various networks has taken place. A similar project has been set up at the sub-regional level. ESAM has partners at the global level (ECPAT, Global March Against Child Labour and Anti-Slavery International) and can share information as well as experience within the network.

ESAM is the coordinator of the Comité de Liaison des Organisations Sociales de Défense des Droits de L'Enfant (CLOSE), a network of 30 NGOs and professionals. Development sees trafficking as being related to the fear of HIV/AIDS and recognises that selling children is an abuse of human rights. It sees the problem as stemming from ignorance and complicity within the community. Its aim is to reduce the incidence of trafficking and sexual exploitation of children, by training youth educators and, through them, increasing awareness of parents and children about human rights. It is forming strategies for the psychosocial education of young persons. ONG-Strategies et Développement's platform is human rights education, which has been extended to cover issues of child trafficking. Such issues are integrated in its educational campaigns at the community level, using a participatory approach which includes the children. Action on trafficking converges with activities in other areas such as HIV/AIDS, delinquency and illiteracy.

Information, education and communication activities include the use of radio and formation of groups of working children. The organisation cites its participatory approach and its multi-professional perspective as being effective, and mentions plans to make this approach regional. There is no direct support for trafficked persons and the organisation is not able to address economic issues or unemployment. WAO-Afrique has identified one root cause of trafficking as the disintegration of social and cultural institutions that support children.

Using a child-centred approach, it aims to encourage the participation of trafficked children in the design for and planning of rehabilitation and reintegration activities. The organisation conducted research in 1997 on human trafficking in Togo, with follow-up research in 2000-2001 on deeper causes of human trafficking, school dropouts, and illiteracy based on testimonies from 500 trafficked children. These reports have provided information for more comprehensive planning of interventions by NGOs and international organisations working on human trafficking in West Africa.

The organisation also produced a training manual, and organised meetings with members of Togo's National Assembly to lobby for the recognition of children as actors in legislative change and for government support to bring children back to school. The target groups of WAO-Afrique span different levels. Activities and strategies are multiple and wide-ranging. The organisation sets up reception centres for children and conducts education programmes, gives training on human rights and offers legal assistance. The organisation has initiated income generation projects and provides credit facilities, legal rights education and literacy classes for parents.

It also assists in acquiring birth certificates for children. At both community and national level the organisation works with associations of truck drivers, conducts sensitisation programmes, debates with and lobbies decision- makers. It works with ministries on the interpretation of legal texts and suggests alternatives.

By involving the communities both in and across the borders WAO- Afrique hopes to have an impact on policy changes and new legislation. The organisation cites its main problems as: high costs to assist children in the reception centre and in the process of reintegration; difficulties in collecting repayment for the credit from the parents; difficulties in disengaging children from the houses of abuse; unclear legal instruments by which to punish offenders; children misidentifying parents; the lack of qualified magistrates and border police and of support for these. The practice benefits much from the use of a participatory approach and the sharing of experiences between young people. Other organisations in Togo are already trying to replicate the practice. APDF sees the demand for prostitution as a major cause of the trafficking of women. By involving the private sector (hotels, bars, restaurants and travel agencies) through information, awareness campaigns and advocacy, the organisation hopes to influence the private sector to cut back on hosting prostitution for economic gains.

Some expected results include the creation of a network between CATW (Coalition Against the Trafficking of Women) and the private sector, and a framework for consultation and action between national coalitions and beneficiaries. Given that government action to redress the situation neither targets the private sector, nor addresses women's issues, APDF's reaching out to actors in the private sector (particularly those segments that might have a traditional interest in commercial sexual service) is a novelty. The organisation sees its practice as having potential for replication if the same problems are identified in another area. It recognises that different social, cultural, judicial and political contexts will make replication difficult.

APDF's exclusionary focus on the abolition of prostitution rather than addressing human trafficking as a broader problem constitutes an important shortcoming; it also lacks the professional ability to take up issues requiring legal reforms. These are left to other networks. APDF seeks to influence policy changes through liaison with national coalitions (national meetings of the CATW) and links global networks (also *per pro* CATW).

WOCON sees trafficking as being related to the ignorance of the community and government's failure to address it. The government is held accountable for the lack of attention paid to awareness and education campaigns in the community; also the lack of measures to address poverty. The organisation acknowledges the diversity of the root causes of trafficking, shaped by a combination of socio-economic and political factors including geographical location as well as historical processes. WOCON aims to eliminate child labour in Nigerian society by withdrawing children from prostitution and domestic work.

The overall objective is specifically related to trafficking. It conducts a 6-month sensitisation programme in a rural community through open air 'outreaches', slogans, town criers, musical bands, radio spots and radio jingles. It reaches out to children, communities, parents, the wider community, traditional rulers and chiefs, law enforcers, transport workers, government officials in ministries. In conjunction with the sensitisation campaign a consultative forum was established. This consultative forum agreed to a 'social contract' that specified the responsibilities of the community to stop the trafficking within that community.

A task force committee was set up within the community to monitor the incidence of human trafficking. WOCON recognises that the short duration of the sensitisation programme is insufficient to change awareness or behaviour. Poverty and the lack of education also aggravate trafficking. WOCON calls on the government to provide more micro-credit funds and more schools generally. The strength of WOCON lies on the use of research findings for planning and targeting; and its use of a participatory approach where the communities themselves monitor the social contract and work with various sectors (government ministries, transport workers, police and the media). Weaknesses include the inability to provide direct support to trafficked persons. Additionally, although WOCON has identified poverty as a root cause of trafficking, it is unable to address the poverty situation. And no training could be given to the task force committee responsible for monitoring the incidence of trafficking. The practice has already been replicated in another border town in Nigeria through ECPAT International, and through the help of UNICEF in another Nigerian town where children were found in illegal quarries.

GPI recognises comprehensive education in sexuality for children as crucial for their empowerment and the prevention of trafficking. It aims to find out why girls are more vulnerable to trafficking than boys and to reduce the incidence of trafficking of girls. GPI activities focus on female children and their parents with some attention to lobbying policy makers and mobilising the media. The activities and strategies include: the provision of comprehensive education in sexuality to female children and adolescents; public awareness campaigns; research and operation of a Gender Development Institute. GPI engages in collaborative work with the Ministry of Education and other NGOs, lobbying government ministries to include such education in school curricula.

Additional GPI centres in two states in the Niger Delta have been created. The girls are regarded as catalysts of change within their own community. One result of the practice is the publication of a book that documents how girls are susceptible to trafficking and contains recommendations for change. The activities of GPI have been adapted by IOM in the training of teachers in Edo State. Some hostility towards the training and awareness that the girls receive has arisen from some parents and those who profit from the trafficking. Also GPI cites its limited reach and its inability to address the poverty situation in the community as major issues of concern.

AWEG accepts that trafficking occurs to 'feed' the sex trade. It believes that women are trafficked also because of their 'compassionate disposition' towards their family and their desire to fend for family members at all costs. Trafficking results from poverty, economic deprivation, and greed. The practice aims to empower women by helping them acquire skills (personally and professionally) to open up opportunities for themselves. Target groups are girls trafficked from Nigeria to Italy as well as returnees from other areas, their families and communities.

AWEG has a number of activities including adult literacy projects, promotion of abstinence among adolescents and information campaigns among adolescents on the risks of being caught up in trafficking. AWEG works along the lines of women's human rights violation, according to which the trafficking of women is considered as one among the many forms of gender discrimination. The organisation propagates this message through information campaigns, such as the publication of 'A Letter to my Daughter' aimed at raising the awareness of the general public.

As an organisation AWEG is unable to address the poverty situation of trafficked persons. AWEG has noted that the Edo State Law against Prostitution and Trafficking criminalises the prostitute along with the traffickers. The criminalisation of prostitution has had adverse effects, such as when trafficked girls feel stigmatised upon return and do not frequent the shelters and the skills-training centres run by the organisation.

Many of the returnees manage to leave again. Similar guilds have not yet been set up elsewhere. RAPCAN recognises that trafficking happens because it stems from a culture of child abuse and exploitation. The organisation holds the belief that ending child abuse will help stop child trafficking. It seeks to prevent and address different patterns of child abuse. The target groups include children, youth, community, parents, associations of truck drivers, government ministries. RAPCAN's key activities include training programmes, legislative changes, curriculum changes and direct support for child witnesses. Training programmes on the prevention of sexual abuse, reproductive health and human rights are organised for adults and children.

The organisation disseminates informative materials related to HIV/AIDS, lobbies and conducts advocacy campaigns among policy makers as part of its work towards changes in legislation and society's treatment of children. A child witness programme is organised to help children who have decided to give testimony providing counselling and support as the child goes through the court procedures. Work with the Ministry of Education seeks to influence curriculum changes to include issues of child abuse. RAPCAN runs a well-maintained resource centre with materials on child abuse and regularly produces resource materials for educational purposes. RAPCAN's strength is its focus on legislative change, based on the recognition that such change will challenge current patterns of child abuse and will lead to societal changes. Trafficking is treated as both cause and result of child abuse.

Save the Children-Sweden has supported substantive research on child trafficking. Its action programmes have benefited from the information obtained. The organisation maintains a database of information on trafficking in the region. The data suggests that children are targets of trafficking for many reasons. Apart from socio- economic reasons such as extreme vulnerability (poverty and illiteracy) in communities, there are gender-specific reasons linked with kinship practices. State-related issues - such as the permeability of borders, the corruption of officials and the extremely high number of children who have no registration of their birth - are also seen as contributing to the incidence of trafficking. Save the Children-Sweden has also noted a marked alteration in the manual labour market arising from the pressure on planters to lower the cost of production.

Employers no longer hesitate to look for cheap labour beyond their borders given the drop in prices in primary commodities in recent years. The organisation builds its practices on three pillars:

1. Strengthening the capacities of all sectors to address trafficking;
2. Advocacy for legislation changes and
3. Support for trafficked persons who return assisting rehabilitation and reintegration.

One basic objective is to attempt to mitigate the abject conditions the children are in under their trafficked status. The efforts towards this end include: advocacy; the training of personnel and trainers; apprenticeships for children; micro-credit facilities for the affected families and families at risk. The target groups of Save the Children-Sweden include individuals, the community, NGOs, networks of child-focussed NGOs. At the grassroots level the organisation helps set up village vigilance committees, provides social workers and psychologists who offer direct assistance to individuals through reunification programmes or placement of returned children with host families.

The organisation conducts training courses for stakeholders including municipal workers, law enforcers, NGO workers and social workers. It functions within a regional network of NGOs whose personnel facilitates exchanges between children across borders. Action is hindered by insufficient capacity – such as social centres to host trafficked children and the lack of specialists in the field.

The lack of knowledge of national and legal instruments among communities and weak coordination between countries also pose problems for the process of reintegration. The strength of the practice is its clear rights-based participatory approach, its multi-pronged and multi-dimensional character. Adequate funding permits the practice to be comprehensive. But the practice is limited in its outreach: micro-credit facilities can be extended only to those directly affected by human trafficking.

The political will of governments is required both for changing conditions of extreme poverty in the communities and resolving open or latent political and ethnic conflicts which aggravate the problem; as well as reforming the socio-cultural traditions which perpetuate it all. Save the Children-Sweden is a member of a regional working group which brings together the principal actors in the region: UNICEF, ILO, UNODC, ECOWAS and others. Being part of a network, Save the Children benefits from the sharing of experiences and can support attempts to replicate the practice in other areas. The organisation works both with the NGO sector as well as with agents of the state to build professional capacity in a variety of areas research, advocacy, social mobilisation and support to trafficked children.

TDH's target groups are primarily NGOs and local organisations already working on issues of the trafficking of children, covering three countries: Burkina Faso, Gambia and Mali. TDH-Germany conducts research on the context of trafficking, assists in the development of local communication plans, sports competitions, and mobilisation of community leaders and local organisations. The focus of TDH-Germany is to bring these organisations together into a network that can coordinate and cooperate with each other. Technically and financially it supports activities such as awareness-raising, conscientisation and advocacy, and care for trafficked children brought in by the different associations. The work of TDH-Germany is linked with the ILO. Its activities include mobilising grassroots communities, awareness campaigns, income generation, education activities, radio broadcasts, popular theatre and support for children's school expenses.

There is no direct support given to trafficked persons and their families. TDH works with state services such as social action and security services. In cases of interception and rescue of trafficked children the organisation involves the communities concerned. Communities choose among themselves who will be members of the vigilance committees. TDH's partners include also the media that uses local languages such as the women's radio created and operated by women in Banfora in Burkina Faso. TDH-Germany publishes an information bulletin (about the anti-trafficking campaign) distributed to associations and partners. TDH considers one of its shortcomings to be the difficulty of working synergetically within a network; and the absence of funds specifically for repatriating trafficked children is another shortfall. TDH recognises the difficulty of addressing economic reintegration of trafficked children and their families as well as the difficulty of addressing the overall poverty situation in the regions from which the children originate.

## FINDING COMMON POINTS

The responses from the organisations reveal a profound understanding of the context and processes of human trafficking in Africa. Occasional discrepancies are found between the understanding shared by these organisations as members of an epistemic community and the way this understanding finds its way into practice at different levels of intervention. A reverse formulation of this statement appears also true: what is being done in practice to resolve a particular dimension of the problem is not always reflected in the explanatory discussions on root causes and policy choices. Trafficking in Women and Children: a By-product of Social Inequality Previous research tended to focus on the processes of trafficking and the conditions in which the women and children found themselves, rather than the causes at deeper levels (structural, institutional, culture and agency).

In recent years a deeper understanding has been developed regarding the conditions in the community and the different supply and demand factors influencing the occurrence of human trafficking. In many instances research has found that community members, parents, women or children still engage in trafficking *in spite of* understanding the risks involved. Often the vulnerability of children to trafficking is an outcome of broader societal neglect. Nevertheless explanations for the continuity and agency of women, children and families of trafficked persons remain inadequate.

The tendency is to place the onus on the trafficked persons. ILO-IPEC (2002:19) notes, "Women and girls may themselves take the initiative to migrate in the hope of earning a decent income, escaping a miserable life or supporting a family back home. In such cases, they are sometimes aware that they are going to work in commercial sex, considering this to be an acceptable short-term remedy to a desperate need to earn a living. They very rarely, however, are aware of the nature of the demands that will be made upon them, the conditions in which they are likely to be held, or the possible long-term repercussions of the activity (including reproductive illnesses and social exclusion)".

Concerning global inequality, most of the analysis of human trafficking tends to be one-sided, concentrating on the supply side only. A number of organisations (ILO- IPEC, UNIFEM, UNICEF, and Save the Children) have acknowledged that trafficking is perpetuated by both the supply and demand sides. Trafficking will continue to happen as long as there is a demand for cheap labour, domestic workers, undocumented workers and undocumented commercial sex workers. Simultaneous intervention to address supply and demand appears imperative.

## CHOICES OF INTERVENTION MEASURES

Intervention measures are dependent on many factors other than an understanding of the situation. A UNICEF report (2002:15) notes: "[t]here is a need for prevention approaches that go beyond awareness-raising to focus on development. There are, for example, no poverty reduction schemes to combat child trafficking in the sub-region other than micro credit schemes in Cameroon and Togo. The costs of awareness-raising activities may be lower than the costs of programmes for poverty reduction. They may be easier to manage and have an immediate impact, while poverty reduction schemes need long-term commitment and maintenance. However, the absence of systematic poverty eradication strategies and the lack of sustained efforts within prevention activities undermine the impact of the entire prevention arsenal".

Although poverty is consistently cited as a root cause at the level of policy rhetoric, it is not consistently addressed at the grassroots levels, where income generation activities (IGA) and micro-credit is not always available. In some cases IGAs are made available to trafficked persons and their families but only after trafficking has occurred and in the context of economic reintegration with the community.

Many organisations have stated that their inability to address the poverty situation in the community is a direct outcome of their institutional weakness, lack of resources, lack of capacity or mandate. Addressing the demand side appears to be similarly out of the reach of many organisations. Clearer links between poverty reduction mechanisms and other human trafficking prevention strategies must be established. A common policy platform for all actors engaged in counter-trafficking efforts at the community level needs to be fostered so as to combine poverty-reduction goals with other goals that will ensure socially meaningful options for returnees and their families.

Awareness programmes without providing alternatives for the community members are unlikely to help bring about change. A number of assumptions behind sensitisation and awareness-raising programmes need to be brought into the open and subject to further inquiry. Mere awareness programmes can indeed contribute to gender discrimination by demonizing the image of the migrating woman and controlling women's mobility more generally. Communities may be aware of the risks of unauthorised migration but may simply continue to engage in the activity with greater awareness of the risks. Dottridge (2004) suggests: " The most effective campaigns to prevent children from being trafficked are based on a thorough understanding of the factors which children and their parents (or others) take into account when considering whether (and when) to leave home. Top down prevention campaigns, which simply impose a message that 'migration is dangerous because of the risk of falling into the hands of traffickers' seem much less likely to be effective".

The UNICEF report (2002) on trafficking in West and Central Africa notes that: "there are wide variations between the awareness-raising campaigns promoted ... and their overall impact in the region is limited by the lack of comprehensive national strategies on trafficking. They often target government officials or public opinion leaders and rarely penetrate into rural areas or the marginalized communities at risk. Information remains sporadic, mainly journalistic and does little to educate families and children". In many cases the primary target group of beneficiaries consists exclusively of either children or women. Men, women and children are rarely addressed at the same time. Simultaneously addressing the trafficking of women, children and men can be a complex intervention, as particular needs and contexts must be accounted for. However, exclusionary practices in the definition of target groups such as children only or women only, can obliterate the suffering of those others including boys and men. The causes and processes of trafficking of women and children are intertwined with wider practices within a community.

Involving the whole community to foster an understanding on human trafficking in general and how it may have different consequences based on gender, age and ethnicity may build a common will to fight it. The delimitation of the 'girl child' as a target group based on the legal definition (under 18 years of age) is not always helpful as it does not always correspond to the sociological definitions of childhood in many communities. A focus on research on 'best practices' as a search for effective solutions should not deflect (or sidetrack) attention from the issues which cause the problem, or locating the key reasons why children and women migrate, why families and parents allow their children to be sent to far off places to work; why women, in spite of understanding the risks of working in commercial sex, still engage in it; why women and girls, in spite of 'awareness programmes', still knowingly go with a middleman into another country/area.

Save the Children-Sweden and TDH- Germany shows that it is possible to have intervention at different levels: international, regional, national and grassroots, by cooperating through networks, even if the diversity of actors involved presents its own challenges.

Networking seems to be generally good in West Africa but not immediately observable in South Africa. Many of the practices are dependent on funding from external sources. Sometimes sustained funding is not available until the practice becomes self-sustaining, which can place innovative action in jeopardy. More sensitivity among funding agencies on the multi-causal nature of the problem and more awareness in communities about the priorities of different funding agencies would be useful in planning for action in ways which creates synergy within a given area.

The need for intervention to address prevention, protection and prosecution simultaneously is articulated at the level of debates. It is not always possible to meet this need owing to a shortfall in resources, institutional capacities and networking in some areas.

Some practices have already been replicated. It is not always clear how the particular context where the practice was replicated has been studied, or how the practice has been adapted to suit the new context, but several organisations are clear about what factors are important for successful replication of a practice. Searching for 'best practices' to address trafficking of women and children in Africa has led to the following observations.

The arenas of action are both social and political. Anti-trafficking organisations and the practices they adopt are bearers of beliefs derived from their moral and cognitive visions. From the institutional standpoint – even if an organisation recognises that the problem of trafficking has multiple roots, makes sure that the planned interventions are 'multi-pronged' and 'multi-level'and employs participatory measures it cannot address the occurrence of human trafficking at all levels. Practical responses need to be scrutinised regarding the discrepancy between field analysis and choice of intervention. Responses from the field suggest that more can be done to learn from NGOs' experiences in order to improve interpretations of human trafficking at the policy level. Furthermore, policy agendas of funding agencies could benefit from more openness rather than closure to negotiations with organisations active *in situ*.

The diversity of forms of human mobility in the contemporary context of global connectivity requires an analytical approach which can explain why tendencies of gender, class, generation and ethnicity as constituents of social structures and human agency have converged to produce what is known as human trafficking. Without adequate explanation, policy tends to lurch in different directions. Reactions premised on human rights concerns have contributed to new international, regional and national legislative frameworks that oppose abusive and exploitative practices in migration. A key concern remains the wide landscape of policy issues underlying the problem, and how policy approaches in diverse areas such as migration management, crime control, labour standards, poverty reduction and particular needs of communities at risk - can be coordinated to curtail practices of human trafficking and ensure human rights protection.

In West Africa existing knowledge on specific features of the trafficking of children and women shows a close interaction between the cultural domain and the changing social, political and economic relations. Sector-specific patterns of trafficking exhibit an interface between local, regional and global forces. Trafficking linked with export-oriented agriculture and commercial services in tourism appear more sensitive of global forces, whereas trafficking linked with domestic services tends to be reacting to national and regional forces. Actors in West Africa have taken steps to build regional networks of knowledge and action to address the context-specific dimensions of the problem. Like-minded organisations have formed alliances through creating and maintaining a database by which to share knowledge. However, deprived of resources and constrained by considerations of funding agencies, the choices of interventions by these organisations are not always determined by what they know. Thus, for example, whereas unsustainable livelihoods may be known to actors on the spot as a key causal issue, criteria for funding tend to shape activities along the lines of awareness-raising, human rights education and changing cultural practices.

The few anti-poverty projects are directed at trafficked persons and only in the context of economic reintegration in the community and without due attention to the significance of the sense of belonging and dignity. Being a multi-causal problem, human trafficking cannot be addressed by one practice. Likewise no single organisation is capable of 'solving' all affiliated problems, nor should it enforce one vision of the problem as global. A combination of practices capable of creating synergetic effects and consolidating policy goals among engaged actors is sorely needed. Finding Best Practices to counter human trafficking begins with the recognition that such practices are elements in a broader process of social transformation. They are initiatives to transform a complex web of social relationships specifically those that are causal related to human trafficking. Social contexts in which the causes of trafficking are progressive and cumulative pose a considerable challenge in determining priorities and boundaries of action. From the perspective of prevention, endorsing a human development approach to ensure the security of livelihood and dignity of identity helps individuals, families and communities to resist risky migration.

When people's capabilities and entitlements are enhanced and when institutions of governance become responsive to their social conditions, voices and anxieties – migration options become less attractive. From the perspective of direct assistance and recovery, more sensitivity should be accorded to the experiences of trafficked persons and returnees. A more contextual understanding of their rights and the practical implications of their well being is called for. Regarding the knowledge base on human trafficking, a resolution of the contention between knowledge networks should be sought. Despite the consensus on key components of human trafficking (poverty, gender discrimination, disorderly migration and organized crime) there is no agreement on the causal relationships between them. Statistical information on international migration does not show trends in human trafficking. Narratives and testimonies of trafficked persons and returnees help us understand the qualitative dimension of the problem but cannot offer insights on its magnitude, scope or structure.

When common sense and/or received wisdom from historical experience fails, and gaps of knowledge of the current situation render policy choices vulnerable to errors, it is inevitable that governments should rely on a consortium of experts who cooperate with each other to maintain a certain level of effectiveness in human rights protection. A plurality of foci of authoritative knowledge offers diverse and potentially richer interpretation as well as fuller representation. To benefit trafficked persons it is important to treat the formation of causative elements of the problem as a two way process. One process involves the learning from data and experience gathered from communities, including trafficked persons themselves. Such data base can be updated and maintained by local organisations.

The other concerns the learning from data gathered on structural processes affecting national, regional and global conditions that might cause specific population groups to be vulnerable to practices of trafficking or might create new routes and destinations. Such a two-way process may foster a holistic approach capable of integrating different dimensions of human trafficking and bringing innovative ideas into the human trafficking policy field. International cooperation can play an important role in promoting this process.

# 5

# Issue of Human Trafficking

All Katya wanted was a good waitressing job. Following the advice of a friend, the young mother left her failing marriage in the Czech Republic for what she was told would be a lucrative job market in the Netherlands. She figured she could make enough money waiting tables there to support her 2-year-old daughter back home. The whole setup turned out to be a hoax. Katya never set foot in a restaurant. The man who was supposed to transport her and four other women took them instead to a brothel in Amsterdam, where she was told she would never see her daughter again if she refused to work as a prostitute. Katya (the name is a pseudonym given to protect privacy) is among the thousands of women and children whom the U.S. State Department is working to rescue from the throws of modern-day slavery. As awareness of the issue is slowly creeping into the consciousness of law enforcement and government agencies throughout the world, Katya's story is one of many being told in an effort to unite affected nations and help destroy the practice of sexual exploitation.

The issue, which is especially timely as countries commemorate International Women's Day on March 8, is one of most underreported human rights issues plaguing the world one that consistently flies under the political radar. The U.S. Justice Department estimates that as many as 800,000 people worldwide are transported illegally each year across international borders for the purpose of modern-day slavery.

Included in this number are some 14,500 to 17,500 people who are taken to the United States from Europe, Eurasia, Latin America and East Asia. The total numbers more than doubles when taking into account those who are trafficked within their home countries. Although some victims must submit to unpaid manual labour, the majority are women and children who are forced into prostitution. Some succumb to border officials demands for sex so they may cross, and then are passed on to pimps and brothels. Others are sucked in by false advertisements promising well-paid job opportunities in foreign markets. Most lose their passports and money in the process. Many are beaten. Among the few who escape, a large number are penalized by authorities, and some are even sent to prison, becoming victims all over again once released.

Many law enforcement officers are not aware of what trafficking is and do not properly assess cases, said Derek Ellerman, co-executive director of the Polaris Project, a Washington, D.C.-based organization that helps victims and survivors. Many police still today will come across a 13-year-old girl who has been forced into prostitution and then arrest and prosecute her, but let off the pimp. The perpetrators prey on vulnerable people living in war-torn regions and nations suffering from natural disasters, where despair and poverty reign. Often, as is the case with many former Soviet countries, sex traffickers are thought to be helped by mail-order bride agencies via the Internet, which make it easy to lure women into what they think will be a marriage but in fact turns out to be prostitution. Among the most recent victims of human trafficking are refugees and orphaned children in countries devastated by the Indian Ocean tsunami.

There are really some terrible cases out there, Ellerman said. It is very violent, and there are some incredibly horrible conditions. This is a very serious problem that is not just in Thailand and South Korea, as many people understand, she added. It is right here in our own backyard. Ellerman talked of residential Latino brothels in the Washington area where 15 minutes of sexual intercourse can be bought for just $30, an accessible price that forces women to perform all day long. In recent years, the work of the U.S. State Department, the United Nations and nongovernmental organizations, or NGOs, has raised public awareness and concern among policymakers. The U.S. Labour Department claims it has helped rescue more than 88,000 children since 1995 through its funding for various programmes.

Still, the movements to fight human trafficking; now in the world's third-largest crime is relatively new. In Russia, where the number of victims is extremely high, the first piece of legislation to outlaw human trafficking was signed in December 2003. Japanese officials just began to crack down on the crime last year after a critical review in the U.S. State Department's Trafficking in Persons Report. Sweden passed a law in 1999. Closer to home, in 2005 the U.S. Government Printing Office added to its long list of records documents that examine efforts to combat illegal drug imports, but the same is not true when it comes to human trafficking, and the agency's basic search engine brings up no such reports on the subject. There is some systematic research available, all of it relatively new.

The United Nations first began collecting data in 1999 through a program dubbed GPAT, or the Global Program against Trafficking in Human Beings. The program tracks smuggling routes and gathers best practices to help policymakers and law enforcement officials combat the organized crime behind trafficking. The U.S. government first delved into the issue in 2000, when the Victims of Trafficking and Violence Protection Act was pushed through Congress to create a new office within the State Department. Other bills are now being pushed through to increase assistance for victims transported to the United States and to help protect children orphaned by the tsunami.

After years of threats and forced prostitution, she was rescued by a friendly cab driver. She is now working at a hospital and studying for a degree in social work. Some people would have been better off if they had never been born. So it seems, if this life is all they have. Take Dara (not her real name). Born in Cambodia, she became an orphan early in life.

Her sister looked after her well. But one day she made a terrible mistake in marrying her off, when only 17. Thinking she was ensuring Dara a good future, she had unwittingly doomed her to a short and brutish life.

For, just three months later, her 'husband' took her to a fishing village. He rented a room in what Dara took to be a guesthouse and disappeared. Next morning to her horror she found out that he had sold her for $300. The guesthouse was a brothel. She survived multiple rapes daily for five years. When she contracted AIDS the brothel owner threw her out. She made her way to a local shelter, and died aged 23. Dara is just one of countless examples of selling and buying human beings.

According to John Miller, director of the US State Department's Office to Monitor and Combat Trafficking in Persons, some 800,000 people cross international borders each year, victims of this vile trade. Of these 80% are women and girls and up to 50% are minors all for the buying, as sex slaves. Sex tourism, according to Miller, is the driving force behind this 'commerce'. Many other victims end up in forced labour on farms or in factories. Human trafficking the world's third biggest crime after illicit arms and drugs deals is big business, he acknowledges, because many countries tolerate it.

Generating up to $10 billion annually for criminal gangs, trafficking, in turn, fuels other criminal activities such as money laundering, drug trafficking, document forgery. However, there are millions more victims trafficked within their own national borders. This form of human trafficking is difficult to monitor. Often it involves individuals who enslave a domestic servant or factory bosses who won't pay their forced-labour workers. While most countries have criminalized forced labour, it is also true that they seldom prosecute offenders, partly because police lack awareness of forced labour issues. But human trafficking is not just a matter of issues or numbers. It is about human beings including minors being subjected to unspeakable perversions daily. Victims of trafficking suffer physical, sexual, and psychological trauma. Frequently they contract sexually transmitted diseases, pelvic inflammatory disease, hepatitis, tuberculosis and other contagious diseases.

It results in unwanted pregnancy and forced abortions. Add to this: rape, physical assault, nightmares, insomnia and suicidal tendencies; substance abuse; even suicide and murder. But the health risks apply more widely than to immediate victims. Sex trafficking can affect the general public because those who go to brothels can become carriers of serious diseases. To effectively combat human trafficking authorities need constantly to improve their knowledge of just what is going on, where it's going on and how it's going on. Also, religious institutions, Non-Governmental Organizations (NGOs), schools, community groups, and individuals with influence within their communities need to cooperate in any effort to eliminate trafficking. Victims and their families are important players in this struggle too.

1. *Prostitution, a form of modern-day slavery*: Prostitution and trafficking of human beings are a form of violence against women and seriously violate basic human rights. However, clearly not every victim of trafficking ends up in prostitution and not all prostitutes have been trafficked. For example, estimates from the International Labour Organization (ILO) indicate that of the 12.3 million people trapped in forced labour about 2.4 million of them are victims of trafficking.
2. *Migration, human rights, trafficking linked*: Links between migration, human rights and trafficking are becoming clearer. Both the UN Protocol on trafficking and the Council of Europe's Convention on Action against Trafficking concur that trafficking is a gross violation of human rights and an offence against the dignity of the human person.
3. *Man-woman relationship*: Men do not always relate to women as equals. Because of violence or its threat, men often assume privilege and power over women reducing them to silence and compliance. This often results in women and children forced out onto the street. Sadly, women too can oppress other women, especially when they are members of criminal gangs involved with prostitution.

4. *Role of the Church*: The Church has a responsibility to promote human dignity – including the dignity of victims of exploitation through trafficking or prostitution. The Church must also encourage people to promote human dignity by eliminating sexual exploitation. The Conference also acknowledged the need for religious congregations, lay movements and institutions to give greater "visibility" and attention to the pastoral care of victims of prostitution. Church action to liberate women of the street: Both men and women should be involved in the fight against trafficking and prostitution, with concern for human rights its driving force. They should try to educate both the traffickers and their 'clients' in human and moral values. The Church should be able to condemn their evil activity in such a fashion that they, the perpetrators, hear it clearly.
5. *Episcopal conferences*: Episcopal conferences in countries where prostitution is fuelled by trafficking should denounce it publicly. They should help promote respect and compassion towards women who have been caught in prostitution.
6. *Role of religious congregations*: Religious congregations should join forces in their efforts to fight trafficking and its consequences. The various projects they sponsor aimed at the repatriation of women caught in prostitution should be adequately financed. International meetings of religious groups involved in this work are to be encouraged. Local clergy should also be involved especially in the Christian formation of young men and in the rehabilitation of sex 'clients'.
7. *Collaboration:* Both public and private agencies should collaborate to defeat sexual exploitation. The media should be involved to ensure effective and correct communication to the public about this problem. The Conference concluded by, among other things, urging bishops to include the topics of sexual exploitation, and trafficking of human beings in their ad limina (five-yearly) visits to the Pope; by advocating education and awareness programmes in seminaries on sexual exploitation of women and minors.

## TRAFFICKING OF WOMEN FOR SEX TRADE

Ruhama a voluntary organization offering support to prostitutes in Ireland has called on the Government to shut down the country's burgeoning trade in lap-dancing clubs. The call follows indications that the number of foreign women trafficked into Ireland to work in the sex industry is increasing. Between 2003-4 Ruhama supported 91 women who were trafficked into Ireland. Most came from Eastern Europe from countries such as Albania and Romania and 91 have been described as the "tip of the iceberg".

The criminal gangs who operate as traffickers use coercion tactics such as constantly are moving the women around the country, threats of or actual physical violence or threatening them with deportation. Women trafficked into Ireland usually end up working in lap-dancing clubs or brothels. Ruhama has contact with over 240 women involved in prostitution in Dublin alone and offers counselling, personal support as well as computer training and employment support. The trafficking and exploitation of South Asian and African children as camel jockeys has burgeoned in the Gulf States as part of the multi-million dollar camel racing industry. Thousands of children, some as young as 3 or 4 years of age, are trafficked from Bangladesh, Pakistan and countries in East Africa and sold into slavery to serve as camel jockeys.

These children live in unsanitary conditions, receive little food, and are deprived of sleep so that they do not gain weight and increase the load on the camels they race. Working in temperatures exceeding 100 degrees Fahrenheit, handlers employ abusive control tactics, including threats and beatings. Some are reportedly abused sexually. Many have been seriously injured and some have been trampled to death by the camels. Those who survive the harsh conditions are disposed of once they reach their teenage years. Having gained no productive skills or education, scarred with physical and psychological trauma that can last a lifetime, these children often end up leading destitute lives. Trafficked child camel jockeys are robbed of their childhoods sand their future.

# 6

# Trafficking vs. Smuggling

U.S. Immigration and Customs Enforcement (ICE), the largest investigative agency, has responsibility for enforcing a wide range of crimes related to border security, including investigations of human trafficking and human smuggling. In fact, ICE is the federal government's lead agency with responsibility for combating human trafficking. An estimated 800,000 men, women and children are trafficked across international borders each year, according to the U.S. Department of State. Victims are trafficked into the international sex trade and into forced labour situations throughout the world. Many of these victims are lured from their homes with false promises of well-paying jobs; instead, they are forced or coerced into prostitution, domestic servitude, farm or factory labour or other types of forced labour.

Victims often find themselves in a foreign country and cannot speak the language. Traffickers often take away the victims' travel and identity documents, telling them that if they attempt to escape, the victims or their families back home will be harmed, or the victims' families will assume the debt. We recognize that men, women and children that are encountered in brothels, sweat shops, massage parlors, agricultural fields and other labour markets may be forced or coerced into those situations and potentially are trafficking victims.

Trafficking vs. Smuggling: What's the Difference?

"Human trafficking" and "human smuggling" are distinct

criminal activities, and the terms are not interchangeable. Human trafficking centres on exploitation and is generally defined as:

- Sex trafficking in which a commercial sex act is induced by force, fraud or coercion, or in which the person induced to perform such act has not attained 18 years of age; or
- Recruitment, harboring, transportation, provision or obtaining of a person for labour or services, through the use of force, fraud or coercion for the purpose of subjection to involuntary servitude, peonage, debt bondage or slavery.

Human smuggling centres on transportation and is generally defined as:

- Importation of people into the United States involving deliberate evasion of immigration laws. This offense includes bringing illegal aliens into the country, as well as the unlawful transportation and harboring of aliens already in the United States.

ICE works with its law enforcement partners to dismantle the global criminal infrastructure engaged in human trafficking. ICE accomplishes this mission by making full use of its authorities and expertise, stripping away assets and profit incentive, collaborating with U.S. and foreign partners to attack networks worldwide and working in partnership with nongovernmental organi-zations (NGOs) to identify, rescue and provide assistance to trafficking victims.

## Victim-Centered Approach

ICE recognizes that in order to successfully investigate and prosecute traffickers, victims must be stable and free from fear and intimidation to be effective witnesses. Equal value is placed on the identification and rescue of victims and the prosecution of traffickers. ICE has more than 300 collateral duty victim/witness coordinators who work with NGOs to assist in the provision of victim services. Short-term immigration relief is provided to certified victims of trafficking in the form of Continued Presence (CP) status.

## ANTI-HUMAN TRAFFICKING SUCCESSES

Sex Trafficking/San Antonio—On June 1, 2007, a San Antonio woman and her two daughters were ordered detained without bond for engaging in sex trafficking of children. The woman, age 59, and her daughters, aged 32 and 29, were arrested and charged with sex trafficking of children by force, fraud or coercion.

Based on the ongoing investigation and the victims' statements, it is alleged that the defendants traveled to Nuevo Laredo, Mexico, to recruit young girls to work as prostitutes in the San Antonio area. The victims in this case were 15, 17 and 22 years old. After arriving in the United States, the victims were told they would have to work as prostitutes for five years to repay the money the defendants had spent.

Allegedly the money was spent on smuggling and other expenses they incurred to prepare the young women to be prostitutes. The victims told ICE agents that they were scared to leave because a male associate of the Ochoa's had threatened them with a gun; he also stated that he could find them and their families back in Mexico, and he would have them killed. The female violators in this case received sentences of time served to 18 months in prison for their convictions for harboring and transporting aliens for financial gain. One of the male defendants was sentenced to 120 months in prison for conspiracy to transport aliens for financial gain and for aiding and abetting sex trafficking of a child. One remaining defendant is scheduled for jury trial in February 2009.

Involuntary Servitude/Michigan—On May 31, 2007, a couple from Cameroon was sentenced for involuntary servitude and related charges. Joseph Djoumessi, 49, was found guilty of conspiracy, involuntary servitude and harboring for financial gain.

He was sentenced to 17 years in prison, to run concurrent with a 9- to-15-year sentence he is currently serving for a Michigan state conviction related to the same crime. A jury also convicted Djoumessi's wife, Evelyn Djoumessi, 42, of conspiracy and involuntary servitude. She was sentenced to five years in prison. The couple was also ordered to pay $100,000 in restitution to the victim. ICE agents in Detroit began an investigation in 2000 after receiving information regarding a young girl who was possibly being held against her will.

A 17-year-old girl from Cameroon was discovered in the Djoumessi home, living under a false identity and in questionable circumstances. The girl had been brought into the United States illegally when she was 14 years old. During the time the girl lived at the couple's home, she was forced "by beating and threats". according to court documents, to care for their children and perform household chores without pay. They also limited her contact with the outside world and did not permit her to attend school.

Labour Trafficking/Long Island, N.Y.—On May 13, 2007, Nassau County Police Department (NCPD) officers encountered a female subject disoriented and wandering around a residential neighbourhood. The NCPD identified her as a possible trafficking victim and contacted ICE agents assigned to the Human Trafficking Task Force who interviewed the victim at the Nassau University Medical Center (NUMC). The victim indicated that she had escaped from a residence in Muttontown, N.Y., where she was forced to stay and work under horrific conditions. Doctors diagnosed the victim with extensive bruising, burns and lacerations, allegedly inflicted by her employer, Varsha Sabhnani.

On the evening of May 13, 2007, ICE agents executed a federal search warrant at the residence in Muttontown and found another female domestic worker hiding in the basement. The second victim denied physical abuse, but witnessed the physical abuse inflicted upon the other victim. Both victims claimed that Sabhnani and her husband verbally abused them and restricted their movements at all times. On May 14, 2007, ICE agents arrested Mahender and Varsha Sabhnani who were subsequently indicted. On December 18, 2007, they were found guilty by jury of forced labour, peonage, document servitude, harboring aliens and conspiracy. In June 2008, Varsha Sabhnani was sentenced to 11 years imprisonment and her husband was sentenced to three years. The jury ordered that their residence, valued at $1.5 million, be criminally forfeited. Proceeds from the sale of the residence will be used to pay restitution to the victims.

Sex Trafficking/New York—The Flores-Carreto family sex-trafficking ring operated between Tenancingo, Tlaxcala, Mexico, and Queens, New York, from 1991 to 2004 and involved brothels in the New York metropolitan area. ICE began its investigation in December 2003 after the mother of a trafficking victim reported to the U.S. Embassy in Mexico City that her daughter had been kidnapped and was being held against her will in New York. ICE discovered that male members of the Flores-Carreto family romantically lured young Mexican women to the United States, where they were forced into prostitution through beatings and threats against their children, who were residing with the traffickers' mother in México. Victims who became pregnant were forced to have abortions.

In April 2005, Josue Flores-Carreto, Gerardo Flores-Carreto and Daniel Perez Alfonso, a brothel manager, were sentenced to 50, 50 and 25 years imprisonment respectively, for multiple offenses related to forced prostitution. In January 2007, Mexico extradited Consuelo Caretto Valencia, the mother of the Carreto brothers, to the United States, where she was charged with conspiring on sex trafficking and related offenses. On July 22, 2008, she pled guilty to sex trafficking and is pending sentencing for that crime. The prosecution has been one of the largest sex trafficking cases brought under the provisions of the Trafficking Victims Protection Act of 2000. The sentences in this case are the longest to date.

## ROOT CAUSES AND RECOMMENDATIONS

Trafficking in human beings, especially women and girls, is not new. Historically it has taken many forms, but in the context of globalization, has acquired shocking new dimensions. It is a complex, multi-faceted phenomenon involving multiple stakeholders at the institutional and commercial level. It is a demand-driven global business with a huge market for cheap labour and commercial sex confronting often insufficient or unexercised policy frameworks or trained personnel to prevent it. Nigeria has acquired a reputation for being one of the leading african countries in human trafficking with cross-border and internal trafficking. Trafficking of persons is the third largest crime after economic fraud and the drug trade. Decades of military regimes in Nigeria have led to the institutionalized violation of human rights and severe political, social and economic crises.

This negatively impacts the development of community participation, especially of women and children, despite international institutions designed to advance their causes. In addition, the oil boom in the 1970s created opportunities for migration both inside and outside of the country. This created avenues for exploitation, for international trafficking in women and children, for forced labour and for prostitution. Nigeria is a country of origin, transit and destination for human trafficking. There is also evidence of internal trafficking. Destinations for trafficked Nigerians include the neighbouring West African countries (Côte d'ivoire, Mali, Benin, Equatorial Guinea, Cameroon, Gabon and Guinea), European countries (Italy, Belgium, Spain, the Netherlands, Germany and the United Kingdom), North Africa (Libya, Algeria and Morocco) and Middle Eastern countries (Saudi Arabia). Recently, South America has also become a point of destination for trafficked persons, particularly Venezuela.

Primarily women and girls, but also boys are trafficked for purposes of sexual exploitation, forced labour and organ harvesting. Poverty is the principle driving force behind this trade, propelling vulnerable people into the hands of traffickers, who belong to both small-scale, local enterprises with extensive criminal networks and to large scale multi-commodity businesses. Nigeria ratified the UN Protocol to Prevent, Suppress and Punish trafficking in Persons, especially

Women and children in 2001 and passed a national law against trafficking entitled "trafficking in Persons (Prohibition) law enforcement and administration act 2003". Nigeria is one of the few African countries that passed such a law. Nigeria also passed the child rights act in 2003, which deals comprehensively with the issue of child trafficking.

Economic empowerment and reintegration programmes have tried to address the problem of human trafficking but they did not achieve the expected results. Awareness-raising activities proved to be more vigorous. Despite theses initiatives, human trafficking remains a critical problem in Nigeria. There is a continuing need for the further ratification and implementation of international legislation along with the use of national legal tools currently available to fight against trafficking in human beings. The persistence of harmful cultural practices, the growth of the reach and influence of organized crime and the persistent loss of young women and children to sexual and forced labour exploitation require concerted and constant attention. to better combat human trafficking in Nigeria, and the attendant damaging effects throughout Nigerian society, will require the energy, talents and resources of government, international organizations, NGOs and civil society.

## HUMAN TRAFFICKING

International 2004 US State Department figures indicate that 600,000-800,000 women and children are trafficked annually across international borders. Approximately 80% are women and up to 50% are minors. The vast majority of those trafficked under 18 years of age are girls. Male minors account for only 2% of trafficking cases. The United Nations estimates a figure closer to 4 million as a total for internationally and internally trafficked people. UNICEF estimates 1,200,000 children were trafficked globally in 2000. Men, women, and children are trafficked for many purposes sexual exploitation, begging, underpaid and exploited forced labour in the agricultural, manufacturing and construction industries, domestic service and organ harvesting.

Transnational organized criminal syndicates and networks are responsible for the bulk of human trafficking, which is linked to a range of other trafficking such as drugs, firearms, consumables, and other criminal activities including money laundering, smuggling and political bribery and corruption. Trafficking in humans is a highly lucrative business. Estimated profits are between US $7-10 billion annually. Crime networks are well organized, flexible and responsive to demand. Weak state structures, resulting from the upheaval of transitional economies, contribute to an environment that favors predatory criminal organizations. Parallel structures that substitute for state security dominate such economies and flourish through fear and intimidation.

The widespread reach of these networks and perceptions of their ability to retaliate against trafficked persons and their families reinforces their clandestine nature, difficulty of investigation and lack of prosecutorial evidence. Armed conflicts destroy livelihoods, severely damage national economies and cause mass population movements. Through heightened insecurity, wars increase the vulnerability of women and children, promote dramatic survival strategies such as prostitution and often involve the abduction of women and children into armed groups/factions. Increased poverty of survivors, particularly widows and female headed-households, is an endemic feature of armed conflicts.

Migration as a response to armed conflict and insecurity results in large number of refugee populations exposing the most vulnerable to an array of dangers including discrimination, sexual violence, intimidation, recruitment into armed forces and trafficking. Stringent entry requirements have increased the regulation of population movements. When would-be migrants fail to meet these requirements, they may resort to illegal means of immigration, giving rise to people smuggling and trafficking. The increase in demand for cheap labour continues to attract people from poorer regions. As a result, with populations moving in search of employment and with the attendant opportunities for exploitation, there is often overlapping between trafficking sources, transit and destination sites.

The commercial sex industry greatly expanded as it was globalized and integrated with other aspects of modernization. The demand factors dominating commercial sex work requires a constant supply of women and children. The commercial sex industry is inextricably linked with tourism, both domestic and foreign, and some countries are specifically promoted for "sex tourism". Widespread gender discrimination that denies women their rights, as well as attitudes that tolerate violence against women and consider women and girls inferior result in objectification and support the existence of trafficking that delivers women and girls into appalling living and working conditions.

Destitute families are vulnerable to persuasion to hire out or sell their children because they lack adequate resources to provide for their family. Girls are most vulnerable to this form of commercial exploitation. Despite international conventions, there remains indifference and a lack of domestic commitments to protect those most at risk through legislation, awareness, information and training of the authorities responsible to provide protection.

Although Nigeria has enormous natural and human resources (Nigeria is the $11^{th}$ largest producer of oil in the world), debt burden and institutionalized corruption takes a serious toll on the country's economy.

Nigeria has been rated one of the six poorest countries in the world with a per capita GNP of about US $280 Dollars for a population of about 133 Million. Nigeria is a country rich in resources but with widespread poverty. Hope of continuing education or working abroad, traditional migration patterns of labour within the country, the practice of children being loaned/sent to better-situated family members to be raised and casual border procedures all contribute to acceptance and expectations of unregulated movement. Poverty is the most visible cause of the vulnerability of women and children to trafficking in Nigeria. An ILO/IPEC report found that 40% of Nigerian street children and hawkers are trafficked persons.

Within Africa, the main destinations for trafficked persons from Nigeria are Côte d'ivoire, Equatorial Guinea Island,

Cameroon, Gabon, Guinea, Mali and Benin. Italy, Belgium, Spain, the Netherlands, Germany and the United Kingdom are the main European destinations. Saudi Arabia is also a country of destination. Road links between northern Nigeria and the Niger republic provide routes to North Africa, the Middle East and Europe. In particular, the Malam Aminu Kano international airport is a key transit point providing international air links for criminal gangs flying trafficked persons to the Middle East and other parts of Europe. Despite the widespread nature of the phenomenon, research on human trafficking is concentrated on southern Nigeria with Delta, Edo and cross rivers States being the main focal points.

Consequently, the northern sector of the country has received relatively little attention. This incorrectly suggests that human trafficking is not a problem in northern Nigeria. The trade in human beings is as prevalent in northern Nigeria as in other parts of the country. Extensive land and sea boundaries are difficult and expensive to patrol effectively. There is an estimated 1,800,000 AIDS orphans living in Nigeria, particularly vulnerable to being trafficked. There exist well-organized and established criminal groups within Nigeria that primarily deal in drugs and smuggled commodities, as well as less organized groups that deal in trafficking of humans. Nigeria ratified the UN convention against transnational organized crime and the UN Protocol to Prevent, Suppress and Punish trafficking in Persons, especially Women and children (the Palermo Protocol) in 2001. There is domestic anti-trafficking legislation in Nigeria: the "trafficking in Persons (Prohibition) law enforcement and administration act" of 2003.

The first internationally agreed upon definition of trafficking is embodied in the UN Protocol to Prevent, Suppress and Punish Trafficking in Persons, Especially Women and Children, Supplementing the UN Convention Against Transnational Organized Crime (2000), as follows: The recruitment, transportation, transfer, harbouring or receipt of persons, by means of the threat or use of force or other forms of coercion, of abduction, of fraud, of deception, of the abuse of power or of a position of vulnerability or of the giving or receiving of payments or benefits to achieve the consent of a person having control over another person, for the purpose of exploitation. Exploitation shall include, at a minimum, the exploitation of the prostitution of others or other forms of sexual exploitation, forced labour or services, slavery or practices similar to slavery, servitude or the removal of organs.

The consent of a victim of trafficking in persons to the intended exploitation...shall be irrelevant where any of the... [fore-mentioned] means...have been used. The recruitment, transfer, harbouring or receipt of a child for the purpose of exploitation shall be considered trafficking in persons even if it does not involve ...[any of the above listed means]. "Child" shall mean any person less than eighteen years of age (Art. 3).

Defines trafficking as a crime against humanity, marked by the intent to deceive and exploit; expands the range of actions considered part of the trafficking process including recruitment, transportation, transfer, harboring, and receipt of persons in end-institutions; addresses a wide range of means used, from blatant force to subtle inducements that capitalize on vulnerability, to achieve 'consent'; Makes consent to the intended exploitation irrelevant, where any of the means outlined in the definition are used; acknowledges men are also trafficked, though it emphasizes trafficking in women and children; recognizes a range of purposes of trafficking, in addition to sexual exploitation; contains rights-based and protective social, economic, political and legal measures to prevent trafficking, protect, assist, return and reintegrate trafficked persons and to penalize trafficking and related conduct; calls for international cooperation to prevent and combat trafficking.

While its human rights provisions needs to be expanded, enriched and made obligatory for all States, this Un Protocol is nonetheless an important step towards locating trafficking within a rights framework. Geographical Dynamics of Human Trafficking in Nigeria Internal Trafficking in the last two decades there has been an increase in the internal trafficking of Nigerian women and children. An increased number of people are trafficked from rural communities (Oyo, Osun and

Ogun States in the South-West; Akwaibom, cross river, Bayelsa States in the South-South; Ebonyi and Imo in the South east; Benue, Niger and Kwara States in the Middle Belt) to cities such as Lagos, Abeokuta, Ibadan, Kano, Kaduna, Calabar and Port Harcourt. Trafficking to these regions is predominantly for exploitative domestic work, farm labour and prostitution, with incidents of human trafficking and forced labour particularly prevalent in Lagos. Cross-Border Trafficking Nigeria as a Source Country internationally trafficked Nigerians come from all parts of Nigeria but some States tend to provide more trafficked persons than others.

These States include Akwa ibom, cross river, Delta, Edo, Imo, Ebonyi, Kano, Delta, Ogun, Oyo and Lagos. West African destination countries for Nigerian trafficked women and children are republic of Benin, Togo, Côte d'ivoire, Equatorial Guinea, Cameroon, Gabon and Guinea where trafficked persons are destined to work mostly as domestic servants and on farm plantations. More specifically, women and children recruited from Shaki in Oyo State are mainly trafficked to Guinea, Mali and Côte d'ivoire to work as hawkers and domestic servants. Recently, Nigerian women and young girls were also trafficked to Benin for prostitution. Most of these trafficked persons find themselves deceived into believing that their destination would be Europe.

Common European destinations for trafficked women and children from Nigeria are Italy, Belgium, Spain, the Netherlands, Germany and the United Kingdom. There is a noticeable and growing trend in the trafficking of Nigerian women and young girls to the United Kingdom to work as domestic servants. An increasing number of young girls claiming asylum in the United Kingdom are, in fact, trafficked persons. Nigerian women and girl's en-route to Europe spend many months in the deserts of North Africa and are forced into labour and prostitution to survive during the journey. About 92% of Nigerians trafficked to Europe for prostitution come from Edo State of Nigeria. Initially, most came from Benin City, the capital of Edo State, and from cities in Delta State. With the mounting anti- trafficking campaigns, however, traffickers are moving away from urban centres and into the countryside. There are also records of recruitment from other Nigerian states, such as Imo, Enugu, Lagos, Ogun, Anambra and Akwa-ibom.

The Middle East is another destination, especially Libya and Saudi Arabia. the recruitment of girls trafficked to Saudi Arabia comes predominantly from the northern part of Nigeria, especially Kano, Kwara Kaduna, Niger, Borno, Taraba, Yobe, Nassarawa, Plateau, Kebbi, Kwara, Sokoto, Katsina, Adamawa, Zamfara, Jigawa, Gombe and Bauchi States. Improved immigration records have helped debunk the erroneous impression that human trafficking for prostitution does not occur in the northern part of Nigeria.

Based on such sources, a paper from the Nigerian immigration Service reported that: "From March 2002-april 2004, the Saudi Arabia authorities deported 9,952 women and 1,231 underage unaccompanied children. Investigations revealed that the majority of the women deported from Saudi Arabia are from: Kano, Borno, Adamawa, Yobe, Nassarawa, Plateau, Niger, Kebbi, Kwara, Sokoto, Katsina, Zamfara, Jigawa, Gombe, Bauchi and Taraba States". Between 1999 and July 2000, traffickers deported about 454 trafficked Nigerians, mostly women and children, from Saudi Arabia. Recently, South America has also become a point of destination for trafficked persons, particularly Venezuela. Nigeria as a Transit Country as a transit country, Nigeria is the centre for distribution of trafficked persons to West Africa and to Gabon and Cameroon.

Some Togolese women and young girls recruited from Dapaong (about 600 km from the capital Lomé) and from Basser, lama-Kara Sokodé and Namtogou in the central region of the country get trafficked to Europe, mainly through Nigeria. Nigeria also serves as point of transit for trafficked persons from republic of Benin to Europe and the Middle East. There are transit camps in Akwa Ibom, cross river and Ondo States. Border States are points of transit for those being taken abroad. This transit may take days, months or years under arduous and deplorable conditions. For example, trafficked Togolese children en-route to Gabon via Nigeria stays in the cross rivers State waiting for boats to ferry them across the seas.

In most cases they lack the necessary means during the wait and some of the Togolese girls prostitute themselves in order to survive. Nigeria as a Destination Country as a destination, Nigeria receives Togolese women, young girls and children from Benin, Liberia, Mali, Burkina Faso and Ghana. Over the years Buzu women from the Niger republic have been trafficked into affluent homes in northern Nigeria to serve as household helpers and concubines. Occasionally, some of the trafficked Buzu women end up marrying their employers who are often affluent business people.

## MAIN AGENTS OF HUMAN TRAFFICKING

1. *Traffickers*: The trafficker is the link between supply and demand, on the one hand increasing supply through the recruitment, deception, transportation and exploitation process, and on the other hand boosting demand by providing easy access to the trafficked persons. This includes recruiters as well as transporters, receivers, pimps, brothel-keepers, corrupt border guards, and producers of false documentation, all of whom benefit as the trafficked persons pass through their hands. The trafficker is often part of the extended family, has links with the family nucleus or is someone known within the local community. Whatever the scale and means of the operation, the process is a systematic, well-organized economic phenomenon, involving the displacement and movement of persons solely to profit from the exploitation of the trafficked person's labour.

   Nigerian traffickers abroad have established mafia-like organizations of control in most destination countries. They are well-connected and operate in cartels and networks which are difficult and risky to infiltrate. They are ruthless and will sacrifice anyone to cover their tracks and remain hidden. They use codes for communication among themselves. Traffickers do not always operate in groups, however, and some engage in solo operations. The high profits and low risks of punishment for human trafficking make it an attractive business. African traffickers face low risk of arrest, prosecution or other negative consequences. They have exploited the lack of rule of law, the non-implementation of existing anti-slavery laws, and corruption of judicial systems. These lapses allow perpetrators to go unpunished. Prosecutions are rare and fraught with difficulties.

2. *The Trafficked Persons*: These include all the women, children and men who are deceived, transported and delivered into the hands of those who exploit them for profit. Poverty, war, lack of information, gender inequality and high demand for cheap labour put demographic populations of women and children at risk.

   The general lack of prospects in rural areas often leads to trafficking, and many of those trafficked come from poor communities. One common dynamic is the following: in times of cutbacks in State services and subsidies, women assume the considerable burden of diminished resources as they are subject to the rigid gender-based division of labour assigning them the household and men tend not to devote their earnings to the household, leaving the women responsible for the survival of their families.

   These women then seek to diversify their sources of income which increases their risk of being trafficked. Furthermore, they are more likely to send their children either to live with other family members in wealthier communities or to seek employment outside of the family network. This thereby increases the risk that those children will be trafficked, as the traditional practice of child fostering has been manipulated by traffickers in order to exploit children.

3. *The users*: The users of trafficked persons are at the end of a long chain. They can be either the users of sex workers or the heads of farms or shops needing access to cheap labour. Sometimes, prospective employers of trafficked persons directly approach the agents who negotiate with the trafficked persons or their relatives.

   According to UNICEF, "very often they do not perceive themselves as part of the trafficking network, although they are, in fact an engine in the machinery of exploitation. Every aspect of the various roles of users requires further research." Users may act as individuals or are networked through access to other illegal activities such as prostitution and sexual abuse of children and forced labour. They may be unaware or unconcerned about trafficking or not perceive themselves as part of the trafficking network.

## MEANS OF TRANSPORTATION

Road transportation is an increasingly popular means of transport for the trafficking of Nigerians to Europe. Traffickers going to North Africa, the Middle East and Europe use the road links between northern Nigeria and Niger. According to Father Don Orestse Benzi at the Pan African conference on Human trafficking (Abuja, Nigeria, 2001): "Until two years ago they used to come to Europe by airplane, now they come by land, by foot and by car, going through various countries to Morocco, through the Gibraltar they arrive in Spain and then by train they reach Italy or other European countries".

Transportation by sea takes place mostly under deplorable conditions. The traffickers use boats or canoes, referred to as "pirogues", to cross oceans and seas without sufficient preparation for the feeding and the well-being of the persons on board. Sea transport is used to traffic persons from Nigeria, Benin and Togo to countries in central Africa such as Gabon, equatorial Guinea, Guinea and Cameroon. Transportation by air is increasingly difficult due to heightened security controls. Nonetheless traffickers still manage to get through without being caught. Those going to Europe have to explain why they are taking the trip, but those going to Saudi Arabia justify their travel under the guise of Islamic pilgrimage. As previously mentioned, the Malam Aminu Kano international airport in Kano, serving the largest city in northern Nigeria, is a key transit point to the Middle East and other parts of Europe.

Human trafficking naturally involves the issue of border controls. Border controls within the Ecowas region are weak and border-crossing relatively easy; the whole area is replete with the unregulated circulation of people moving informally from one country to another. Strengthening border controls is a potential strategy, as less porous borders make the traffickers' job far more difficult. One should note, however, that tighter borders simultaneously increase demand for the illegal transport provided by traffickers among migrants and smugglers. Thus, any controls must be implemented carefully and intelligently.

Purposes of Trafficking in Human Beings, especially Women and Children in Nigeria, persons are trafficked for prostitution, to work as domestic servants, bus conductors, and street traders. They are exploited in agricultural work, brass melting, stone digging and scavenging. Prostitution Nigerian women and children are trafficked both internally and externally for sex. In the last decade, thousands of women and young girls were trafficked into the sex industry, especially into Europe, so that many people in Nigeria came to equate trafficking with prostitution alone and not with other forms of labour. Traffickers recruit girls from countryside markets, salons and other public places. Usually such persons are instructed not to tell their parents that they are planning to travel out of the country.

With the help of corrupt immigration officers, traffickers switch pages from stolen passports having valid visas with those of the trafficked persons, giving fake names, ages and other particulars. The trafficked persons are then coached to claim that they have been traveling in and out of the country, whereas they may never have even left their villages. Upon arriving at their destinations, they are deprived of their travel documents and made to sign agreements to pay back their Madams. In addition, prior to their travels or on reaching their destinations trafficked persons' body parts such as pubic hairs, finger nails, menstrual flows, as well as underwear and photographs are taken from them and sent to Juju priests in Nigeria to ensure obedience. Many of the girls are also coerced with threats to kill their parents and other relatives if they do not cooperate.

Prostitution in Nigeria is perceived as an aberrant and immoral act and is considered a sin, especially according to the religious teachings of Islam and Christianity prevalent in the country. In the northern part of Nigeria, the penal code is fashioned along Islamic laws and criminalizes prostitution. In the southern part of Nigeria, the criminal code does not criminalize prostitution but does prohibit the operation of brothels and forbids anyone from living on the earnings of prostitutes. Overall, the degree of tolerance of prostitution differs from community to community. For example, many communities in Edo State trivialize the issue. Trafficking for prostitution is only publicly recognized as an external phenomenon while internal trafficking for prostitution, which has been going on for decades, is not publicly recognized.

Extensive literature on the trafficking of Nigerians for sex in Europe and the Middle East has drawn national and international attention to the issue. Interventions targeted at the known sources of recruitment for trafficked persons often focus on Edo State, to the disadvantage of other parts of the country also implicated.

1. *Domestic Help*: Urban migration and poverty have saturated the labour market, especially the informal labour market, and led to the systematic reduction of the cost of labour. As a result, cheap labour in the informal sector, particularly domestic labour, grew as the economic crisis obliged every member of the family to work outside their homes to sustain family finances. The following narratives capture the experiences of trafficked children in Nigeria for domestic help.

   Elizabeth, a native of Benue State in the Middle Belt of Nigeria, never had any form of education because her parents were poor. Her brother brought her to Lagos along with other girls for domestic service work. She is employed by a Madam to work in a food joint. With this "Madam", she earns naira 2, 000 (US $15) monthly. The money is kept by her brother for her father in Benue State, for the upkeep of the family. Elizabeth wakes up at 4.30 a.m. and is asleep by 1.30 a.m. She is running a 21 hour work day, 7 days a week. She is also responsible for taking care of the house on return from the restaurant. Often her employer beats and curses at her. Obviously, Elizabeth is under a lot of pressure, she has not seen her brother since she started work and her Madam told her that she had a two-year contract with her. The young girl summed up her feeling like follows: "I wish I had a place I can go to. This suffering is too much to bear."

Bisi, now 14 years old, is the only child of her mother. She has worked as house help for three years. Her father has three wives, and Bisi's mother left her because she did not have enough money to care for her child. Bisi left her last Madam because she was raped by one of the Madam's children who also warned her not to tell anyone. She became pregnant and moved to another Madam. "I was too afraid to tell them who impregnated me because my Madam will not believe me and Uncle Bayo will kill me... nobody can care for me like my parents". Pre-pubescent girls are recruited from States in the north with a promise to their parents that they will be trained or will work and accumulate a dowry for when they get married. Girls, some as young as seven years old, are thus brought to places like Lagos and Ibadan and given out as domestic servants, beggars or street traders.

They are usually paid n 3,000 (around US $ 23) a month, half of which goes to the traffickers as a "fee". One such female trafficker was intercepted by the police in Lagos in March 2005 with 40 girls between the ages of 7 and 17 years old. "Diya" or "Blood Money" a form of trafficking currently under investigation takes place in the northern part of Nigeria and involves the luring of young children to Saudi Arabia to be killed for blood money known as "diya". The method is quite simple: the trafficker, often female, takes a child trafficked to Saudi Arabia to go shopping; when she spots an affluent Arab's car, she pushes the child in the path of the car to get run over and possibly killed. There are two types of penalties for anyone who kills another human being in Saudi Arabia.

The first is the death penalty; the second is the offering compensation to the relatives of the dead victim, if the relatives accept ("diya"). The trafficker opts for the second option and obtains an equivalent of about naira 3,500,000 (local currency, equivalent to some US $27,000). The trafficker returns to Nigeria and informs the parents of the trafficked child that the child died of natural causes. The trafficker pays the parents about naira 100,000 an equivalent (about US $775) as the wages of the child while in Saudi Arabia. Parents do not typically probe the trafficker's story, often accepting the death of the child as the will of Allah.

Many simply accept the supposed wages. There is little research on this form of trafficking, but our interviews suggest that those recruited are women and children from poor family backgrounds and rural communities.

2. *Begging*: Another type of trafficking in northern Nigeria is the trafficking for organized begging. Physically challenged or disabled persons, such as the blind and crippled, are lured into the begging business in major Nigerian cities, such as Lagos, Ibadan, Kano and Kaduna. Recently, this type of trafficking has spread beyond the country's borders to the Middle East, in particular to Saudi Arabia. Contractual beggars are often adults of both sexes. Physically challenged or handicapped persons are hired on a daily basis for begging assignments with a token fee of often no more than Naira 500 (some US $3.8). There are rampant abuses involved with this kind of arrangement.

   The 'investor' only releases the trafficked person when he has made sufficient profit. The physically challenged are often carried on their back, in a wheel burrow or wheel chair and taken around town from sunrise to sunset, often under harsh weather and dangerous traffic conditions. Furthermore, experienced adult beggars traffic children under their custody. These children are then compelled to lead the handicapped into organized begging. They are forced to do this for practically nothing or without any financial reward other than the daily meals that may be handed out to them along the streets. These trafficked children who lead beggars across the major cities of Nigeria are denied access to formal education and proper social upbringing in 1995, the Saudi Arabian authorities deported 18 Nigerian men for running a ring that trafficked in women and beggars.

3. *Baby Harvesting*: In States like Abia, Ebonyi and Lagos, many cases have been reported to clinics, doctors, nurses and orphanages who help pregnant teenagers and other women who do not want to keep their babies after birth. They care for these women during pregnancy and provide money and shelter. Upon delivery the babies are sold to couples who pay a premium for the babies of their choice. The young mothers are paid off after having signed papers repudiating their claims on the babies or swearing oaths of secrecy. Officials recently handled a case of two sisters who approached a doctor in Lagos with an offer to sell the unborn child of one of the sisters. They demanded US $3875 and US $ 2325 for a baby boy and baby girl respectively.

   Later they raised the price of a baby girl to US $3100 because of "the rising cost of living". Another case was that of the Good Shepherd orphanage which engaged in the illegal adoption of babies. Young girls with unwanted pregnancies were sheltered at the orphanage and their babies sold at birth, with official cover from the administration. There is no trace of many of the babies that are sold, and one cannot be sure exactly how they are used. The supply and demand equation is typically described in terms of "push" and "pull" factors. These factors have a global resonance, but vary in local emphasis and scale. While armed conflict distorts and magnifies conditions of hardship and insecurity and creates fertile conditions for trafficking in all commodities, it is ultimately poverty, high unemployment and lack of opportunity, the quest for a means of survival, that is the engine driving trafficking in humans.

   The push/pull factors - two sides of the same coin - factors that make women and girls particularly vulnerable are rooted in systemic gender discrimination. It is important to remember that these explanatory factors can be mutually reinforcing and that some of the causes can also be the consequence of others. More research is required into the mechanics of these causes. Women and girls are more vulnerable to being trafficked because of factors contributing to supply (push factors) unequal access to education that limits women's opportunities to increase their earnings in more skilled occupations; lack of legitimate and fulfilling employment opportunities particularly in rural communities; sex-selective migration policies and restrictive emigration policies/laws, instituted often as a "protective" measure, limit women's legitimate migration.

Most legal channels of migration offer opportunities in typically male-dominated sectors (construction and agriculture work); less access to information on migration/job opportunities, recruitment channels, and a greater lack of awareness of the risks of migration compared to men; disruption of support systems due to natural and human created catastrophes; and traditional community attitudes and practices, which tolerate violence against women. Factors contributing to demand (pull factors) women's perceived suitability for work in labour-intensive production and the growing informal sector which is characterized by low wages, casual employment, hazardous work conditions and the absence of collective bargaining mechanisms; the increasing demand for foreign workers for domestic and care-giving roles, and lack of adequate regulatory frameworks to support this; the growth of the billion-dollar sex and entertainment industry, tolerated as a 'necessary evil' while women in prostitution are criminalized and discriminated against; the low risk-high profit nature of trafficking encouraged by a lack of will on the part of enforcement agencies to prosecute traffickers (which includes owners/managers of institutions into which persons are trafficked); the ease in controlling and manipulating vulnerable women; lack of access to legal redress or remedies, for victims of traffickers; and devaluation of women and children's human rights.

Push Factors Poverty although Nigeria has enormous natural and human resources (Nigeria is the largest oil producer in Africa and the eleventh largest in the world), it is rated as one of the poorest countries in the world with a GDP per capita of about US $1,000 (2005 est.) for a population of about 130 Million. There is massive unemployment and a general lack of opportunities for economic ventures, low standards of living, devalued local currencies and a failure to meet the health, food, and habitat and security needs of the people. Populations living in political and economic instability often seek to migrate elsewhere in search of better opportunities. The destination of that migration is usually into bigger cities. The rural areas of Nigeria, where the bulk of the population resides, are not industrialized. There are few job opportunities or institutions of higher learning. Consequently, even when the children do receive some education up to secondary school, there are no jobs at the end of their schooling nor additional institutions for them to attend. The economic situation is such that most parents are unable to care and properly feed their families. Parents subject their children to various forms of labour, including trafficking for economic gains. Urban migration in Nigeria is not only internal. It also involves migration from poorer neighbouring countries, especially from West Africa facilitated by the ECOWAS agreement on free movement of goods and persons. Political and economic instability in Nigeria's northern neighbouring countries (Chad, Mali and Niger) creates an influx of the displaced into Nigeria. The massive migration from rural communities to urban centres has had a negative impact on society. In urban centres it has created a vast supply of human capital, especially in the informal labour market (domestic labour in particular), that greatly outweighs the demand. This has led to a systematic reduction in the cost of labour. During the dry season, or "cin rani", there is also a mass movement of peasants from the north to the South and newcomers to this seasonal trek are particularly vulnerable to traffickers. Traffickers promise lucrative job opportunities in the cities.

The majority of dry season migrants who fall prey to traffickers are unskilled males. They often migrate to work on plantations in Côte d'ivoire, the republic of Cameroon and Gabon. When they end up in the cities, most of the unskilled migrants find work as security guards or watchmen of workplaces and the homes of the affluent. Due to poor wages and exploitative contracts, these migrants often end up in perpetual bondage, unable to return home. There are also historical relationships that have degraded with the economic downturn: witness Edo State. There were myriad business transactions between some of the natives from Edo State with Italians when the Nigerian economy was buoyant. These Nigerians visited Italy to buy gold, shoes and clothes to sell in Nigeria.

When the Nigerian economy began to dwindle, some of these businessmen and women stayed longer to pick tomatoes for quick returns before returning home. As the economy in Nigeria worsened and the tomato picking was taken over by immigrants from Eastern Europe, the sex industry became a more lucrative venture for Nigerian women. People from Edo State started trafficking from among their own families, friends and communities as they felt it was safer to recruit from sources they knew.

Perversion of Cultural Traditions in Nigeria, as in much of Africa, the childcare is the responsibility of the extended family. This practice provides social balance and is meant to cushion the effects of poverty among the extended family members and to stop the cycle of poverty by placing the children of the poor with wealthier relatives for proper care and upbringing. In recent years, this form of cultural or traditional fostering has been exploited by traffickers to recruit children.

Sometimes, the parents or guardians solicit the help of traffickers themselves; this often happens out of ignorance as to what the conditions will be for the children, and in the naïve hope that they will be well-educated or will acquire other skills for future advancement.

4. *Manipulation of Religious Rituals*: Some forms of trafficking are underplayed and not typically regarded as human trafficking. in northern Nigeria, for example, human trafficking is often disguised as institutionalized migration known as "peripatetic scholarship" or "almajirci" and sometimes through religious pilgrimage, called "hajj" or "umra" (a lesser form of pilgrimage).

   Traditional scholarship, "almajirci", when conducted in the pupil's hometown, is subject to parental care and does not fall under the definition of trafficking. It can, however, involve the movement of large numbers of pupils, often teenage males, by an Islamic teacher (or Malam) during the dry season from their hometown to somewhere far away from home and sometimes even unknown to the parents. The pupils learn from the scholar as they move from one town to another. They are often inadequately prepared for such a journey. The Malam is frequently too poor to sustain his family or the pupils entrusted to him. Consequently, both the Malam and his pupils often rely on the benevolence of the community in which they happen to be guests. In most instances, the Malam lives on the support of his pupils who beg or perform menial tasks for food sellers and shopkeepers in public places and motor parks all over northern Nigeria.

   The rationale for traveling to the city, the quest of Islamic knowledge, is often forgotten when hunger and neglect begin to take their toll. Unfortunately, both the benefactors and the pupils are often unaware that this constitutes an aberration from international norms: this "almajirci" is like trafficking because of the servitude and exploitation that goes along with it. Though not all Koran teachers in the northern Nigeria are involved in this practice, which is becoming old-fashioned and quite unpopular, it remains common among teachers in the rural areas. Children and young women are also lured into exploitative migration and sex work via their desire to go to Saudi Arabia for pilgrimage. This is another example of Islam being manipulated for the purpose of trafficking.

Young girls from nearly all the northern states are potentially vulnerable, contrary to the common belief that trafficking for commercial sexual exploitation is limited to the southern part of Nigeria. In the north, religion is used as a means to lure the innocent just as it is in the South, where the majority of trafficked persons are Christians. Traffickers and sponsors also exploit religion to ensure that trafficked persons honor agreements and pay their debts. Recruited girls and women are sometimes forced to swear oaths of secrecy before voodoo priests in traditional shrines. This practice of oath-taking has greatly complicated the investigation into incidents of human trafficking from Nigeria to Europe. Oaths of secrecy are administered to the soon-to-be trafficked persons and their families at the point of recruitment in Nigeria, especially in Edo and Delta States. These traditional oaths involve the use of body parts of the trafficked persons, such as blood, fingernails and hair from the genitalia or the head.

Traditional priests prepare ceremonial drinks in their shrines that are taken by the future trafficked persons and their relatives. This traditional oath-taking is designed to instill fear, promising death, madness or terrible harm in the event that the trafficked persons reveal the trafficker's secrets. According to Father Oreste Benziin, the trafficked girls are made to repeat several times "if I don't pay I will go crazy or I will be killed". The concoctions taken during the oath are also believed to help attract sex customers while protecting the trafficked persons from contracting HIV, or to prevent detection by immigration authorities. Some returnees cited the taking of these ceremonial drinks as a reason for their having the confidence to go in the first place, thereby illustrating their psychological potency; believing in their efficacy they will neither claim to be trafficked nor reveal the identity of their traffickers.

The churches where the oaths are administered are referred to as "spiritual churches" where special prayers are also made for members to succeed in business ventures.

5. *Harmful Cultural and Social Realities*: A significant portion of females in Nigerian society could be seen as culturally submissive. Despite recent urbanization, many traditional social norms remain intact, and even well-educated women can still have marginal status. Women cannot inherit property, even if they are the only remaining heir. Thus, women are trapped within a rigid hierarchy where the will of men is to be respected. This makes them extremely vulnerable to the manipulation and influence of traffickers. Another area requiring further investigation is the impact of broken homes on the vulnerability of children to trafficking. Profiles of trafficked persons interviewed revealed that most of the trafficked children were products of broken homes and/or orphaned children. In 2003, there were 7,000,000 orphans in Nigeria, which represents 10% of all children between 0 and 17 years old.

   Whereas in the past parents cared for their children regardless of marital status, today many abandon their children when the marriage ends in separation. Lack of Information traffickers usually recruits the vulnerable with promises of better conditions elsewhere. The typical bait is a job opportunity with higher earnings than those available in the local community. Traffickers also use the opportunity of further education or the acquisition of skills. They promise potential marriage or guarantee jobs overseas, mostly in the informal and unregulated sectors, such as hairdressers, nannies or domestics. In the case of children, traffickers approach the families in rural communities with promises of education, better living conditions and lucrative work. The traffickers or their agents sometimes add incentives such as a provision of money or clothing. The majority of trafficked persons are unaware of the forms of labour to which they will be subjected.

Most people trafficked to Europe for prostitution did not foresee entry into the sex industry. A study on the impact of the reintegration programme of the ALNIMA project of TAMPEP in Nigeria showed that most of the women and girls trafficked to Italy were in-fact shocked by the nature of the job they had to perform there. As for the trafficked persons who were aware of the nature of their future job, they were either ignorant of or failed to anticipate their lack of freedom or the extreme conditions of servitude and human rights abuse they were to encounter. This ignorance is in part a catalyst for the escalation of human trafficking in Nigeria there is also an ignorance of the health dangers lying at the core of human trafficking. In March 2002, a study on the plight of domestic workers in Lagos conducted by Banke Akinrimisi found that over half of the respondents were ignorant of HIV and AIDS and other sexually transmitted diseases, including prevention.

Despite the recent increase in awareness-raising programmes about HIV and AIDS by the government, NGOs and international agencies, the curbing of the spread of the disease has been marginal due to the economic and socio-cultural factors already mentioned. The general public in Nigeria lacks overall knowledge of the human trafficking phenomenon. Most people interviewed for the study, while admitting that they recently became aware of the issue of human trafficking, hold different perceptions as to what it actually entails. Other respondents were clearly ignorant of what constitutes human trafficking, especially child trafficking. With regards to the trafficking of women for sexual purposes, the general perception is that those trafficked are adult women who knowingly choose sex work and thus should face whatever consequences they encounter.

When interviewed, a Nigerian lawyer in Enugu State said the following about her understanding of the issue of human trafficking: "We talk about human trafficking when we have grown up ladies, who we call adults who should know what is right and what is wrong and they decide to go into prostitution. they have at times what we call pimps or madams who take care of them and make sure that they get what they call 'customers' who when they visit them they are paid and the madam or whoever is in charge gets his or her own cut". Trafficked women working in prostitution are regarded as immoral and are presumed to have contracted HIV and AIDS. This stigmatization is particularly felt by those deported from European countries after they were trafficked for prostitution or sexual exploitation.

The probability of these former trafficked persons getting into serious relationships is diminished and they may never receive marriage proposals. In addition, they are not likely to find employment which only worsens their economic condition and drives them once again into the hands of traffickers.

6. *Peer Pressure*: Children fall victim to human trafficking because of peer pressure and lack of alternative opportunities within their impoverished home communities. They often seek out traffickers on their own initiative and are thus recruited. At a consultative forum with strategic stakeholders in the Shaki community in Oyo State of Nigeria, a child explained how peer pressure makes them more vulnerable to traffickers. He attributed the peer pressure to the desire for an opportunity to enjoy the good things of city life and/or for adventure saying, "I am really very attracted to travel to the city and do whatever it takes because when my primary school classmate Bose came back from Lagos she had nice clothes to wear and told us that at about 8.pm she usually watches the soap opera 'Super Story' on television. Now we do not have electricity or television in our house and I will like to go to Lagos to be able to watch the programme which Bose described so well."

   Consequently, some children run away with friends to find and be recruited by traffickers so as to "enjoy" the big city life.

7. *HIV and AIDS orphans*: HIV and AIDS wreak havoc in the country. In 2003, 26% of all orphans were orphaned due to AIDS. Consequently, most of these children left on their own are easily recruited by traffickers. A vicious cycle thus ensues: HIV and AIDS prevalence increases the number of persons trafficked as illustrated in the case of the AIDS orphans. Simultaneously, trafficking increases the number of HIV infections. In general, women and girls are more vulnerable to HIV and AIDS infection, thus trafficked girls and women are most at risk. In the case of those trafficked for purposes of commercial sex work, vulnerability is increased in myriad ways: trafficked persons are unable to insist upon condom use. Trafficked persons may be forced to perform those sexual practices most associated with AIDS transmission.

   Trafficked persons are forced to have sex with multiple partners. Violence in commercial sex is common, especially where women or children are forced to have sex against their will. Injuries sustained during forced sex may increase vulnerability to HIV transmission. The physically immature bodies of young girls are extremely vulnerable to sexual injury. Such injuries increase their risk of infection. Many trafficked persons have other sexually transmitted diseases (STDs) due to forced and unsafe sexual activities. This heightens the risk of contracting HIV by up to a factor of 10. The vulnerability of trafficked persons to sexually transmitted diseases is compounded by their inability to receive medical testing, treatment, counseling or other health services. Their inability to understand or speak the language in a foreign land, their high poverty and their lack of freedom may also impede access to health care.

   Weak Legal Framework human trafficking has flourished due to the lackluster attitude of law enforcement and a weak legal framework which mainly focuses on trafficking for sexual exploitation. Generally, law enforcement agents are ill equipped and lack the technical know-how and gender sensitivity to handle cases. Trafficked persons often allege that some Nigerian officials collude with traffickers by assisting them with forged documents and then facilitate their movement across borders and through ports. Law enforcement agents are usually reluctant to investigate violent crimes, especially those against women and children who are unable to pay the costs of investigations or bribe the investigating officers. Thus, perpetrators of rape, sexual assault, domestic violence and human trafficking largely go unpunished in Nigeria.

As for foreign trafficked persons, they are often treated as illegal immigrants and deported without thorough investigation. As a result, a combination of corrupt officials, complicit authorities, and weak laws combine to guarantee impunity for traffickers while increasing the plight of trafficked persons. Many non-governmental organizations and women's right organizations continue to protest against the government's inability to prosecute well-known traffickers: the conviction of traffickers is quite rare, and even if convicted they are typically released within a short period of time. Restrictive Migratory Policies the global economic inequality between the northern and southern hemispheres is another important factor underlying human trafficking. Because of their relative wealth, those from the north can easily migrate while those from the South, coming from relative poverty, face stronger migratory barriers.

When, in the 1970s, the Nigerian economy was booming, Nigerians had easy access to many countries in the north. For those businessmen and women from Edo State who spent huge sums of money in Italy, an Italian visa was not difficult to obtain. Today, migration for Nigerians is much more difficult. More generally, people living in states of deprivation seek to improve their lives. This creates opportunity for exploitation by traffickers who capitalize on their misfortune. Restrictive migratory policies contribute to human trafficking in Nigeria as migrants often rely on traffickers offering false hopes of future gains. Moreover, the intensification of border controls in wealthier countries elevates the risks associated with illegal migration, thereby creating demand for the perceived sophistication of human traffickers. Thus, the greater the barriers to migration, the more sought after and expensive the traffickers' services and the more lucrative the trafficking business becomes. It should therefore be explored whether the creation of more open and legal channels of migration to western countries might not greatly reduce human trafficking.

## PULL FACTORS NEED FOR LOW-SKILLED LABOUR

The global reach and scale of trafficking in humans is the "underside of globalization". Globalization has created powerful market demand for cheap, low-skilled labour in sectors such as agriculture, food processing, construction, domestic service, labour-intensive manufacturing, home health care, sex work, the service sector in general, and the entertainment sector (circuses, begging, camel jockeying). Such demand exists in both industrialized and developing countries. The types of work where trafficked labour is used tend to be located in sectors where it is easier to maintain highly exploitative working conditions that are gross violations of human rights and labour standards, in locations and conditions that are difficult to monitor. High Profits Modern day slavery thrives because of its profitability.

The UN estimates it generates US $7-$10 billion annually, the third largest profits behind arms dealing and narcotics. It is also easier to move human cargo across borders than drugs or weapons which are seized when found. Human beings can be constantly re-used and re-trafficked not so for drugs. Trafficking is, by definition, a complex, clandestine, underground business, constantly changing and evolving both in response to demand and to remain sufficiently flexible to elude arrest and prosecution. Low Risk By its very nature trafficking is secret and dangerous, (which helps explain the inadequacy of reliable information). victims for retaliation by traffickers or recrimination within their families and villages (which often provided the funds for the journeys they anticipated and take the woman to a job that could help support the family) and the stigma of prostitution. As a result few will bear witness against the traffickers.

Fear and mistrust of police, the lack of documentation and fear of complicity also play a part in maintaining the victim's silence. Most victims are poor, illiterate, from marginalized populations and are ignorant of their rights. Traffickers exploit not only bodies but the deepest anxieties and disadvantageous life conditions of the victims. The adoption trade, the demand for organs and body-parts and the need for child-soldiers in armed conflict are other common pull factors that would require more research to conclude if they apply for the Nigerian case. The infrastructure and trends associated with a rapidly globalizing world such as increasingly open borders, better transport and increased overall migration flows complement the forces of supply and demand that underlie trafficking. Globalization has provided the impetus to both those who wish to migrate and those who traffic.

## LEGAL FRAMEWORK AND HUMAN TRAFFICKING

The main network of collaboration for West African countries is the ECOWAS Plan of action of 2002. This Plan calls for countries to ratify and fully implement crucial international instruments of ECOWAS and the United nations that strengthen laws against human trafficking and protect trafficked persons, especially women and children. This plan is made up of the following actions: Prevention and awareness raising Protection and support of trafficked persons collection, exchange and analysis of information. Specialization and training establishment of efficient mechanisms of travel and identity documents delivery. Monitoring and evaluation of the initial Plan of action at the sub regional level, Nigeria is a leading member of ECOWAS and has endorsed the ECOWAS interim Plan of action to combat trafficking in human beings

2002-2003. Nigeria is also committed to upholding the Plan of action as specified in the Libreville common Platform Declaration to combat trafficking in West and central Africa. Nigeria also subscribed to the OUAGADOUGOU action Plan to combat trafficking in human beings especially women and children adopted on 28th November 2002.

Additional agreements with other governments in the region have also been reached. There is a Memorandum of Understanding (MoU) between the governments of Benin republic and Nigeria, which compels the two governments to:

- Work out effective cooperation on human trafficking;
- Identify, investigate and prosecute agents and traffickers;
- Protect trafficked persons and return them promptly to their countries of origin.

This process began in Lagos in March 2004. A second meeting was held in Cotonou in June 2004. An inter-country commission should be created as well as mechanisms of collaboration in the struggle against trafficking. More recently in July 2005, Côte d'ivoire, Liberia, Burkina Faso, Guinea, Niger, Mali, Nigeria and Benin signed a multilateral agreement on child trafficking in West Africa. The Nigerian government also recently started working with destination countries such as Italy and Great Britain in its bid to protect trafficked persons and punish traffickers. Memorandum of Understanding was signed in November 2004 between Nigeria and Great Britain, allowing for the extradition of offenders to their home countries to face appropriate charges and punishment. Nigeria also signed a Memorandum of agreement with Italy in September 2000. This agreement established a comprehensive legal framework for the repatriation of illegal Nigerian immigrants, and especially women, from Italy to Nigeria.

According to this agreement, the Italian government provides technical training for Nigerian policemen while also helping in the fight against HIV and AIDS. The HIV and AIDS programme focuses on Nigerian women involved in prostitution who were illegally trafficked into Italy. Since these women are repatriated to Nigeria, the programme provides them with psychological and medical support, thus encouraging them to consider repatriation as a way of starting a new life. National Legal Instruments certain chapters of the constitution provide protection for vulnerable groups including women and children. However, the sanctions against infringements of these provisions are too weak. Criminals are frequently allowed to escape serious human rights abuses with impunity. The result is a distrust of the legal system and its punishments. Consequently, there is a need for strong institutional tools to identify and punish human traffickers. The convention on the rights of the child was ratified by Nigeria and implemented by the child rights act of 2003. The child rights act deals comprehensively with the issue of child trafficking in Nigeria.

Unfortunately, this act has not been adopted by all the States of the Federation and so its effectiveness cannot be fully measured. Trafficking in women was criminalized in Nigeria by the criminal code in 1904 and the penal code in 1960. However, the criminal penal codes did not deal with the issue comprehensively enough, failing to accurately define what constitutes trafficking and leaving its various forms unaddressed. Instead, they only defined those offences related to the external and internal trafficking for prostitution and slavery.

Section 279 of the Penal code reads: "Whoever imports, exports, removes, buys, sells, disposes, traffics or deals in any person as a slave or accepts, receives or detains in any person against his will any person as a slave shall be punished with imprisonment for a term which may extend to fourteen years and shall also be liable to a fine". Nigeria is one of the few countries in Africa to have passed a national law against trafficking, the "trafficking in Persons (Prohibition) law enforcement and administration act 2003" enacted by the national assembly.

This law addresses the issue of human trafficking in Nigeria in a comprehensive manner. It also establishes the "national agency for Prohibition of traffic in Persons and other related Matters" (NAPTIP), which the Nigerian Government set up in august 2003. Section 4 of the Nigerian trafficking law empowers the NAPTIP to coordinate all the laws on trafficking in persons in the country. Thus, all laws on human trafficking at the state level became subordinate to the national law on trafficking.

Although Nigeria's trafficking law provides a unified approach for the first time, it is not without its shortcomings. The law adopts the definition of trafficking in persons as contained in the Palermo Protocol but deals more extensively with trafficking for prostitution and sexual exploitation than with trafficking for other forms of labour. This greatly limits its scope. Moreover, there are lapses in the provisions of the Nigerian trafficking law for the protection of trafficked persons and witnesses. It thereby falls short of the recommended human rights standard approach.

While it is noteworthy that the law criminalizes the transport of potentially trafficked persons by any commercial carrier with knowledge of the trafficking transaction, no commercial carrier has ever been charged. Though still young and in need of necessary infrastructures for the effective execution of its mandate, NAPTIP has succeeded in effecting some arrests and prosecutions.

In august 2004, for example, the agency prosecuted and convicted a woman trafficker in the Benin City High court in Edo State of Nigeria and as at February 2006, NAPTIP's efforts have yielded seven convictions: three in Benin City and two in Kano, two in Ijebuigbo Ogun State. There are also multiple cases pending that raise public awareness. NAPTIP also collaborates with the Nigerian immigration office, the police and NGOs and has established offices across the country.

To date a total of four offices have been created: one each in Lagos, Benin city, Uyo and Kano. Two shelters were also set up in Lagos and Benin City in addition to a mini-shelter in Abuja. There is also a national anti-child trafficking network operating in 22 states of Nigeria with the support of the United

States Department of State and UNICEF.

Finally, both the police and immigration service have established anti- trafficking Units located at exit and entry points for trafficking and the Kano immigration command now issues annual reports of repatriations through the Kano airport. NAPTIP carries out the following actions: research projects to discover new and emerging trends and while better clarifying the old, preventive measures, awareness raising campaigns, deterrent strategic arrests, investigation, court prosecution and conviction of offenders, team approach to complex, multi-dimensional, multi-faceted and underground criminal activity, bilateral and multilateral efforts. NAPTIP works closely with foreign embassies and consulates in Nigeria and Nigerian embassies and consulates abroad, ECOWAS and the United nations.

## COUNSELLING AND REHABILITATION OF TRAFFICKED PERSONS

Legal Instruments at States Level in accordance with the national law allowing individual states the right to amend, Edo State recently added new provisions to the criminal code. These provisions had some positive effects: for the first time they made it a crime for third parties, i.e. sponsors and traditional priests, to facilitate the secret oath ceremony and/ or to participate in it. Unfortunately, the Edo State amendment also criminalized prostitution, thereby alienating trafficked persons working in prostitution. Since the adoption of this law, there is no evidence that trafficking for prostitution in Edo State has been reduced. In fact, as of April 2004 the majority of repatriated trafficked persons for prostitution from Europe and West Africa were from Edo State. Also, 25 trafficked Nigerian women were recently deported from the republic of Benin and 23 of them were from Edo State. There have been no convictions since the enactment of this law.

The amendment also provided for compulsory STDs and HIV tests for deported trafficked persons. This provision violates international human rights standards which permit testing for HIV only with the informed consent of the individual nonetheless, state liaison offices are given details of trafficked persons including their HIV and AIDS status for record purposes and "there is a standing order that such deportee victims should be prevented from traveling outside Nigeria." Anti-migratory policies such as not issuing passports to single females from Edo State below the age of 25 years have not had any effect on the trafficking of Edo girls. Instead, traffickers have found other means of getting passports and visas for trafficked persons. However, the policy has succeeded in discouraging and frustrating women from Edo State from traveling out of the country to pursue legitimate ventures, violating their fundamental rights. With an increased awareness of human trafficking, other Nigerian States are creating laws in response.

There is already a law in Enugu State against child abuse that bans child trafficking. Efforts are also underway to arrest and prosecute traffickers. Unfortunately, few cases have been fully prosecuted. Poverty is a major cause of human trafficking and measures addressing poverty are crucial. Though the Nigerian government has created many programmes to alleviate poverty the results have not had a significant impact on the people, particularly women and children. During the military rule that lasted until 1999 there were successive Government initiated policies and programmes such as the People's Bank, the National Directorate for Employment (NDE) and the Family economic advancement Programme (FEAP). Since civilian democratic rule, the following programmes were also introduced: the national Poverty eradication Programme (NAPEP), loans for the purchase of shares in companies, micro-credit for farmers and small and medium scale entrepreneurs.

More recently, the Nigerian government introduced the National economic Empowerment Development Strategy (NEEDS) to address the economic situation of the people and each State is simultaneously developing States Economic Development Strategies (SEEDS). Women are rarely involved in the planning, implementation and monitoring of the various government programmes that address poverty. Consequently, the programmes fail to take into account the needs of women.

Thus, the government is struggling to implement the roads, potable water, housing and electricity that enhance the economic productivity of women, especially in the rural communities, because it is doing so without their input. These failures undermine the political will to reduce poverty in the country. Other factors also impede the access of women to the programmes for economic advancement. These include large family sizes, lack of education, lack of land ownership, and various forms of institutionalized and cultural violence against women's rights. Although the Nigerian constitution technically guarantees the socio-economic rights of its citizens, it is difficult for women to challenge the infringements of their rights in the courts.

Another major challenge lies in the effective implementation of programmes addressing the needs of children. Since the 1990s there have been policies for free education that have not been effectively implemented. As a result, parents still pay fees for classes, uniforms and supplies. In 2003, the federal government adopted the Universal Basic education (UBE) policy.

The UBE policy made it free and compulsory for every child to attend school up to the junior secondary level. It also punishes the parents or guardians of children who are found on the streets and not attending school during school hours with imprisonment. Since the adoption of this policy, however, no parents have been arrested or prosecuted despite the thousands of children, including trafficked children, found hawking on the streets. None of these trafficked children have been questioned as to their parents or guardians. The UBE policy has the potential to help prevent child trafficking. If the UBE policy were to be correctly implemented, more children could be put back into the classroom and removed from states of extreme vulnerability to traffickers.

This law is still at the experimental stage, however, and many states complain about inadequate funding. International organizations as well as foreign governments have actively cooperated with the Nigerian government and NGOs to alleviate poverty in Nigeria.

Agencies such as UNICEF, ILO, UNIFEM, USAID, DFID, the European Union commission and the British council have various programmes that tackle the problem of poverty in the country. As for the NGOs, their efforts are manifold. Seed loans, grants for shares acquisition, micro-credit, skills training, initiation of accounting for women's work in the GDP, personal empowerment and adult literacy education schemes are just some of the programmes offered.

Research and the Creation of Awareness the Government recognizes the role that a lack of awareness plays in the escalation of human trafficking in Nigeria and established the national agency for Prohibition of traffic in Persons and other related Matters (NAPTIP), an agency charged, among other things, with the research of, and raising of awareness about, the issue of human trafficking in the country.

Until recently in Nigeria, research on trafficking in persons was either inadequate or unavailable. Media reports were the main sources used to estimate the extent of trafficking in persons and those reports often underestimated the issue.

The overall lack of adequate gender-specific data and statistics on the prevalence of trafficking in persons still makes it difficult to monitor the evolution of the phenomenon and design strategies to combat it. in March 2005, the Women's consortium of Nigeria (WOCON) and Women Advocates Research and Documentation center (WARDC) were among the four non-governmental organizations in Lagos commissioned by the international labour organization's action Program against Human trafficking and Forced labour in West Africa (ILO/PATWA) to conduct a baseline study in Lagos on trafficking in persons for the purpose of child labour.

Such studies are of tremendous value and enhance the available data on human trafficking in Nigeria, thus allowing for awareness-building campaigns based on solid facts. International organizations, in collaboration with NGOs, have also implemented awareness-raising campaigns to prevent human trafficking in Nigeria. The project "trafficking from Nigeria to Italy: Program of action against trafficking in minors and young women from Nigeria to Italy for the purpose of sexual exploitation" implemented by the United Nations Interregional Crime and Justice research institute (UNICRI), in collaboration with United nations office on Drugs and crime, and supported by the Italian Ministry for Foreign affairs (Italian Development cooperation) is particularly noteworthy.

This project raises awareness across Nigeria and Italy. In particular, it includes: a campaign in Italy in cooperation with RAI (Italian national television) for the production of a video spot targeting both the male/potential clients of trafficked persons and audience at large (broadcast on the RAI channels starting on 3 April 2004); three campaigns in Edo State (Nigeria), one of which is specifically intended to reach minors.

A network of six local NGOs (coalition against human trafficking) was created for the organization of this campaign. It includes the committee for the Support of the Dignity of Women (COSUDOW), the international reproductive rights research action Group (IRRRAG), the African Women empowerment Guild (AWEG), the national council of Women Societies (NCWS), idea renaissance and Girls Power initiative (GPI). Apart from the use of training and education workshops and materials, both the Government and NGOs use the media, newspaper, on-line journals, radio and television, to sensitize the population to the issue of human trafficking.

A television drama entitled "IZOZO" runs on national television under the sponsorship of two NGOs and deals with human trafficking. Radio programmes and informational announcements are aired by some NGOs in Benin City, Edo State and other parts of Nigeria. The Government agency NAPTIP also airs informational announcements on television and radio nationwide.

Reintegration Programmes to date, there is no significant programme for the reintegration of internally trafficked or repatriated children. As for foreign children trafficked to Nigeria, the policy is that of a quick return to their home country without adequately assessing their needs or choice or willingness to return.

Many trafficked children have lost touch with their home or may not have any left. Lacking the necessary social services, many trafficked children do not receive the necessary assistance to help recover from the abuses suffered. This help is essential though because deported trafficked persons are at a higher risk of being re-trafficked and are often severely traumatized. NGOs, in collaboration with their international partners, have attempted to facilitate the reintegration of trafficked persons and their relatives through education, both formal and informal, skill acquisition and the establishment of income generating cooperatives and seed grants.

Between 2001 and 2003, the international labour organization (ILO)/ international Programme for the elimination of child labour (IPEC) in collaboration with Nigerian NGOs engaged in a programme for the removal and rehabilitation of children involved in the worst forms of labour such as domestic work, prostitution, bus driving, street children and beggars. Most of these children had been trafficked.

The programme also targeted the economic empowerment of parents and relatives of trafficked children. Similarly the ILO/IPEC, under its capacity-building programme, targeted the trafficked children and their parents through the provision of formal education and skill acquisition as well as income generation and support. These efforts helped to reintegrate some trafficked persons and to prevent further human trafficking by improving the economic conditions in rural areas.

Some of the children returned to schools and have since continued with their education. Parents in rural communities of Idiroko and Ajegunle in Ogun State of Nigeria also started businesses producing tie-dyed cloth in commercial quantities as members of cooperative groups. Cooperative groups producing bar and powdered soap as well as body cream also formed in Nkalagu, Ntezi and Ezilo in Ebonyi State and have turned a profit. These activities generate income and improve the local economy, thereby making the community less susceptible to traffickers.

Trafficking has a complex socio-economic and political

basis linked to larger, global processes. It is not simply a social or moral problem to be treated with casual initiatives, as they do not address poverty or related issues of vulnerability and discrimination in strategic or sustainable ways. Trafficking is a development concern, which requires a balanced, layered and integrated approach, built on a foundation of rights-based principles and standards. UNESCO focuses its recommendations on the prevention side of the fight against human trafficking.

Prevention requires long-term thinking and interventions on three levels, primary (stopping things before they happen), secondary (limiting the number of cases that occur) and tertiary (limiting the extent of the cases and their damaging impact). The following recommendations are proposed in compliance with this requirement:

Further ratify international legal instruments aimed at protecting human rights and combating human trafficking, including the convention on the Protection of the rights of all Migrant Workers and Members of their Families (1990), the optional Protocol to the CRC on the Sale of children, Child Prostitution and Child Pornography (2000) effectively implement all of the ratified international laws and regulations, in particular the Palermo Protocol (2000), the UNCRC, the ILO convention no. 182 and the CEDAW, in order to provide an environment conducive to the elimination of human trafficking in Nigeria. The focus must be on all forms of trafficking including trafficking in children and not limited to trafficking for prostitution and sexual exploitation.

Implement the Memorandum of Understanding signed between the Federal Government and transit and destination countries. Continue regional and international cooperation between NGOs and government institutions and honor the existing bilateral agreements to uphold international human rights.

Harmonize laws against trafficking at the regional level, especially between English and French speaking countries and encourage all the countries in the region to enact laws to fight trafficking in persons where they have not done so. Adopt and implement the child rights act of 2003 in all Nigerian States. Revise anti-trafficking measures and laws so as to address all forms of trafficking as well as the protection of trafficked persons. Replace anti-migratory policies with policies that inform and empower citizens migrate safely. At the national level it may be too early to rush into immediate reform as the laws are still in an early stage, thus some further experience is necessary in order to identify grey areas.

Link up local law enforcement agencies with Interpol when dealing with the more complex problems associated with human trafficking. Give a human face to the poverty alleviation programmes with active participation and access available to all, especially women at the lowest level of poverty. Implement a peer review mechanism at the ECOWAS level to ensure that every member state is working hard to improve its economy in order to eradicate poverty. Carry out more policy-oriented research on the various manifestations of human trafficking in Nigeria, in particular on socio-cultural factors increasing vulnerability. There is a need for the different agencies including the Hajj Board, the Department of immigration and the police to check the harmful effects of the annual pilgrimage on human trafficking in Nigeria.

Develop concerted and clearly articulated strategies to combat human trafficking in Nigeria along with a national plan of action and reliable information with the active collaboration of all strategic stakeholders such as the government, NGOs, international agencies, as well as representatives from urban and rural communities. Create anti-trafficking watchdog committees in rural areas across Nigeria. Such efforts should require the cooperation of community based organizations (CBOs) and law enforcement agents such as the Police and immigration Departments. Give funds to all anti-trafficking agencies including NAPTIP, the police and immigration to support their actions and improve efficiency. This measure would enable NAPTIP to ensure speedy prosecution of trafficking cases.

Establish witness protection programmes to encourage and protect trafficked persons who act as witnesses. Set up policies to create jobs for young graduates and school dropouts in Nigeria. The skill acquisition programmes of the government must be designed to meet the needs of the Nigerian people create resource centres for the skills acquisition of rescued trafficked persons. Develop facilities and social services for the reception, protection and reintegration of trafficked persons to prevent as much as possible the re-trafficking of the trafficked persons. Further strengthen NGO networks and build alliances with migrant workers, including those in domestic work or prostitution, for the protection of the trafficked persons amongst them.

Raising and training in cooperation with UN agencies (UNESCO, UNICEF), implement the Universal Basic Education (UBE) Programme, which mandates free and compulsory education for every child up to junior secondary school level. Establish a community education program for the prevention of child abuse and trafficking, with children as the main actors of the program. The initiative should consist of awareness-building in schools and elsewhere through drama, song, dance, sports, speeches and debates on harmful practices using children. Develop awareness raising and educational courses about HIV and AIDS and human trafficking to better inform the public about the mutually reinforcing effects of these two phenomena. Train community leaders regarding the manipulation of religious practice in human trafficking. Train community leaders on gender issues to address the perceptions of the role of women and men and how those perceptions relate to the phenomenon of trafficking. Involve traditional and religious leaders in the fight against trafficking and forced labour as these phenomena are often linked to customary practices and beliefs.

Train paralegal staff to work in communities to assist trafficked persons. Provide adequate training for police officers to sensitive them about trafficking, in particular regarding the causes of trafficking, the modus operandi of syndicates, the profile of trafficked persons and traffickers and how to identify and investigate the legal and social implications of the problem within and outside the country. Educate recipient communities of repatriated trafficked persons so that they accept them without unnecessary and unfair stigmatization. This would prevent the re-trafficking of the repatriated persons. Populations vulnerable to trafficking are growing in Africa, which increases the supply of potential victims for traffickers and the damaging effects on all segments of African society.

Some of the outcomes are likely to be: Irretrievable depletion of human capital negative effect on labour markets, denial of access to education necessary to break the cycle of poverty and illiteracy that creates trafficking conditions. National labour force ill-equipped to compete in global economy where success is based on skilled workers. Fewer people left to care for elderly and sick. Loss of human resources elsewhere, to other countries, undermining public health AIDS cost to public health system, exposure to AIDS, STD, violence, dangerous working conditions, poor nutrition, addictions.

Decreased participation in child immunization programmes, Psycho trauma from experiences, Life of crime, addiction and sexual violence. Breakdown in social fabric loss of family support network makes trafficking easier, undermines relationships, weakens ties of family affection and influence, interrupts passage of cultural values and knowledge from one generation to the next, thus weakening the core of African society. Victims increasingly will have nowhere to go. Crime links to other criminal networks, drugs, weapons. Profits funneled into other criminal activities, car theft rings, drugs, terrorist groups.

# 7

# Combating Human Trafficking in India

The United Nations' definition of human trafficking is "The recruitment, transportation, transfer, harboring or receipt of persons, by means of the threat or use of force or other forms of coercion, of abduction, of fraud, of deception, of the abuse of power or of a position of vulnerability or of the giving or receiving of payments or benefits to achieve the consent of a person having control over another person, for the purpose of exploitation". Put into simpler words, human trafficking is modern-day slavery. Through an American's eyes this concept is more than hard to grasp. Does this really happen? Yes, sadly it does, not in just poor, undeveloped nations but all around the world. The United Nations agency named International Labour Organization (ILO) estimates that there are 12.3 million people held against their will in servitude at any given point in time. Other organizations estimate the number to be as high as 27 million.

The victims of human trafficking are those who are the most vulnerable and weak, young women and children. According to U.S. Government-sponsored research activity conducted in 2006, 600,000 to 800,000 persons are trafficked across international borders annually. Disturbingly, the research also shows that 80% of trafficked persons were women and girls and 50% of the victims were minors. It must be understood that some human trafficking crimes cross national borders, but it would also be considered human trafficking to hold, or harbor, a person in a country against their will. It should also be known that some servants voluntarily become servants out of lack of job skills and opportunity.

However, in some cases, the servants move into an environment that was not as advertised. They may become forced to stay in this environment and work for their "employers" for no wages or in inhumane conditions. This would also be considered human trafficking. The underlying theme of human trafficking is that the "trafficker" exploits, coerces, frauds, or forces the victim against their will into servitude at the gain of the trafficker. Thus this financial gain brings in the business factor to these atrocious crimes. The United Nations estimate that an approximate five to seven billion US Dollars per year is generated globally. This number is quite large and serves as justification of why human trafficking thrives in countries that are facing poverty and social injustice.

## FORMS OF SERVITUDE

Now that we have a definition of human trafficking and understand the make-up of those directly affected, what form does "servitude" take? The scope may be wider than we have documented, but for the most part there are two major sectors. The victims are either subject to labour exploitation, sexual exploitation, or both. Labour exploitation, also referred to as "labour trafficking", includes mostly men and children, but also women. The forms of labour exploitation include bonded labour, involuntary servitude, domestic servitude, and child labour. People in these situations are subject to unsafe, inhumane working conditions. The positions can be paid, but usually are unpaid. Often, the labours are beaten on a regular basis adding to their woes. In general, forced labour often occurs when employers find gaps in employment law and uses these gaps to exploit their victims. Immigrants, in particular, are very vulnerable to forced labour because of the number of laws surrounding their employment.

Let me discuss each form of labour trafficking. Bonded labour occurs when the employer uses a bond or debt, to keep the worker in service. The worker will receive a debt or inherent a debt as part of their initial employment. The worker must stay working for the employer until the debt is paid off. The concept of "inheriting debt" has kept workers in servitude for multiple generations. Involuntary servitude exists when a worker has a perception that they cannot escape their work for fear that they may be physically beaten or be prosecuted through legal action. The common factor in these situations is that a threat is made that keeps the worker trapped. Domestic servitude is different from involuntary servitude in that the worker is working for a person or family in their home. Wealthier families may be the perpetrators in these cases. Children are most vulnerable in these situations and are held in servitude through emotional or sexual abuse. This type of labour trafficking is extremely hard to identify and track. Child labour overlaps with the first three categories. By definition, it involves a minor and it is particularly troubling that some children are sold by their own parents into a forced labour situation.S

Sexual exploitation, or sex trafficking, affects almost wholly women and children. By the United Nation's definition, "sex trafficking means the recruitment, harboring, transportation, provision, or obtaining of a person for the purpose of a commercial sex act". Commercial sex act means that something of value is given in exchange for the act. Commercial sex trade is a booming business, so much of the human trafficking that exists today involves such services. Many of the sexual exploitation cases involve working in street prostitution, organized brothels, strip clubs, live-sex shoes, pornography businesses, etc. Other sexual exploitation cases take the form of private homes, where the woman or child is forced to live and work with the offender. The victims of sexual exploitation are often lured in with the promise of a good job in another country in exchange for the acts, kidnapping, fraudulent marriage proposals or even sold in to the business by family members. Child Sex Tourism, a specific type of commercial sex trade that is a fast growing problem, involves a person travelling to another country in order to engage in this act.

By its very nature, human trafficking is something that is not publicly identified, so how can quantify how much corruption is taking place? I am not sure that there is a real answer to that question. You can not measure what you can not see. We have no doubt that human trafficking takes place wherever someone sees there is a need for cheap labour, sex and money; therefore it exists in every country in the world. Many organizations around the world have taken on extensive research projects to attempt to identify the scope of the problem, none have been completely successful. Most all of the reports have been questioned as to reliability and accuracy, as should be expected due to the reason above. With that being said, multiple reports point to India as a "source, destination, and transit country". The huge population and location seem to be contributing factors to this statement. It is less liking that someone would be caught trafficking among the population.

The number of borders India shares with its neighbours adds to the problem. China, Nepal, Bangladesh and Pakistan all have been identified as countries with a significant amount of human trafficking. It is also arguable that many industries in India require manual labour, which is also a factor. The Trafficking in Persons Report published by the United States' Department of State identifies India as a country having both labour trafficking and sex trafficking issues. The number of persons trafficked is estimated to be in the millions. Again, these are very vague statistics as no organization has actually been able to quantify the problem. Looking for more data on the subject, I did find a second report published by the United Nations Office on Drugs and Crime (UNODC) that ranks India as a country of high origin for human trafficking. This same report also ranks India as a high destination country.

A high origin country means that people from India are trafficked to other countries, while a destination country would refer to people from outside India being brought into the country and harbored there. From these reports, it is safe to conclude that there is a problem in South Asia, including the country of India. At a briefing in Washington, D. C. Ambassador Mark P. Lagon, Senior Advisor on Trafficking in Persons, was quoted saying, "India has the world's largest labour trafficking problem with hundreds of thousands of sex trafficking victims and millions of bonded labourers including forced child labourers. In India, there is no national anti-trafficking effort, no recognition of bonded labour on an official level and poor efforts against sex trafficking. The world's largest democracy has the world's largest problem of human trafficking". This briefing took place at the release of the 2007 Trafficking in Persons Report.

While Lagon is certainly qualified to have an opinion on India's trafficking problem, I believe his statement is in conflict with the Trafficking in Persons Report published by the State Department. In that report, India is on the "Tier 2 Watch List", while the worst of countries are on the Tier 3 List. If indeed India does of the world's largest labour trafficking problem, then it should have been included on the Tier 3 List along with the other 16 countries on that list. Nonetheless, I do feel confident that India does have a significant problem to be placed on the Tier 2 Watch List. The Trafficking Victim Protection Act of 2000 is the U.S. law that was created to attempt to combat human trafficking. It lays out the criteria for which "list" a country will be placed on.

A country on the Tier 2 Watch List, also known as the "Special Watch List". is a country where the number of victims of this crime is significant or is significantly increasing, the government of the country has not produced concrete evidence to demonstrate their combat towards the severe forms of trafficking over the prior year, and the country is making significant efforts to comply with the minimum standards. India has been on this list for four consecutive years, including 2007. The specific reason given for this is that the Indian government has not recognized the country's huge bonded labour population. Non-governmental organizations (NGOs) estimate that between 20 million to 65 million bonded labourers are held in India. Another reason is that the government has not taken action to prosecute or punish three government officials that were found to be involved in trafficking-related corruption.

## INDIA'S EFFORT COMBAT HUMAN TRAFFICKING

In September 2006, the Indian government responded to the trafficking issue by creating a central anti-trafficking law enforcement "nodal cell". The nodal cell is a federal two-person department responsible for collecting and performing analysis of data related to trafficking, identifying the causes of the problem, monitoring action taken by state governments, and holding meetings with state-level law enforcement.

In 2007, three state governments established anti-trafficking police units, the first of this kind in the India. In October 2006, the central government passed a law banning the employment of children in domestic work. In July 2006, the Maharashtra government was given authority by the Supreme Court to seal brothels. The government already has laws in place to prohibit bonded and forced labour, set in place by the Bonded Labour Abolition Act, the Juvenile Justice Act, and the Child Labour Act.

Despite the legal efforts that are taking place, enforcement of the law leaves room for desire. In 2006, for the entire country of India, only 27 convictions for trafficking offenses were reported. From October 2006 to December 2006, 1672 child labour violations were reported, but no one was criminally prosecuted. Also in 2006, 685 suspected sex traffickers were attained, but no convictions were reported. Two specific examples given in the Trafficking in Persons report pertain to rescue missions. In New Delhi, 234 children were rescued by police from embroidery factories and rice mills.

The owners of these businesses did not receive punishment. Forty-three government-run rescue missions freed 275 victims of commercial sex trafficking, however the government did not report any convictions on those accounts as well. NGOs and human rights activists are left to fill the void of the government's negligence. Without a significant amount of funds, how much of an impact can NGOs have? On individual lives their impacts are huge, but when you look at society as a whole the crisis is too big, the Indian government must step up and address this issue.

## POTENTIAL EFFECTS ON THE ECONOMY

If the government does not address the human trafficking problem in a more effective manner, the impact on India's economy will be tragic. Being on the Tier 2 Watch List should serve as a warning to India if they value their relationship with the United States. Countries that are downgraded to the Tier 3 List face potential sanctions from the United States government. In addition as stated in the Trafficking in Persons report, "governments subject to sanctions would also face U.S. opposition to assistance from international financial institutions such as the International Monetary Fund and the World Bank".

## RECOMMENDATIONS FOR CHANGE

The United States has taken a hard stance on human trafficking. The U.S. government does not see human trafficking as a problem related to any certain country, but rather has a global issue that must be resolved. "We must eliminate modern-day slavery" is the mindset administration has taken. Countries struggling with the issue, like India, should take advantage of the help the United States is willing to extend.

The United Nations also has taken a similar stance, showing that humanitarian aid is available; it is solely a matter of showing that the Indian government is making a serious effort to address the issue. I recognize the fact that the Indian government must be overwhelmed with issues that need attention, but in my opinion few are more important than protecting your own people. Outside of government intervention, there are other actions that can help. NGOs must not give up the fight. People like Kailash Satyarthi, an Indian activist against child labour who has set free over 75,000 bonded labourer children, must passionately continue in their missions.

People in the education field can teach ethics training in Indian Business Schools that may prevent future business owners from pursuing "cheap forms of labour". Multi-national enterprises that enter the Indian economy can lead by example. They can refuse to do business with companies that knowingly engage in the inhumane practices of employing bonded labourers. Indians and Americans both live in democratic societies that value freedom, we must work together to ensure that all of our citizens can enjoy freedom and that each person's human rights are respected.

## CHILD ABUSE

The UN Convention on the Rights of the Child which India ratified in 1992 requires member states to take affirmative action in protecting children from all forms of sexual abuse, neglect, exploitation, torture or any form of cruelty. Currently Indian laws are inadequate to identify and punish offences against children. Child abuse, especially sexual abuse, is a serious problem in India. It has devastating effects on the victim. It is estimated that between 30 and 50 per cent of Indian children are sexually abused. India has approximately 300, 000 to 500,000 child prostitutes. There is no separate legislation to deal with child sexual abuse and the existing laws are inadequate. An average of 44,476 children is reported missing every year, out of which 11,008 children remain untraced. Most of these children end up in brothels. These children are taken to Mumbai, Delhi and the tourist beaches of Goa, Puri, Mahabalipuram and Kerala where paedophile tourism is on the rise.

### THIRD LARGEST CRIME

Trafficking in children, underage girls and young women is the third largest organised crime next only to illegal trade in drugs and arms. Pakistan, Malaysia and Indonesia, some of the countries closely associated with piracy, drug dealing, and gun running, are also associated with human trafficking. India with a large number of poor is a source of women and children for trafficking. In spite of this, only 65,602 persons were arrested during the five-year period of 1997-2001, out of which 87 per cent were females. Traffickers, transporters, brothel owners, clients and other such exploiters are largely untouched by the law; as prosecution is rare. While there are strong laws relating to rape of female children, the rules of evidence and the inordinate delay in prosecution often leads to vital evidence going missing and witnesses turning hostile. There are no effective laws dealing with abuse of male children.

This lacuna in the law has ensured that there is no disincentive to commit abuse of male children in India. The Immoral Traffic (Prevention) Act, 1956 as amended in 1986 widened the scope of the law and enhanced penalties for offences involving children and minors. The act deals primarily with trafficking in women and children at brothels. It does not cover the trafficking in children at beaches, hotels and guest houses. One of the biggest lacunae in the Act is that even if minor children are found in a brothel, they are passed off as the children of prostitutes and mostly have to be released without any proper procedure in place to determine if this is true.

## PENAL CODE

The Indian Penal Code, 1860 has several provisions to deal with the use of criminal force against women and female children: Sections 354, 366, 366 A, 366 B, 372 (selling minors for prostitution), 373 (buying minor for the purpose of prostitution) and 375. Abuse of male children is covered under Sections 372 and 373. In addition Section 377 may be invoked. Punishment may extend to 10 years. There is no minimum punishment for procuring, buying or abusing a minor male child; a male child is not treated as a victim of rape, nor is there any presumption of lack of consent as is statutorily done in the case of a girl. Section 375 provides inter alia that sexual intercourse with a female child under the age of 16 is rape regardless of whether it was with her consent or not. The only exclusion is in case the minor is the wife of the person accused of rape and is above 12 years of age. Enhanced punishment is provided for rape of a female child below 12 years.

The Section does not apply to the rape of a male child by another male as Section 375 clarifies that only a woman can be raped. This has been upheld by the Supreme Court in the case of Sakshi 2004. Section 377 covers several offences: non-consensual assault of a male child; non-consensual assault of a male adult under threat of death; sodomy of a female child; sodomy of an adult female; unnatural sexual relations with animals; and consensual homosexual relations. Several gay rights activists have been campaigning for deletion of Section 377 from the IPC. While consensual homosexual relations are covered under Section 377, this is only a small part of the entire gamut of offences covered by the section and any hasty move for deletion of the section will leave many victims of crime without any legal recourse.

As Section 377 has no minimum punishment, the offenders are normally released on bail and then become absconders. By contrast, Section 375 gives a minimum punishment of 7 years. When a minimum punishment is prescribed, it is assumed that the crime of rape is a heinous one and, therefore, a minimum term of seven years is prescribed. There is no such presumption in Section 377 even if a minor male child is brutally sodomised although the police may at their own discretion add on other sections. It is also imperative that child sexual abuse and non-consensual sodomy be separated from the wider issue of gay rights based on consensual relations between adults. All these are covered under Section 377 of the IPC. The Law Commission has been studying the matter for the last five years, but no new laws have been passed. Meanwhile, instances of trafficking in children continue.

## JUVELINE JUSTICE

The only existing legislation on children, the Juvenile

Justice Act 2000, deals primarily with children in conflict with the law and their rehabilitation. It does not provide adequately for children in need or identify offences against child victims. Enforcement of even the existing laws for protection of children are weak. While the issues have been deliberated for the last 15 years, no new laws have been passed to protect children and punish those who abuse them. Child abuse is a threat to the social fabric of a nation and will have disastrous consequences for India unless a more humane approach to children is adopted by the state by defining child rights and enacting positive measures to protect child rights.

Almost all countries have legislation to protect children. The United Kingdom (Sexual Offences Act 2003 dealing extensively with the rights of children), the United States, Sri Lanka, Thailand and Malaysia, among other nations, have adopted a child rights approach. Under this approach, any transgression of a child's rights, violence and other forms of physical and mental torture, is a punishable offence. The government should enact a separate child abuse law clearly defining the rights and remedies for children. Microsoft Chairman Bill Gates announced that the Bill and Melinda Gates Foundation will donate US$100 million to help India's fight against HIV/AIDS. While the country's HIV/AIDS levels are considered to be low, experts claim that they are beginning to rise and will continue to do so if preventative measures are not more widely introduced. The money will be used in targeting mobile populations, such as migrant workers and truck drivers, as they cross borders frequently and accelerate the spread of the disease.

Hopefully, this recent donation will also raise the profile of a population that has been victimized while increasing AIDS cases: young girls trafficked from Nepal to India. Sex trafficking is greatly fueling the HIV/AIDS epidemic and will continue to decimate the female population of this region in years to come. It is estimated that 200,000 Nepalese women and girls are trafficked to work as prostitutes worldwide and approximately 12,000 are trafficked to India each year. Internationally, trafficking in persons is considered the third largest illegal trade after drugs and arms, with an annual profit of $5-7 billion. In August, high-ranking police officials from South Asian countries met in Kathmandu, Nepal for the South Asian Association for Regional Cooperation (SAARC) Police Conference to discuss how to combat terrorism and the trafficking of women, children and drugs.

One goal of the conference was to strengthen regional cooperation by bringing together the regional police bodies of the South Asian member countries, which include Nepal, Bangladesh, Bhutan, India, The Maldives, Pakistan and Sri Lanka. At the conference, a regional police umbrella body—now referred to as SAARCPOL—was proposed to aid in combating the crimes discussed. SAARCPOL will be a regional forum that would coordinate all the SAARC countries in dealing with crime, terrorism and human and drug trafficking. The idea behind forming SAARCPOL follows from that of the creation of other regional organizations like EUROPOL and ASEANPOL, the regional bodies of European and South East Asian countries. Nepal Inspector General of Police Pradip Shumsher J.B. Rana told Agence France Presse, "[c]rimes like terrorism, drug crimes, [and] trafficking in women and children have discredited the human civilization of our region today".

He also remarked that since India had high-ranking officials present at the conference, he expected the results of the convention to be significant. But as of yet, none have been reported. The conference and the development of the regional police body appear to be a positive step in tackling the huge trafficking problem in South Asia, and the member countries have already implemented programs to assist trafficked victims and educate the public about the problem. However, they still have not made any substantial efforts to combat and prevent the crimes from actually occurring.

In an interview with the Digital Freedom Network (DFN), Sumnima Tuladhar, Information Coordinator for the Child Workers in Nepal Concerned Centre (CWIN), stated that child sex trafficking in Nepal is "one of the most inhuman crimes against children". She cited the causes of the problem as "poor economic conditions, unfair labour relations, bad governance, social discrimination and conservative social systems including patriarchy, which leads to acute gender disparity".

Nepal and India have a porous border that makes it almost impossible to track and stop trafficking. No passports or other forms of identification are required to pass through the borders, allowing traffickers and their victims to easily migrate.

Also, the towns along the borders of India and Nepal are filled with busy markets that cater to people from both countries, thereby creating a natural market for smuggling and prostitution. According to a trafficking report by Human Rights Watch/Asia, these markets serve "as a nexus for brokers and agents who take advantage of the crowds' anonymous travelers, the guest lodges, and the easy access to transportation". Nepal is a mostly mountainous region made up of many small villages. Although some urban areas of Nepal have undergone increased industrialization with the help of India, there has been little change in the rural economy.

According to the Human Rights Watch/Asia trafficking report, 90 percent of Nepal's population resides in rural areas and are dependent on subsistence agriculture. Most of those in rural areas are cut off from the educational and economic opportunities afforded in the more developed areas. As a result, they become easier prey for traffickers. Sometimes unaware of the traps of traffickers and enticed by money, parents encourage their daughters to leave home to accept jobs elsewhere or the girls themselves may leave home to find work to help support their family back home. Often, traffickers falsely promise parents that their daughter will be taken to work at a factory to provide financial support for the family. And in some cases, parents unwittingly marry their daughters off to a trafficker.

## THE PATH TO PROSTITUTION

After these young girls are trafficked, they are sold into Indian brothels and immediately forced into submission by being gang raped, starved, locked in isolation, beaten and forced to use drugs. If the girls resist, they are beaten further and often bound and gagged during the initial rape. After months of physical and emotional torture, isolation, and rape, the girls break down and fully submit to their new life. Their lives as young girls with bright futures fade. They are lost in a foreign land where they know no one, have no money, and cannot trust anyone. A case report by CWIN tells the story of two teenage girls, Maya and Parvati, who were offered a job in a carpet factory by their relatives.

The two girls were from the mountainous region of Sikharbesi village in the Nuwakot district, which is located northwest of Kathmandu. The girls worked in the factory for about six months, but then were coerced by an older woman to accompany her to Mumbai.

The impoverished girls were impressed by the woman's clothing, cosmopolitan style and promises of a better, more glamorous life. Visiting Mumbai was like a dream come true for the girls as they considered it to be "the ultimate city of joy". But Maya and Parvati never made it to Mumbai. The woman sold them to a brothel in Sonagachhi, Calcutta, where they were tortured and forced into prostitution. Sonagachhi is one of the largest "red light districts" in the world.

## AIDS IS A LOOMING CATASTROPHE

The spread of HIV/AIDS in this region is exacerbated by the illegal sex trade and is affecting the population and health of this region, especially females. Contraception is often not available in the brothels, increasing the rates of pregnancy and sexually transmitted diseases (STDs). According to a 2001 World Bank report, "Nepal will see an AIDS catastrophe by the end of the decade unless immediate and vigorous action is taken to combat human trafficking". In this region, there is a commonly believed superstition that a virgin girl can rid a man of STDs, including HIV/AIDS. Because of the superstition, there is a high demand for young virgin girls, and consequently the age of girls being trafficked is as young as 10 years.

Virgin girls are considered a hot commodity to brothel owners and customers, and they are valued as two to three times the average "price". To increase their profits, some brothel owners are known to offer the same girl out as a virgin several times, forcing these young girls to be raped up to 14 times per day.

Unfortunately, most of the girls die young or become extremely ill from malnutrition, abuse, neglect, STDs, most notably HIV/AIDS, and emotional breakdown. The average life span for these young females is only 30 years. And because of these statistics, the traffickers are constantly busy finding new prospects to replace the ones they lose to disease, death, and maturation.

## THE CHALLENGE OF ENDING TRAFFICKING

Sex trafficking in Nepal and India is further enabled by the virtual neglect of the crime by police and government. In addition to the porous borders allowing traffickers to cross freely with their victim's right under the noses of the border patrol, the police and government officials are often participants in the transactions themselves. Poverty and lack of judicial responsibility entice officials into complicity.

Nepal's Human Trafficking (Control) Act of 1986 states that if traffickers caught, have to spend 5-10 years in prison. But since the small chance of being caught is not much of a deterrent for traffickers, the business continues to thrive. While such efforts as the recent SAARC meeting are clearly positive efforts to combat this crime, much more still needs to be done at the local, national and international levels to save girls from a life of abuse and slavery.

The process of change in the South Asia region is moving forward at a slow pace. Tuladhar stated what is required for greater action against trafficking, "we need to empower and make people aware in the grassroots and ensure dignified lives to people in general to challenge trafficking in women and children". However, this crime will only continue until some of the basic issues surrounding its perpetuation—such as the suppression of women, superstitious ignorance, extreme poverty and lack of education—are alleviated.

Most recently, the international community has identified and attempted to combat trafficking with the UN Protocol to Prevent, Suppress and Punish Trafficking in Persons, Especially Women and Children (2000), onto which Nepal and India have yet to sign. However, both countries have ratified or signed treaties for human trafficking, such as the Convention on the Elimination of all Forms of Discrimination Against Women (CEDAW) and the Convention on the Rights of the Child (CRC) and the Worst Forms of Child Labour Convention, 1999 (No. 182). While Gates's donation offers hope in eradicating this growing business, India and Nepal need to step up to take responsibility and acknowledge the magnitude of this issue before it can be corrected.

# 8

# 21st Century Form of Slavery

Most of us think of slavery as something that took place hundreds of years ago, but slavery is still taking place on a large scale in the 21st century. These modern day slaves are the victims of the growing international practice of human trafficking. As this form of modern-day slavery continues to become a global problem, it is becoming better known (International Organisation for Migration, 2003). The aim of this is to provide an overview of the depth and breadth of the problem, and to consider some ways in which it may be combated. The UN defines trafficking in persons, also known as human trafficking as the recruitment, transportation, transfer, harbouring or receipt of persons by means of the threat or the use of force or other forms of coercion, or abduction, of fraud, of deception, of the abuse of power or of a position of vulnerability or of the giving or receiving of payments or benefits to achieve the consent of a person having control over another person for the purpose of exploitation.

Exploitation shall include, at a minimum, the exploitation or the prostitution of others or other forms of sexual exploitation, forced labour or services, slavery or practices similar to slavery, servitude or the removal of organs. Trafficking differs from smuggling in that whereas the trafficking of human beings involves the exploitation of the migrant, people smuggling simply implies the procurement, for financial and material gain, of the illegal entry into a state of which that person is neither a citizen nor a permanent resident. While the predominant form of slavery -chattel slavery- that was prevalent throughout history (and still exists today) involved legal ownership, human trafficking is the predominant form of slavery today.

Trafficking in persons does not necessarily involve legal ownership over the people in question, but uses other mechanisms to control the victims, and to extract labour from them, whether in the form of labour in sweatshops or sexual exploitation and forced prostitution. The mechanisms used are force, fraud or coercion. This modern form of slavery is not only viewed as a transnational crime, but also an enormous violation of human rights. Today, trafficking in persons is a fundamental and crucially important challenge in the areas of human rights and law enforcement. While human trafficking has a devastating impact on individual victims, its impact also undermines the safety and security of all the nations it touches as it is a global health risk and it fuels the growth of organised crime.

## ORGANISED CRIME

Trafficking in people (and people smuggling) has become the third-largest source of profits for organized crime after drugs and arms, generating billions of dollars each year. A growing number of criminal networks world-wide are showing an increased sophistication with regard to moving large numbers of people at higher profits than ever. In fact, these have become the most profitable crimes in the world today. UNICEF put the global value of human trafficking at over $12 billion a year. Economist Jagdish Bhagwati refers to the rotten trade, that is all kinds of trade in bads - arms, drugs, stolen goods, hazardous and toxic products as well as traffic in babies, bodies and slave labour as opposed to ordinary and normative trade in goods.

The number of victims of trafficking began to grow in the 1990s but the clandestine nature of trafficking as an organised crime makes it difficult to determine the extent of the problem or to discern accurate figures of how many people are affected by this phenomenon Boe observes that the trade in human beings Aids more pervasive than we think and much more than meets the eye.

Conservative estimates indicate that there are 700 000 to 2 million people trafficked each year. Other sources suggest that the number could be between 1 and 4 million. The majority of the victims are women and children; 35 percent are under the age of 18. People trafficking and smuggling syndicates are still benefiting from weak legislation, huge profits and the relatively low risk of detection, prosecution and arrest compared to the other activities of transnational organised crime.

Ellerman states that in terms of risks to the traffickers, to the actual organised crime groups, sex trafficking presents a much lower risk than either arms deals or drug trafficking. It is speculated that sex trafficking will take over drug trafficking in the next decades as the second largest criminal industry as, unlike drugs, bodies can be sold several times. Traffickers are easily able to take advantage of the vulnerabilities created by war, endemic poverty, minimal education, unemployment and a general lack of opportunity for the majority of the population. This means that traffickers usually prey on individuals who are poor, frequently unemployed or underemployed and who may lack access to social safety nets predominantly women and children in certain countries.

Victims are often lured by false promises of good jobs and better lives and then forced to work in brutal conditions. Victims are forced to toil in sweatshops, construction sites, brothels and fields. Many victims are subjected to threats against their person and family, violence, horrific living conditions and dangerous workplaces. Some victims have responded to advertisements believing that they will have a good job waiting for them in a new country. Others have been sold into this modern-day form of slavery by a relative, an acquaintance or family friend.

## THE GLOBAL DIMENSIONS OF TRAFFICKING

Human trafficking is characterized by three stages:

- Recruitment,

- Transportation, and
- Exploitation.

Countries are classified as countries of origin, transit or destination. In the country of destination, trafficked persons are usually exploited by their recruiters for financial profit, and are sold or leased to others.

Such persons usually hold their victims under conditions of physical captivity and use of force, threats, debt bondage, and coercion to subject them to different forms of exploitation. While victims of trafficking are primarily from developing countries like Asia, Eastern Europe, the former Soviet Union, Latin America and Africa, trafficking is also found in developed countries, in countries where governments abuse human rights and in countries where the government's human rights record is generally excellent. Countries of origin are generally marked by economic and political instability.

The trafficking of persons leaves no country untouched. The widespread global nature of the practice is well documented by Global March:

Afghanistan, Albania, Algeria, Argentina, Armenia, Australia, Austria, Azerbaijan, Bahrain, Bangladesh (about 40.000 children from Bangladesh are involved in prostitution in Pakistan) Belarus, Belgium (both a transit point and destination for trafficking in women and children), Belize, Benin, Bhutan, Bosnia and Herzegovina, Botswana, Brazil, Brunei and Darussalam, Bulgaria, Burkina Faso, Myanmar (Burma), Cambodia, Cameroon, Canada, China, Hong Kong, Macau, Taiwan, Columbia, DR Congo, Costa Rica, Cote d'Ivoire, Croatia, Cyprus, Czech Republic, Denmark, Dominican Republic, Ecuador, El Salvador, Equatorial Guinea, Eritrea, Estonia, Ethiopia, Fiji, Finland, France, Gabon, Germany, Ghana, Greece, Guatemala, Haiti, Honduras, Hungary, India, Indonesia, Iraq, Ireland, Israel, Italy, Japan, Kazakhstan, Kenya, Korea (DPR), Korea (Rep), Kosovo, Kyrgyzstan, Laos, Latvia, Lebanon, Lesotho, Libya, Lithuania, Luxembourg, Madagascar, Malaysia, Maldives, Mali, Mauritania, Mauritius, Mexico (the number one centre for the supply of young children to the USA. The majority are sent to international paedophile organisations), Moldova, Mongolia, Morocco, Mozambique, Nepal (carpet factories employ children common sites of sexual exploitation by employers and recruitment centres for Indian brothels), Netherlands, New Zealand, Nicaragua, Nigeria, Norway, Pakistan, Panama, Philippines, Poland, Qatar, Romania, Russian Federation, Saudi Arabia (An estimated 1 000 to 1 5000 children smuggled to Saudi Arabia from India during the Haj season). Singapore, Slovakia, Slovenia, South Africa (an IOM report (2003a) released early this year states that South Africa has become a key hub for slavery in Africa), Spain, Sri Lanka, Sudan, Surinam, Swaziland, Sweden, Switzerland, Tanzania, Macedonia, Thailand, Togo, Turkey (a major destination and transit country), Uganda, Ukraine, United Arab Emirates, United States of America, Uzbekistan, Venezuela, Vietnam, Yugoslavia, Zambia.

Forty five of Africa's fifty four countries are involved on human trafficking and South Africa is a major receiving and transit destination. South Africa, despite boasting one of the most progressive constitutions, does not have legislation outlawing trafficking in humans for sexual or any other forms of exploitation.

## TRAFFICKING OF WOMEN AND CHILDREN

The most lucrative part of trafficking involves sex trafficking, and the trafficking in women and children for the sex trade has emerged as an issue of global concern which is facilitated by porous borders and advanced communication technologies and is becoming increasingly transnational in scope.

Sex trafficking includes forced prostitution, bride trafficking, child prostitution and child pornography. Girls as young as twelve years old are sold to traffickers where newcomers, usually virgins, are repeatedly raped. This is the seasoning process where the victim's spirit is broken so that she becomes easier to control. The cage brothels in Bangladesh are well documented - where victims are kept in cages.

Commenting on the tender age of the victims, Gedda (2003:1) observes that the victims of sex trade see little of life before they see the worst of life: an underground of brutality and fear.

According to Anti-Slavery International the trafficking of children has assumed frightening dimensions. Child trade is a huge business, with billions of US dollars in annual turnover worldwide. ECPAT International, a Thailand-based international based NGO which monitors the commercial sexual exploitation of children reports that despite many efforts by dedicated groups and individuals the sexual exploitation of children is a phenomenon that is increasing in scope.

Thousands of children are being reduced to commodities in a trade in human misery. They are bought and sold to satisfy perverted sexual appetites, to provide slave labour, or, worst of all, to be harvested for their organs and body parts so that the rich and their children can live at their expense. The flow of organs and other body parts tends to imitate the flight of capital from the impoverished South to the North.

It would appear that, regardless of the continent, wherever child traffickers see potential for their business, their recruiting methods follow a similar pattern. Recruiters target impoverished rural areas in the poorest countries - make friends with the parents, give false promises of jobs and education for the children in the cities and pay money to the parents. Often parents, knowing what is waiting for the children, let them go. Very often children are sold by their own parents or other relatives. Although children are trafficked largely for sexual exploitation, they are also trafficked for many other kinds of exploitation: Many children and minors are end up working in slave like conditions as household servants, in plantations or on construction sites; others are forced to join organized begging groups. Global March (2004:5) reports that about 50-100 boys, aged about 8-15, some even younger, are being trafficked from Bangladesh to the Gulf States for use as camel jockeys in the Gulf States.

More and more reports are coming in of children being kidnapped and killed for the removal of organs for transplant, skin for use in witchcraft or making magic charms or for sacrifice in traditional rituals - the case of the torso of a young boy, 'Adam found in the Thames in London was well documented. As with trafficking in general, the sexual exploitation of children takes place in both developing and developed countries. While poverty is often a catalyst in sexual exploitation, it does not adequately explain the commercial sexual exploitation of children addiction to drugs, discrimination against girl children and simple materialistic greed are others. The armed conflict which is taking place in parts of the world also contributes largely.

Children are often separated from their parents in the chaos of conflict and displacement; still others are left as orphans. Unaccompanied children are vulnerable and at risk of sexual abuse or exploitation. Escalating incidents of conflict around the world have left ever growing numbers of children exposed to exploiters.

Disappearances have been reported from refugee camps in Kosovo and Africa. Children have been trafficked from conflict situations to work in relatively safer countries, from Myanmar to Thailand, from Georgia to Turkey. A wide range of individuals and groups contribute to the commercial sexual exploitation of children. In addition to the child sex offender, persons involved in the commercial exploitation of children may include parents, family members, community leaders, private sector and organised criminal networks. Deception is often involved; however, some parents knowingly sell the children to traffickers.

A German mother and her boyfriend offered the woman's 8 year old daughter for sale on the auction site eBay. An Internet user alerted police when she say a picture of the girl with the sales pitch Ayou can play with her and Areal working toy and a starting price of 1 Euro.

A recent article in the Guardian newspaper reported the case of a retired Italian couple who had been arrested for buying a three year old Albanian boy, paying $6 000 to the trafficking gang that specialised in under age merchandise. The boy had allegedly been traded for a colour TV set by his father. In a typical child-trafficking scenario, the recruiter may earn between $50 and $20 000 per child delivered to an employer. Profit varies according to the source countries. An African child trafficked to the US might net between $10 000 and $20 000 according to the US Immigration and Naturalisation Service.

Community leaders in some countries are often indirectly or directly involved and are aware of agents recruiting in their villages, but ignore them in order to receive the money. (NGOs in Nepal are countering this by introducing a community surveillance system, mobilising over 13 000 local women and also teachers and local authorities). More and more it is becoming apparent that organised criminal networks are involved in procuring and channelling vulnerable young women and children towards coercion and exploitation and in perpetuation of such exploitation. The reasons are clear the profits are substantial: It has been established that trafficking for prostitution, controlled by organised crime rings from the former Soviet Union, is a multi million dollar business. Because of the criminal and hidden nature of the practice, it is difficult to determine the number of children who are victims of commercial sexual exploitation.

## THE IMPACT ON VICTIMS

Commercial sexual exploitation seriously compromises a child's right to enjoy and lead a productive, rewarding and dignified life and has life threatening consequences for the physical, psychological, spiritual and social development of children.

The most immediate danger exploited children face is physical violence where beatings and rape are daily occurrences. Children are even more vulnerable to sexually transmitted diseases like HIV infections and AIDS, as their body tissues are more easily damaged.

They are not in a position to receive education about AIDS and safe sex practices much less negotiate safe sex practices like the use of condoms. In one instance, seventy percent of girls rescued from a brothel in Italy were infected with HIV. Kristof (2004e) observes that at its worst, the trafficking system takes innocent girls, imprisons them in brothels to be raped repeatedly and leaves them dead of AIDS by their early 20s - and yet there is far less international effort to save these children that to save the Brazilian forest. Women and children who are survivors of the modern form of slavery have little recourse to the sort of specialized care necessary for persons who have been exploited physically and sexually.

## THE TRADE IN HUMAN ORGANS

Organ trafficking has become an international trade. A simple query on the Google search engine produces numerous Web sites professing to sell various body parts for up to $125 000 and the commodified kidney being the primary currency to date. Organ transplantation today is a significant and established part of therapeutic medicine, with good and improving survival rates for patients and transplanted organs. Organ transplants differ, however, from most other medical procedures in that they must be removed from the body of a living or dead human being. The spread of transplant capabilities has created a global scarcity of transplantable organs.

The scarcity of transplantable organs together with the legal principle that has gained legislative approval throughout most technologically advanced societies, that that the removal of an organ from a living or deceased person for transplant purposes must be a free and altruistic act of generosity and the consequent criminalisation of the sale or purchase of organs for transplantation have given rise to a large-scale circumvention of laws governing human organ transplants, particularly by organised crime.

The criminalisation of the sale of purchase of organs for transplantation by nearly all Western nations, however, have resulted in a worldwide shortage of organs in the face of an escalating global demand that as Foster (1997:140) points out, has been exacerbated by advances in pharmacology better immunosuppressant drugs, and by improved medical transplant procedures. In the Middle East, for example, from the Gulf States to Israel, transplantable cadaver organs are extremely scarce owing to religious reservations, both Jewish and Islamic (about the ontological status of the brain dead donor) and to the elaborate religious protocol for the proper treatment and burial of the dead.

The global shortage of transplantable organs has networks of organized crime (and so called body mafia) have given rise to ambulatory organ buyers, itinerant kidney hunters, outlaw surgeons, medical technicians, makeshift transplant units, and underground laboratories. For the last twenty years organized programs transplant package tours (transplant tourism) have carried affluent patients from Israel, Saudi Arabia, Oman and Kuwait initially to India for transplant and later to Turkey, Iran and Iraq and, most recently Russia, Romania and Moldova where kidney sellers are recruited sometimes coercively from army barracks, prisons, unemployment offices, flea markets, shopping malls and bars.

Transplant package tours are arranged in Europe, North America and Japan to take transplant patients to China where their surgery is arranged, with the complicity of Chinese doctors and surgeons to coincide with public executions that provide the primary source of high lucrative transplant organs. Condemned prisoners are reportedly incubated and surgically prepped for harvesting minutes before execution. In India, trading a kidney for a dowry has become a common strategy for parents to arrange marriage for an otherwise economically disadvantaged daughter. One-kidney shanty towns have sprung up on the peripheries of Manila and Thailand to service the needs of Saudi and Japanese transplant patients and in recent years, a growing number of North Americans.

Indeed, the poor man's and women's kidney has become the ultimate collateral against debt and destitution in many parts of the world. Scheper-Hughes (2003:199) sees the division of the world into two distinctly different populations of organ suppliers and organ receivers as a kind of globalised apartheid medicine that privileges one class of patients, organ receivers, over another class or invisible and unrecognised non-patients, about whom almost nothing is known. Scheper-Hughes (2003:199) observes that in general, the circulation of kidneys follows the established routes of capital from North to South, from poorer to more affluent bodies, from black and brown bodies to white ones and from female to males.

Women are rarely the recipients of purchased or purloined organs anywhere in the world. Willing seller and willing buyer apart, the number of people especially children who are tricked or coerced into parting with a kidney, or killed for their organs is growing. Malunga (2004) observes wryly that in South Africa, where there is a thriving illegal market for internal organs, "We already have enough problems with hi jackers taking us to the cleaners for our vehicles. Now we will have to worry about our eyes or our kidneys or livers being sliced out for a quick transplant".

There was a report in a South African newspaper, *This Day*, earlier this year of a nun at a Mozambican orphanage who had reported to the authorities that children were disappearing from the orphanage in fact, were being kidnapped and killed for their organs. In the Pretoria News of Monday18 May 2004, a few lines appeared Brazilian Catholic nun Maria Elilda dos Santos, who last year accused a South African farmer of child and human organ trafficking in Mozambiques Northern province, Nampula province, has left the country claiming Mozambican authorities pressured her to leave. Marina Rini of Terre des Hommes (cited by Tyler 2003) says that as we know that gangs offer children for sale dead or alive. We can only conclude that the missing children die or are killed for their organs.

## THE ROLE OF CIVIL SOCIETY

Despite the number of anti-trafficking organizations, Ellerman (2002:9) speaking of the position in the United States, reports that progress in dealing with trafficking is painfully slow. This he attributes to the fact that initiatives have been top down. Legislation may be passed but at the level where trafficking actually takes place, which is in the local communities, there is little or no awareness, there is no funding and there is no training. He argues further that the key issue is not only to make community members aware of the issue and talking about the issue but getting police and local government aware of the issue, especially local law enforcement.

Given the struggle of developing countries to end human poverty and strive toward the attainment of the Millennium Development Goals, state-provided social services in the large majority of countries do not lie in the near future. The prevention of human trafficking requires several types of interventions (Human Trafficking.org 2004:1). Some are of low or moderate cost and can have an immediate impact, such as awareness campaigns. The Stiftelsen Kvinnoforum (1998:13) observes that civil society will have to bear the brunt of the responsibility of filling the gap of social services needed. There are very few Non Governmental Organizations (NGOs) that take on the issues of trafficking and the sexual exploitation of women and children.

The four areas in which work is needed are:

1. Organising social support and practical assistance for victims of trafficking (rescue campaigns for sex slaves, safe shelter, legal aid, money for basic needs, medical services, counselling).
2. Advocacy work and campaigning on national and international levels in the fields of legislation and litigation, social policies, assistance programmes and strengthening political commitment to combating trafficking in women, for example campaigns to add to the definition of refugee status the notion of sexual oppression.
3. Public relations, documentation and information services, training and educational programmes;
4. International networking aimed at long term strategies.

Social movements have, over the years, been successful in breaking the silence about many social ills. Through collective efforts, such movements create awareness; build shelters, safe houses and crisis shelters.

# 9

# Trafficking for Commercial Sexual Exploitation

## DISTINCTIONS BETWEEN HUMAN SMUGGLING AND HUMAN TRAFFICKING

This fact sheet will explain the differences between human smuggling and human trafficking. Because these are complex crimes, it is not always readily apparent when a "human smuggling" case crosses into the realm of a "human trafficking" crime. Understanding the basic principals outlined in this fact sheet will assist the reader in identifying the subtle differences between each of these crimes. For this discussion, the terms "human trafficking" and "trafficking in persons" refer strictly to "severe forms of trafficking" as defined in 22 USC 7101.

As in any other area involving complex crimes, it is important to gather and examine as many relevant facts as possible, compare the fact pattern against relevant statutes, and when necessary, seek expert legal advice in making determinations. Trafficking in persons and human smuggling are some of the fastest growing areas of international criminal activity, according to the United Nations. It often involves a number of different crimes, spanning several countries and involving an increasing number of victims.

Trafficking in persons (TIP) can be compared to a modern day form of slavery. It involves the exploitation of people through force, coercion, threat and deception and includes human rights abuses such as debt bondage, deprivation of liberty and lack of control over freedom and labour. Trafficking can be for purposes of sexual exploitation or labour exploitation. According to U.S. Government estimates, 600,000 to 800,000 victims are trafficked globally each year and 14,500 to 17,500 are trafficked into the United States. Women and children comprise the largest group of victims. Trafficking victims are often physically and emotionally abused. Although TIP is often an international crime that involves the crossing of borders, it is important to note that TIP victims can be trafficked within their own countries and communities. Traffickers can move victims between locations within the same country and often sell them to other trafficking organizations.

While there are significant differences between TIP and human smuggling, the underlying issues that give rise to these illegal activities are often similar. Generally, extreme poverty, lack of economic opportunities, civil unrest, and political uncertainty, are factors that all contribute to an environment that encourages human smuggling and trafficking in persons. Although there are similarities in the conditions that give rise to TIP and human smuggling, there are distinct differences in the expectations and treatment of persons being smuggled and the victims of human trafficking. Additionally, there are significant statutory differences between TIP and human smuggling.

## HUMAN SMUGGLING

Human smuggling is the facilitation, transportation, attempted transportation or illegal entry of a person(s) across an international border, in violation of one or more countries laws, either clandestinely or through deception, such as the use of fraudulent documents. Often, human smuggling is conducted in order to obtain a financial or other material benefit for the smuggler, although financial gain or material benefit are not necessarily elements of the crime. For instance, sometimes people engage in smuggling to reunite their families. Human smuggling is generally with the consent of the person(s) being smuggled, who often pay large sums of money. The vast majority of people who are assisted in illegally entering the United States are smuggled, rather than trafficked.

Smuggled persons may become victims of other crimes. In addition to being subjected to unsafe conditions on the smuggling journeys, smuggled aliens may be subjected to physical and sexual violence. Frequently, at the end of the journey, smuggled aliens are held hostage until their debt is paid off by family members or others. It is also possible that a person being smuggled may at any point become a trafficking victim. The Immigration and Nationalization Act, Section 274(a)(1), (2), provides for criminal penalties under Title 8, United States Code, Section 1324, for acts or attempts to bring unauthorized aliens to or into the United States, transport them within the U.S., harbor unlawful aliens, encourage entry of illegal aliens, or conspire to commit these violations, knowingly or in reckless disregard of illegal status.

## TRAFFICKING IN PERSONS

On October 28, 2000, Congress passed the Victims of Trafficking and Violence Protection Act of 2000 ("VTVPA"). The VTVPA is a comprehensive statute that addresses the recurring and significant problem of trafficking of persons for the purpose of committing commercial sex acts, or to subject them to involuntary servitude, peonage, debt bondage or slavery. It also is designed to increase the protection available to victims of trafficking and other types of violent crimes. It is an attempt to address these issues on a national and international level and affects many government and non-government agencies and organizations. Unlike smuggling, which is often a criminal commercial transaction between two willing parties who go their separate ways once their business is complete, trafficking specifically targets the trafficked person as an object of criminal exploitation.

The purpose from the beginning of the trafficking enterprise is to profit from the exploitation of the victim. It follows that fraud, force or coercion all plays a major role in trafficking. It may be difficult to make a determination between smuggling and trafficking in the initial phase. Trafficking often includes an element of smuggling, specifically, the illegal crossing of a border. In some cases the victim may believe they are being smuggled, but are really being trafficked, as they are unaware of their fate. For example, there have been cases where women trafficked for sexual exploitation may have knowingly agreed to work in the sex industry and believed that they would have decent conditions and be paid a decent wage. What they did not realize is that the traffickers would take most or all of their income keep them in bondage and subject them to physical force or sexual violence. Or, the victims may have believed they were being smuggled into the United States where they would be given a job as a nanny or model, later realizing that the so-called smugglers deceived them and that they would be forced to work in the sex industry.

Conversely, persons being smuggled may sometimes willingly enter into "contracts" with the smugglers to work off a smuggling debt. Unless the aliens' labour or services are enforced through the forms of coercion set forth in the trafficking statutes, such deferred repayment does not make these people trafficking victims. However, a work-based debt can be an "indicator" of trafficking, and such a situation could trigger further examination to determine whether the aliens are victims of trafficking or extortion. According to The Trafficking Victims Protection Act of 2000, severe forms of trafficking in persons always includes the recruitment, harboring, transportation, provision, or obtaining of a person for one of the three following purposes:

1. Labour or services, through the use of *force, fraud or coercion* AND resulting in involuntary servitude, peonage, debt bondage or slavery; OR

2. Commercial sex act, through the use of *force, fraud or coercion*; OR
3. If the person is under 18 years of age, any commercial sex act, whether or not force, fraud or coercion is involved.

Human trafficking does not require the crossing of an international border it does not even require the transportation of victims from one locale to another. Victims of severe forms of trafficking are not all illegal aliens; they may, in fact, be U.S. citizens, legal residents, or visitors. Victims do not have to be women or children - they may also be adult males. While trafficking victims are often found in sweatshops, domestic work, restaurant work, agricultural labour, prostitution and sex entertainment, they may be found anywhere in the U.S. doing almost anything profitable to their handlers. Victims may not even recognize that they have been victimized, or may be forced into protecting their exploiters, so self-proclamation of their status is not required.

The Trafficking Victims Protection Act of 2000 also provides tools to combat trafficking in persons both worldwide and domestically. The Act recognizes the need to protect the victims while gaining their cooperation by providing a safe haven. Section 107(c)(3) reads: "Authority to Permit Continued Presence in the United States.Federal law enforcement officials may permit an alien individual's continued presence in the United States, if after an assessment, it is determined that such individual is a victim of a severe form of trafficking and a potential witness to such trafficking, in order to effectuate prosecution of those responsible, and such officials in investigating and prosecuting traffickers shall protect the safety of trafficking victims, including taking measures to protect trafficked persons and their family members from intimidation, threats of reprisals, and reprisals from traffickers and their associates".

**Table 9.0: Differences between human trafficking and smuggling**

| *Trafficking* | *Smuggling* |
|---|---|
| Must Contain an Element of Force, Fraud, or Coercion (actual, perceived or implied), unless under 18 years of age involved in commercial sex acts. | The person being smuggled is generally cooperating. |
| Forced Labour and/or Exploitation. | There is no actual or implied coercion. |
| Persons trafficked are victims. | Persons smuggled are violating the law. They are not victims. |
| Enslaved, subjected to limited movement or isolation, or had documents confiscated. | Persons are free to leave, change jobs, etc. |
| Need not involve the actual movement of the victim. | Facilitates the illegal entry of person(s) from one country into another. |
| No requirement to cross an international border. | Smuggling always crosses an international border. |
| Person must be involved in labour/services or commercial sex acts, i.e., must be "working." | Person must only be in country or attempting entry illegally. |

In some cases it may be difficult to quickly ascertain whether a case is one of human smuggling or trafficking. As will be illustrated in the scenarios below, the distinction between smuggling and trafficking are often very subtle, but key components that will always distinguish trafficking from smuggling are the elements of fraud, force or coercion. However, under U.S. law, if the person is under 18 and induced to perform a commercial sex act, then it is considered trafficking, regardless of whether or not fraud, force or coercion is involved.

## CASE EXAMPLES AND SCENARIOS

- Sonia was invited to come to the United States by family friends and told that she could work for them as a housekeeper, and they would pay her $100.00 a week. Sonia was provided with fraudulent documents and departed for the United States with her new employer. She knew that this was illegal, but she needed the money and was willing to take the risk.

Sonia was smuggled into the United States. She left willingly with full knowledge that she was entering the United States illegally. Upon arriving in the United States, Sonia was kept in isolation, she was given a place to sleep in the basement and told not to speak to anyone or she would be turned over to the Immigration Service. Sonia was never paid for her work and felt that she had no one to turn to for help.

Was Sonia smuggled or trafficked? At this point Sonia was restricted from leaving the house, threatened with deportation if she attempted to talk to anyone and forced into involuntary servitude. Sonia is a victim of trafficking.

- A recruiting agency in India was looking for welders to work at a company in the United States for $10.00 an hour. The agency charged each perspective worker a non-refundable $2,500.00 application fee. Enroute to the United States the workers were given contracts to sign. The contracts obligated the workers to work for the next six months for less than $3.00 per hour. They were told to sign the contracts or they would be sent back home. The workers felt that they could not back out because they had invested all their savings, and were already on their way to the United States. Once they arrived, they were confined to the factory grounds and the owner of the company kept their passports.

Were the workers smuggled or trafficked? The workers were victims of severe forms of trafficking in persons. The workers were transported for the purposes of labour through the use of fraud and coercion, which resulted in the workers being subjected to involuntary servitude. Confiscation of the workers' passports by the employer also caused the workers to believe that they were forced to stay with the company.

- Local law enforcement authorities executed a search warrant at a brothel and arrested three 17-year-old girls for prostitution. The Department of Family Services notified Immigration and Customs Enforcement concerning the illegal immigration status of the three juveniles. Immigration and Customs Enforcement Agents interviewed the three juveniles and learned that they were smuggled into the United States.

Were the girls smuggled or trafficked? The girls were trafficked into the United States. All three girls were juveniles and were performing commercial sex acts. Since the girls were under 18 years of age, they would be considered victims of severe forms of trafficking, regardless of whether or not they have consented to participate or paid to be brought illegally into the U.S.

- A husband and wife in the United States convince their relatives in India to allow their daughters to travel to the United States to receive an education. The husband and wife are the aunt and uncle to the girls and have promised the girls' parents that they would provide housing and support for the girls. In order for the girls to receive a student visa, their aunt and uncle enrolled the girls in school. The girls are granted student visas and allowed to enter the U.S. to receive an education.

Once the girls arrive in the U.S. their aunt and uncle immediately tell them that they won't be attending school. The aunt and uncle never intended to have the girls attend school and only enrolled them for the purpose of fraudulently obtaining the entry visas. At this point, the girls have unwittingly been smuggled into the U.S. through the use of visa fraud. During the next several weeks the girls are locked in a basement and continually told that if they try to leave they would be arrested for their involvement in the visa fraud.

Eventually their uncle takes the girls to local motels where they are made to clean rooms and provide janitorial services. The girls are never paid for their work, all their identification has been taken away and they are continually reminded that they could be arrested for their involvement in visa fraud. Because the girls are being held against their will through coercion and intimidation and are being forced to work for no pay, they are now victims of trafficking.

An estimated 800 000 women and children are trafficked each year across international borders, 80% ending in forced sex work. This estimate does not include those trafficked within their own countries or missing children. Human trafficking for commercial sexual exploitation (CSE) is a gross violation of human rights and has been described as a modern form of slavery.

The United Nations (UN) estimates that the trafficking of women and children for CSE in Asia has victimized over 30 million people. India has been identified as one of the Asian countries with a severe CSE trafficking problem. The U.S Department of State has put India on the Tier 2 Watch List, for the fourth consecutive year. It has also warned India that it could be downgraded to a Tier 3 category, thereby exposing itself to international sanctions, unless it improves its record on trafficking.

This presents an overview of the trafficking of women and girls for sexual exploitation (CSE) in India; identifies the health impacts of CSE; and suggest strategies to respond to trafficking and related issues. To our knowledge, this article is the first condensed and comprehensive paper on CSE in India. For the purpose of this paper, trafficking is defined as 'the act of recruitment, transportation, transfer, harbouring or receipt of a girl or women for the purpose of exploitation' (Palermo Protocol art. 3; Council of Europe Convention art. 4). Underage children are children below 18 years of age.

Key words describing or related to human trafficking for commercial sexual exploitation and its health impacts, as well as their synonyms, were identified via MeSH (medical subject heading) (e.g., sex trafficking, trafficking of women and girls, female sex workers, female prostitution) and guided the literature search. A manual search of the reference lists of the retrieved documents was also performed. We contacted the publishers or organizations of documents that were not retrievable on the internet or the university library. All together, we reviewed 261 articles. Additionally, we sent this paper to NGOs working with women who have been sex-trafficked in India for their comments and review.

The clandestine and transnational nature of trafficking and the reluctance of those involved to discuss the topic make accurate assessments of the magnitude of CSE difficult. A recent government commissioned by the Department of Women and Child Development (India) estimated the number of persons trafficked for CSE in India to be around 2.8 million, an increase of 22% from an earlier estimate. The majority of trafficked persons are young women or children who have been forced into sex work as a result of poverty, often before they were 18 years old. Published literature further points to an increasing demand for younger children and virgins, partly fuelled by the fear of HIV/AIDS; the emergence of new sources and destinations for trafficked persons; and an increase in the overall sophistication of trafficking networks, many of which are controlled by organized crime syndicates or insurgent factions.

This has been illustrated in Nepal where the traditional trafficking of Nepalese girls to Indian brothels had been taken over by Nepalese rebel groups in order to fund their fight against the state. The magnitude of the problem may partly be accounted by the different forms of sexual exploitation in India. The most common form of sex work involves young women and girls from economically deprived and marginalized groups ( *Dalits*) who have been 'recruited' by brokers, sold to pimps or brothel owners (most of whom are ex-prostitutes)and forced into prostitution. Brokers may be community members known to the victims or the victims' families pretending to help families; agents seeking the help of a local person to approach families and victims; individuals willing to kidnap potential victims; and family members (e.g., parents or husbands). Recruitment strategies include: false promises of employment; approaching debt-bonded families and persuading them to part with their children to pay for their debts; abduction; and arranged marriages whereby young women and underage girls are 'married' to grooms willing to pay poverty-stricken parents a dowry.

Once married (marriage makes this form of trafficking particularly difficult to challenge under the law) wives are either forced into prostitution directly by their husbands or abandoned/divorced and sold to a broker who resells them to a brothel. This practice has been documented in Bihar, West Bengal, Chhatisgarh, Orissa, Uttarakhand and Hyderabad. Common destinations for women and girls forced into 'arranged' marriages include Punjab, Haryana, Uttar Pradesh and the United Arab Emirates. Customary prostitution is also prevalent in India. It includes socially (if not legally) accepted forms of prostitution, religious and tribal prostitutions. Victims of religious prostitution are pre-pubertal girls from scheduled castes ( Devadisi, Jogini, Nailis, Muralis, and Theradiyan) who are dedicated to different deities. After a few years of concubinage with temple priests, they are sold or auctioned to traffickers for CSE. The market value of girls tends to fall after puberty.

This form of prostitution is mostly practiced in Karnataka, Maharashtra, and Andhra Pradesh. Tribal prostitution involves girls from different ethnic tribes ( Bedia, Nats) who used to entertain feudal lords. Overtime, many of these tribal communities have been forced to engage in prostitution for economic reasons. Tribal prostitution is prevalent in Andhra Pradesh, Rajasthan, Maharashtra, West Bengal, Chhattisgarh and Manipur. However, Orissa, Bihar, and Uttarakhand have also emerged as supply states for tribal prostitution. Victims of customary prostitution are generally forced into prostitution at a very young age (9–13) by family members (parents or brothers) who act as agents of the victims. Approximately 16% of persons forced in the sex trade are in prostitution as a result of customary practices.

Another form of sexual exploitation includes sex tourism (ST). ST includes the sexual exploitation of young boys and girls by international and Indian tourists. Street children are particularly vulnerable to this type of sexual exploitation. Costs per sexual act vary from 50 to 200 Indian Rs (about 1 to 5 US$) and can reach up to Rs 1000. (about 25 US$) when victims remain with their clients overnight or longer. Sex tourism is prevalent in the 'pink triangle', the Agra-Delhi-Jaipur belt, as well as south and south-west India: Goa, Maharashtra

(Mumbai), Karnataka (notably, in some of the new tourist spots like Gokarna and Karwar), Kerala (in Kovallam and other new popular destinations such as Cochin, Kumily, and Varkala), in Tamil Nadu (Mammallapuram), and in Orissa (particularly Puri). Himachal Pradesh and Rajasthan are emerging as new destinations for sex tourism.

Sex tourism may be facilitated by travel agencies, tour operators, hotels and associated business. There is also some evidence of young boys being imported from the Gulf countries into Southern India and forced into prostitution. In the last 15 years, CSE has been characterized by two changes. Females from upper castes are increasingly becoming victims of CSE. Prostitution is no longer primarily confined to traditional brothels and can be found in new venues, such as mobile brothels, dance bars, escort services, friendship clubs, massage parlour and huts or bath establishments along the national highways ( the Kolkata,-Siliguri-Guwahati-Shillong highway, the Dehli-Kolkata-Chennai-Mumbai highway, the Solapur-Hyderabad highway; the Grand Trunk Road between Bangladesh and Pakistan).

## INTERNAL AND TRANSNATIONAL TRAFFICKING

India is a source, transit, and destination country for women and girls trafficked for CSE. Interstate trafficking represents 89% of trafficking for CSE in India. The biggest supply states include: Andhra Pradesh (16/23 districts affected by trafficking for CSE), Bihar (24/38 districts affected by trafficking), Madhya Pradesh, West Bengal, Karnataka (16/27 districts affected by CSE), Tamil Nadu, Maharashtra and Uttar Pradesh. They are followed by the states of Orissa, Rajasthan, Assam and Jharkhand. Bihar, Maharashtra, and Madhya Pradesh have also the dubious distinction of being the states that procure the largest number of minor girls. The biggest buyers of minors include West Bengal and Maharashtra. Main destinations include Delhi, West Bengal (Kolkata), Maharashtra (Mumbai), Gujarat, Punjab and Haryana (the last 2 states being particularly popular for 'arranged' marriages).

Cities like Mumbai, Delhi, Kolkata, Bangalore, Hyderabad, and Chennai have the largest concentration of prostitutes.

Trafficking from neighbouring countries into India account for about 10% of trafficking for CSE. Bangladesh and Nepal are the biggest suppliers, respectively accounting for 2.17% and 2.6% of the international traffic for CSE into India. An estimated 10,000–20,000 Bangladeshi women and girls are trafficked every year into India. Total estimates of Bangladeshi persons trafficked for CSE into India vary between 200000–300000. Trafficked victims are initially kept in West Bengal, Assam, Orissa or Tripura. There, they are 'graded' according to their age, beauty (light or dark skin) and sexual status (virgin), initiated into commercial sexual customs, and sent to new destinations, including New Delhi, Agra, Mumbai, Kolkata, Goa or Pakistan (Karachi and Lahore).

Estimates of Nepali persons trafficked into India vary from 100 000 to 200 000. Human Rights Watch (2005) estimated that 6,000–10,000 Nepalese were trafficked into India annually. Other studies have suggested similar numbers (5,000–11,000). Seventy per cent of trafficked victims, most of them under 16, come from ethnic minority groups (Tamang, Gurung, Magar, and Sherpa) who live in remote hill villages or poor border communities. Trafficked victims are sold to brokers from amounts as small as 200 Nepali Rs. 200 (US$4.00) who then deliver them to Indian brothels for amounts ranging from 15,999 to 40,000 Rs (US$ 500–1300). India is also a transit country for Nepalese and Bangladeshi women trafficked to Pakistan, Western Asia and the Middle East and for women trafficked from the Russian Federation to Thailand.

It does not include non-brothel based prostitution or prostitution into small urban and rural red light areas. The literature also indicates that India is a destination country for women trafficked from Bhutan, Myanmar, Kyrgyzstan, Pakistan, Europe, Russia and Thailand. Data on India as an international supply country are scarce. However, evidence suggests that children from Karnataka, Andhra Pradesh and Madhya Pradesh are trafficked to the Gulf States, England, Korea and the Philippines for CSE. As well, the United Nations reported trafficking for CSE from India to Western Asia (the most prevalent), Kenya, The United Arab Emirates, The United States of America and to a lesser extent to Bahrain, Bhutan, Canada, France, Germany, Kuwait, Malaysia, Netherlands, Pakistan, Saudi Arabia, Singapore, Thailand, Turkey, The United Kingdom, and The United Republic of Tanzania.

Trafficking for CSE is a demand-driven phenomenon, facilitated by traffickers, who find trafficking highly profitable and low risk, and the availability of vulnerable populations. Vulnerability results from a range of inter-related economic, social, political, and familial factors ( poverty, lack of sustainable livelihoods, structural inequities) and creates the supply needed by traffickers to meet the nature of the demand. In most cases, trafficking results from the interface of multiple risk factors. For example, trafficking in Manipur has been fueled by years of civil unrest, the presence of armed forces, drug trafficking from neighbouring Myanmar, and poverty.

## Sexual Exploitation and HIV/AIDS

There is little evidence on the morbidity and mortality of persons engaged in commercial sex. Overall, adult HIV prevalence in India is 0.36% (2–3.1 million people infected), with 85% of HIV transmitted via heterosexual contacts, except in the northeastern states (Nagaland, Manipur and Mizoram) where the primary mode of transmission is injection drug use. Estimated HIV prevalence is greater among males (0.43%) than among females (0.29%). HIV in India continues to be primarily concentrated in high risk populations (i.e., females or males in prostitution and injecting drug users). Estimated adult HIV prevalence was greater than 1% in Manipur (1.67%) and Nagaland (1.26%) in 2006. HIV prevalence among women in prostitution (WP) in 2003, 2004, 2005 and 2006 was respectively 10.3%, 9.4%, 8.4%, and 5.4. In 2006, HIV among WP was very high in Nagaland (16.4%), followed by Maharashtra (12.8%), Manipur (11.6%), Mizoram (10.4%), Karnataka (9.6%)and Andhra Pradesh (8.8%). Overall, 8 states had greater than 5% HIV prevalence among WP, while 9 states had HIV prevalence between 1 and 5%.

Other studies on specific sub-populations found higher HIV prevalence rates than the ones previously mentioned. For example, a recent study on 287 repatriated Nepalese who had been trafficked in Indian brothels indicated that 38% of the study population was HIV+. In other studies, HIV prevalence among WP ranged between 43 to 54% of the study population. However, the higher HIV prevalence rates in these studies may be due to the small sample size or the selected sample (WP attending STI clinics). The aggregate data mask the heterogeneity of the epidemic. This heterogeneity reflects the influence of multiple factors, such as the types of prostitution in different states ( brothel versus non-brothel based), the age at which trafficked persons had their first sexual contacts and/or were forced into CSE, the clients (regular vs. one-time clients) and broader contextual variables (the ability of regional and local health care systems to prevent and respond to STIs).

HIV prevalence among WP was 45% and 26%, respectively in Mumbai (Maharashtra) and Mysore (Karnataka) and 13%, 27% and 44% in Kolkata, Siliguri and Panjipara in West Bengal in 2004–2005. However, there are rural districts (e.g., in Rajasthan and Karnataka) where the epidemic is just as advanced as in urban areas. Furthermore, younger WP (25 years of age or less) are more at risk of acquiring STIs than older ones. Higher infection rates among younger WP may be associated with the integrity of the genital lining when they are subjected to repeated trauma during sexual intercourse, facilitating higher HIV transmission. Additionally, younger WP may find it more difficult to negotiate condom use with their clients, leading to unprotected sex.

A limited number of studies have looked at STIs other than HIV among WP. These studies (N sizes ranging from 113 to 5574) also suggest that 48–80% of WP have symptoms of STIs. Most common symptoms include vaginal discharge (13–83%), vaginal warts (3–14%), vaginal ulcer (4–25%), Trichomonas (3–40%), Candidiasis (9%) and Gardenella (3%). Overall, brothel-based WP reported less signs of STIs than non-brothel-based WP, except in one study. Interestingly, this study also found that home-based WP was less at risk of acquiring HIV than brothel- or street-based WP.

Inconsistent condom use may partly explain STI prevalence. About 50% of the 5574 WP who participated in a national survey used a condom every time with all their *paying* costumers during the 30 days preceding the survey. Consistent condom use with *paying* clients was lower than the national average in Nagaland and Mizoram (23%), Bihar (24%), Assam (27%), Haryana (28%), Rajasthan (34%), and higher than the national average in Kerala (74%) Maharashtra (72.5%), Goa (69%), Delhi (63%), and Madhya Pradesh and Orissa (65%). Brothel-based WP reported more consistent condom use than non-brothel-based WP (57 vs. 46%). However, overall only 20% of WP reported consistent condom use with *non-paying* partners during the 30 days preceding the survey, with the exception of WP in Delhi, Manipur, Karnataka, and Orissa where consistent condom use with *non-paying* partners was higher than the national average. Less than 10% of WP in West Bengal, Bihar, Haryana, Maharashtra and Punjab reported using condoms consistently with non-paying partners.

Consistent condom use with first-time clients was also generally lower than with regular customers. Furthermore, while the national survey indicated that over 70% of WP insisted on using condoms with their clients, only 38% refused to have sex with clients who objected to using condoms. This number is somewhat alarming since 45% of the WP's clients (N = 5684) reported having more than one STI symptoms in the 12 months that preceded the national survey. Also alarming is the fact that only 6.8% of the WP's clients reported using condoms consistently with their regular or lifetime partners. WP's reasons for not using condoms consistently included clients' and partners' objection, complexity of condom negotiation under certain circumstances (with drunk clients, pimps or the police), lack of access to free or purchased condoms, lack of financial resources to buy condoms, lack of privacy in stores when buying condoms, and social stigma associated with condom purchase. However, recent studies have highlighted more fundamental issues.

Lack of funding has hindered the National AIDS Control Organization (NACO) in rolling out an adequate number of interventions targeted at WP.

As a result, interventions only reached a small proportion of high-risk individuals, even though the number of WP exposed to STI information/education has steadily increased over the years. Furthermore, the rigidity of financing mechanisms (USAIDS only fund programs promoting abstinence and condom use but does not fund condom procurement), a lack of strategic planning, a top-down approach to targeted interventions that failed to include the needs, experiences, and perspectives of those working at ground level, including WP, programs that narrowly focused on behavioural changes to the detriment of initiatives focusing on life-skill development and human rights issues have undermined the overall success of condom use interventions. Too often, prevention messages were framed in a moralistic approach promoting abstinence and neglecting the reality that WP may be not able to leave prostitution. Overt and covert discrimination against WP from district hospital personnel and other healthcare workers also prevented WP from seeking necessary health care.

Discrimination strategies included denial or delay of treatment, early dismissal, HIV test without WP's consent and breach of confidentiality re-test results. The national surveillance survey highlighted that 13.5% of its sample of over 5500 participants did not seek any treatment when they had STI symptoms, while 16% took home-based remedies and another 5% borrowed prescriptions from friends based on self-diagnosis of symptoms. Further compounding these issues, NGO outreach workers have described a repeated pattern of harassment from the police, including unjustified arrests and coercion, as a major challenge to HIV/AIDs prevention.

Although we did not find data on diseases other than STIs among WP, it is likely that the prevalence of chronic diseases among WP is high. These would include pelvic inflammatory disease, chronic pelvic pain, ectopic pregnancy, chronic liver disease and hepatocarcinomas secondary to hepatitis, COPD, asthma and bronchiolitis due to the living conditions, highly polluted environments and moldy dwellings with poor air quality and tobacco smoke. Chronic digestive problems and nutritional deficiencies due to poor nutrition can also be expected. Furthermore, the experience of one of us (H. V.) who has worked as a counselor with rescued victims of CSE for 12 years in India suggests that victims of CSE also suffer from post-traumatic syndrome, severe depression, feelings of helplessness and hopelessness. This has been supported by recent findings on trafficked women.

The number of women and children trafficked for CSE in India is large. Trafficking in India has become an international business and, unless stringent action is taken, is unlikely to slow down, given the enormous potential profits for organized crime syndicates and independent traffickers. Women and children have a right to be protected from any forms of trafficking and to be treated with dignity. This requires a comprehensive anti-human trafficking strategy embedded in a human rights approach since violations of human rights are both the cause and consequence of human trafficking. Such as approach requires the systematic development and implementation of policies and programmes that address the socio-economic, political, environmental and cultural factors that increases vulnerability to trafficking at the local, regional, state, national, and international levels.

India's recent effort toward the harmonization of the anti-trafficking legal framework in India, Nepal and Bangladesh and its new/revised Child Marriage Prohibition Act (2007) are steps into that direction. However, accrued efforts towards the promotion of gender equality in the family, community, and society at large, the facilitation of women's economic empowerment (via job training, job creation and income-generation schemes) and women's ownership and control of productive resources, the development of wider social welfare networks, the enforcement of safe migration policies and a zero-tolerance level for corruption are also needed. For example, a wider number of border guards, police and health practitioners should receive specific training related to trafficking.

As many others, we suggest strengthening the Immoral Trafficking Prevention Act, India's legal response to trafficking, in accordance to the United Nations Protocol to Prevent, Suppress and Punish Trafficking in persons, Especially Women and Children (2000) and the UN Recommended Principles and Guidelines on Human Rights and Human Trafficking (2002). Comprehensive anti-trafficking policies not only address the root causes of both supply of and demand for trafficked persons, but they also include the protection of and assistance to trafficked persons, appropriate enforcement mechanisms, and adequate sanctions against traffickers. Protection and assistance to the victims should include compensation for victims of trafficking; necessary medical care; provision of free legal assistance; and the rehabilitation and reintegration of rescued victims in consultation with trafficked victims and countries of origin.

With respect to health, a human rights approach posits that women in prostitution have the same rights to health and safe environments as any other human beings. It requires that STI prevention move away from stereotypical and moralistic notions of prostitution to a broader understanding of the complex nature of human trafficking for CSE; be sensitive to and inclusive of the experiences and perspectives of WP; and extend the locus of responsibility for HIV/AIDS prevention from WP to those participating in or facilitating this business, namely clients, regular partners, the families of WP, brothel owners, pimps, and law enforcement. Interventions also need to address the stigmatization and discrimination against WP at all levels of society (media, law enforcement, health care, communities), as exemplified by the Sonagachi project launched in Kolkata in 1992.

Harassment and ostracism drive epidemics underground and undermine the reach and effectiveness of prevention efforts. This means not only improving the quality of STI interventions for vulnerable women and their partners but also increasing STI monitoring, prevention and intervention efforts at male sexual workers and men having sex with men. In the context of the global AIDS epidemic, sex between men is significant because it may involve anal sex a practice that carries a higher risk of HIV transmission than vaginal sex, when no protection is used. Evidence suggests that more people become infected with HIV through male-male sex than via any other transmission route. In India, recent estimations of HIV prevalence among MSM varied from 6.41 to 11.8%. However, this group has largely been ignored due to the reluctance of the government to acknowledge and monitor MSM. In fact, sex between men is considered a criminal act in India. As a result, MSM often hide their same-sex relations from friends and families.

Many have wives, or have sex with women as well as men, transmitting HIV to their female partners if they are infected. The impact that HIV may have on MSM is therefore not an isolated problem, but one that is linked to the country's wider HIV epidemics, and one that needs to be addressed with greater efforts.

# 10

# The Immoral Traffic (Prevention) Act

Human Trafficking is modern form of slavery, whose victims are mainly women and children. It is the second largest criminal industry in the world and it is the fastest growing. No country today is free from human trafficking. According to UN estimates nearly 2 million women and children are abused and trafficked globally every year, and millions more are trafficked within their home countries. This commerce in human life generates crores of rupees each year-much of which is used to finance organized crime.

## TRAFFICKING AND INDIA

The size of the problem Thousands of Indians, especially women and children, are trafficked everyday to some destination. They are forced to live like slaves. They survive in brothels as sex workers, in dancing bars, child soldiers, as child brides, in factories doing hazardous work, guesthouses, farms and in the homes of well off Indians, with no control over their bodies and lives.

They are also being trafficked for illegal adoptions, organ transplants, working in circus, for begging and for the entertainment industry especially as camel jockeys. Like slavery, trafficking offers huge profits. Transactions in prostitution itself are worth Rs. 185 million a day; Rs. 370 billion per year.

Human trafficking is globally the third largest transnational crime after arms and drug trafficking, and comparatively the least risky. Story of Anju (name changed): Ms Anju, a 15 year old girl belonged to a village in Ranchi district of Jharkhand. She, along with her friends, was promised job in Delhi by the local agent near Ranchi. In July 2003, she, with her friends, boarded Mori Express which brought them to Punjab via Delhi. From the railway station they were brought to the house of Mr. Jawahar (name changed) of a village in Nawanshahar who confined her in a room with 7 more girls. The girls were sent daily to different people for domestic and farm work. A week after Ms Anju landed in Mr. Jawahar's house, his son tried to rape her during the day when no other women were present in the house.

The same evening she managed to escape from the house and hid herself in the fields. The next day she was noticed by a Bihari labourer who took her to the *Sarpanch's* house of the nearby village. She stayed with them for few days and then met some other migrant labourers in Nawanshahar who brought her to the police. A case FIR No.198 dt.5.8.2003 was registered under Sections 342/370/374/376/420/120-B IPC and 18 of Bonded Labour System (Abolition) Act, 1976 by police against Mr. Jawahar and his son on the statement of Ms Anju. On investigation it was found that Mr. Jawahar was working as the agent for distribution of labour from Jharkhand in Punjab for the last 4 years.

The agents from Jharkhand used to send young girls, boys and couples to Mr. Jawahar who, in turn, sent them to local people who needed domestic and farm help, and took a commission of Rs. 2000/- to Rs. 4000/- per person. Girls hired as household and as farm help were paid monthly salary of Rs.600/- to 800/-, while men were paid Rs.1000/- to 1200/-. They were not paid 3 months salary and the same was kept as a commission by Mr. Jawahar. After working for a year in the allocated houses, these labourers returned back to Mr. Jawahar who sent them to different households after taking his fresh commission. According to the investigation, Ms. Anju was sexually exploited by her agent from Jharkhand while she was staying with him in Delhi en-route. She was handed over to her parents who took her back to their native village.

Organ Trafficking in India: A case study of a donor of Punjab Kidney Scam Donor, a 17 year minor, belonged to a poor family in a small town in Punjab. Once when he had gone to visit Golden Temple in Amritsar where he met a middleman. The middleman, on the pretext of teaching him driving, forcibly abducted him and took him to the residence of a police inspector in Chandigarh.

His hair was trimmed and his identity was changed to Raju, a resident of Jalandhar. He was shown as a migrant in the records and then his case for kidney transplant was cleared by the Authorization Committee.

The Authorization Committee headed by the Principal, Government Medical College cleared the case on 6$^{th}$ June, 2002 without any verification for obvious reasons. He was operated upon in one Hospital in Jalandhar by two doctors and his kidney was removed and transplanted on to police the inspector.

Before removing his kidney, he was kept in illegal confinement in Jalandhar and threatened with dire consequences if he reported the matter to the police. His kidney was removed at gunpoint. In the affidavits it was shown that the "age of Raju was 22 years and he was working as a domestic help with the recipient police inspector for the last 10 years. As his parents had expired and he had no siblings, he wished to offer his kidney for transplant purely out of love, affection and humanitarian grounds without any payment in return". The victim was however even denied the promised sum of Rs.40, 000/-.

The parents of donor are alive and he has 2 brothers. A case vide FIR No.118/02 was registered in this matter in the PS Kotwali under Sections 95A, 363, 367, 368, 420, 468, 469, 471, 506, 120B IPC and 18, 19, 20 of Transplantation of Human Organs Act, 1994.

Victim of Coerced Marriage: Story of Miss Bala (name changed) Ms. Bala, a 15 year old girl, belonged to a village in

Nadia district of Bengal. She was the youngest member of a poor Bengali family and had studied up to 2 nd class. Her father used to beat her mother, and left her with 2 sons and a daughter. Her eldest brother was unemployed and the other brother worked in a hotel. Her mother worked as a domestic maid in other people's houses and earned about Rs. 400/- per month.

A close neighbour from her village "Krishna didi" told her mother that she would get Ms Bala a job in Delhi which would fetch her about Rs. 3000/- per month and her mother allowed her to travel to Delhi with Krishna and some other relatives. They stayed in Delhi in a jhuggi belonging to Krishna's relative for 10 days after which they went to Rewari. Krishna was married to a local carpenter in a village in Rewari and she had a daughter and a son from the marriage. She owned a *pucca* house of her own. She told Ms. Bala that she will get her married to a boy in the village and forced her to do so. Krishna had earlier sold two girls from their village for marriage in Haryana. Ms. Bala was confined for a month by Krishna and was pressurized to get married to the man selected by her. Ms. Bala managed to escape to visit a nearby Hanuman temple and narrated her story of confinement and marriage to the priest, who, in turn, informed the Police.

Police raided the place and arrested Krishna and lodged her in jail, and registered case u/s 363, 366, 372, 511/506 IPC. Ms. Bala was rescued and shifted to Nari Niketan, Karnal by order of the Court on 28/01/2004. Today Ms. Bala is totally blank about her future as she does not want to go home and her mother also has not responded to official letters sent by the Nari Niketan authorities.

## Size of the Problem

The fact is no one knows the full truth. These are just estimates:

- 27 million people are enslaved in some form worldwide – more than at any time in history
- Number of slaves trafficked from Africa to Americas in 400 year long Atlantic Slave Trade 15 million

- Up to 4.000.000 people are said to be trafficked annually, the majority of whom are women and children.
- UN estimates of number of persons illegally trafficked across borders in 1990s, per year 2 million
- Worldwide trafficking is growing fastest in East Europe. Former Soviet Union today is the largest source of women for the sex industry.
- It is estimated that about 500 000 Russian women are trafficked every year to over 50 destination countries.
- Human Trafficking today is the 2nd largest crime (after Drug trafficking). India is a source, transit and destination country for victims trafficked for sexual and economic exploitation.

Women and children are trafficked into India from Bangladesh and Nepal en-route to the Middle East nations. About 89 percent of trafficking in India is inter-state. Every day, about 200 girls and women enter into prostitution mostly against their will. Estimates of women involved in sex trade in India ranges from 100000 to 800000 Of over 2 million commercial sex workers [CSWs] in India up to 25 percent of (3, 00,000 - 5,00,000) are below 18 years of age. Mumbai has more than 2, 00,000 CSWs, 20 percent of them below 18 years of age. The HIV/AIDS threat has fuelled the demand for younger girls because of the popular myth that virgins are a cure for HIV/AIDS and increase the male potency. Every year over 22,000 women and 44,000 children are reported missing in India. Of these, more than 5,000 women and 11,000 children are not traced. 60% of the rescued girls said that they were deceived into the trade. Only 11% said that poverty was the reason.

Earnings:

- The average purchase price of a woman/girl is Rs. 10,000/ - .
- On an average the rescued girls said that they met 6 clients a day.
- On an average the girls earned about Rs. 3000/- per month.

- On an average a girl gets to keep only 1/3rd of income generated by her.
- One girl generates around Rs. 1, 00,000 per year for others.

Trafficking means trade in something that should NOT be traded - drug trafficking, arms trafficking etc. Human trafficking is the criminal practice of exploitation and trading in people. This crime is:-

- Very lucrative/profitable.
- Has very low risk.
- The majority of trafficking in persons (approximately 95%) is controlled by organised criminals.
- It has a major humane overtone.
- It is a crime in which victims suffer over a very long period.

Human Trafficking has three components. It is: the act of: recruitment, transportation, transfer, harbouring, or reception of persons By means of: threat, use of force, coercion, abduction, fraud, deception, abuse of power or other weakness of victim. For exploitation: which includes, prostitution, sexual exploitation, forced labour, removal of organs, etc. One element from each sub group must be present for it to be defined as Human Trafficking.

It is for basically two purposes:

A. *Sex Trafficking:* By use of force, fraud, coercion a women is made to indulge in commercial sex and can be seen in brothels, dance bars, massage parlours, pornography, etc.
B. *Labour Trafficking:* By use of force, fraud, coercion a person is made to provide involuntary labour service or is paid less than his due.

Criminal Activity from Human Trafficking is:

- Against the state as it causes corruption, money laundering, tax evasion, forgery of documents;
- Against the victims as it leads to illegal detention; bonded labour; kidnapping; murder; injury; sexual assault; rape; torture; cruelty; forced abortion; forced marriage; sale of organs, etc.

In Human Trafficking we always have: A source/origin from where the trafficking starts. This is where the recruitment for human trafficking takes place.

- *Transit*: This involves bringing victims from their villages, etc., to places where they can be exploited. All forms of transport are used for this purpose. It also covers providing temporary shelters through a series of safe houses - places which are used to transport the victim from one place to another.
  Destination is the place/places where the exploitation takes place.

## Causes of Trafficking

Some important causes are:

- Poverty & Economic Hardship.
- Increased Wealth Gap.
- Un-ending demand for prostitution.
- Increased opportunity to travel.
- Free market but no effective laws to tackle trafficking.
- Growth of Criminal Networks.
- Technology especially Internet and satellite channels.
- Difficulty in prosecuting due to the silence of victims.

*Some social causes are:* Lack of education, especially among women and children, harsh/ abnormal family environment including breakdown of marriage, low status of women in general, increase in violence - especially against women, breakup of joint family resulting in absence of social safety net, sexual 'revolution/freedom' resulting in casual attitude towards exchanging sex for money and extraneous reasons like natural disasters e.g. drought, famine, earthquake, war, etc.

Who are the Traffickers? Traffickers can be:

- Organized crime syndicates with international links.
- Gangs trafficking arms, drugs.
- Smugglers of contrabands.
- Small group with loose structures (including family of victims).

- Marriage/Modelling agencies.
- Gangs who forcibly take/sell orphans/children.
- Friends/acquaintance usually a former victim.
- Groups promising lucrative jobs.

The Characteristics of Traffickers are:

Organized criminal group of three or more persons, " existing for a period of time", acting in consort ", with the aim of committing serious crime, " in order to obtain directly or indirectly ", financial or other material benefit. How are victims trafficked? Traffickers use:

- Force: Rape, beating, constraint, confinement.
- Fraud: Giving false and deceptive offers of employment, marriage, better life, etc.
- Coercion: Threats of serious harm to victims or their families if the victims do not obey. How organized is this Crime?

The organized nature of this crime can be judged from the fact that:

- Someone locates and recruits the victim.
- Someone 'escorts' the victim.
- Someone 'neutralizes' the official machinery.
- Someone who knows and makes arrangements in local places.
- Someone keeps the victims safely
- Someone provides logistic support to the movement of victims - food, housing, etc.
- Someone collects the payment for providing the victims.
- Someone is responsible for moving the victim from one place to another
- Someone makes 'investment' in the whole activity, especially when they are sent outside the country.
- Someone watches the movement/activity of police and immigration authorities.
- Someone collects the fees in the country of destination.

- Someone makes the earnings legitimate/ white.
- Someone enforces order and discipline in the entire activity.

## LAW

Human trafficking is not comprehensively defined in any Indian law. However there are many laws where reference to different forms of trafficking is made. Indian Laws: Human trafficking is basically dealt with by four laws in India: the Indian Penal Code, 1861; The Immoral Traffic (Prevention) Act, 1956; Juvenile Justice (Care and Protection of Children) Act, 2000 and Bonded Labour System (Abolition) Act, 1976.

### Indian Penal Code

- Section 292 & 293: Obscene material Sale, distri-bution etc.
- Section 341: Punishments for Wrongful Restraint.
- Section 342: Punishment for Wrongful Confinement.
- Section 361: Kidnapping a minor from lawful guardianship.
- Section 362: Abducting any person.
- Section 363: Punishment for Kidnapping.
- Section 363A: Kidnapping or maiming a minor for purposes of begging.
- Section 365: Kidnapping or Abducting with Intent Secretly and Wrongfully to Confine Person.
- Section 366: Kidnapping, abducting or Inducing Woman to compel her for Marriage, illicit intercourse, etc.
- Section 366A: Procuration of Minor Girl.
- Section 366B: Importation of Girl from Foreign Country.
- Section 367: Kidnapping or Abducting In Order To Subject Person To grievous Hurt, Slavery, etc.
- Section 368: Wrongfully Concealing or Keeping in Confinement, Kidnapped or Abducted Person.
- Section 369: Kidnapping or Abducting Child under Ten Years with intent to steal from its Person.

- Section 370: Buying or Disposing of Any Person as a Slave
- Section 371: Habitual Dealing in Slaves.
- Section 372: Selling Minor for purposes of Prostitution, etc.
- Section 373: Buying Minor for purposes of prostitution, etc.
- Section 374: Unlawful compulsory labour.
- Section 376: Punishment for rape.
- Section 376(f): Rape of woman less than 12 years of age.
- Section 377: Unnatural offences.

## The Immoral Traffic (Prevention) Act of 1956

This is the most important law to curb trafficking and has been dealt with separately. The Bonded Labour System (Abolition) Act of 1976: It prohibits forced or bonded labour. The National Human Rights Commission of India monitors its implementation. Young Persons (Harmful Publication) Act 1956: Prohibits distribution of material related to crime, violence and vice. The Juvenile Justice (Care and Protection of Children) Act, 2000: This Act explicitly provides for effective social rehabilitation and reintegration of all juveniles in need of care and protection and makes explicit provisions for punishment for employment of juvenile or child for begging, giving intoxicating liquor or narcotic drug or psychotropic substance to juvenile or child, exploitation of juvenile or child employee.

## Transplantation of Human Organ Act, 1994

It provides for the regulation of removal, storage and transplantation of human organs for purpose of treatment and for the prevention of commercial dealings in human organs.

## The Child Marriage Restraint Act, 1929

The Act provides for age of marriage 21 for male and 18 for female.

- Section 3: It is an offence for a male above 18 years but below 21 years to get married.

- Section 4: It is an offence if a male above 21 years married a girl below 18 years.
- Section 5: Whoever performs conducts or directs any child marriage commits an offence.
- Section 6: Parent or guardian in charge of the minor, promoting or permitting, or negligently failing to prevent child marriage commits an offence.
- It is a cognizable offence but no Court can take cognizance of any offence under this Act after the expiry of one year from the date on which the offence is alleged to have been committed.
- The Court may issue an injunction against any of the persons mentioned in Section 3, 4, 5 and 6 of this Act prohibiting such marriage.

In ITPA, prostitution is defined as sexual exploitation or abuse of persons for commercial purposes. As per this definition, prostitution is not confined to only women. Homosexuality is also brought under this definition. It includes not only exploitation of one person by another but also abuse of one's own self for commercial purposes. Exploitation or abuse for purposes other than commercial is not covered under this definition.

*Section 3 of ITPA*: Running a brothel or letting premises for running a brothel is offence under Section 3. Brothel is defined as a place where sexual exploitation for abuse is carried on for the gain of another person or for the mutual gain of two or more prostitutes.

Prostitution, per-se, is not an offence by itself. Nature and type of evidence possible in the given situation: -

1. You are required to establish the ownership of the premise. This can be done by examination of Land deeds; by examination of registration documents, lease deeds; by examination of receipt of payment of rent or cess/tax for water, electricity, telephone etc.; by examination of voter's list, ration card, and bank accounts.
2. To prove that the premise is being used as a brothel.

This can be done by statement of witnesses; statement of victims; by newspaper reports that the place is being used by brothel; recoveries from the premise; earlier police records.

If a person allows premises to be used as a brothel, the law presumes that he had the knowledge of the place being used as a brothel if any of the relevant documents is produced as evidence.

*Section 4 of ITPA Offence of Living on the earnings of the prostitute: Living on the earnings of the prostitute being above the age of 18 years is an offence under Section 4. Even husband or adult children can also be accused under this section:*

Living on earnings related to prostitution of a child or a minor is a more serious offence. Nature and type of evidence possible in the given situation 1) In this we have to establish that a person is getting income from prostituting others; or, a person is living with a prostitute; or, a person is habitually found in the company of a prostitute; or, the person aids, abets or compels a prostitute; or the person acts as tout, pimp on behalf of a prostitute.

To prove this we need to use income statements, receipts of payments, vouchers of expenditure, books of accounts, other documents which are maintained in the ordinary course of business to establish that he has unexplained source of income.

The association with prostitutes will link this income with the earning of prostitutes. Presumption will be drawn against the person that he is living on the earnings of prostitution

*Section 5 of ITPA:* Procuring or inducing or taking any person for the sake of prostitution whether the victim accompanies willingly or unwillingly is an offence under Section 5.

If the offence is committed in respect of children or minor it is a more serious offence. Nature and type of evidence possible in the given situation 1, we have to establish that the person was taken away to be used for prostitution.

To prove it we need the following type of evidence:

- The age of the trafficked person.

- The statement of victim to bring out how the consent was obtained.
- Whether it was under pressure, through coercion, threat, deceit, etc.
- That the trafficker/exploiter had displaced the victim from the community of the latter.
- The intention or knowledge of the trafficker/exploiter can be established by his contact/association with the brothel or the persons in the brothel.
- Medical examination of the trafficked person.
- Medical examination of the abusers to establish the act of sexual assault.
- The details of the destination point, brothel or such other places where sexual exploitation takes place under the cover of other activities (massage parlour, etc).
- The details of the source point from where the person was trafficked or attempted to be trafficked.
- The transit points, halting places, etc.
- The mode of transport, statement of transporters, travel documents like train ticket, etc.
- A map showing the entire trafficking route and the places of exploitation and the role of exploiters.

*Section 6 of ITPA:* Detaining a person in premises where prostitution is carried on is an offence under Section 6 Certain important presumptions are provided in this section for the benefit of prosecution in proving the cases under this section.

It shall be presumed that she is detained in place of prostitution if:

- A child of the victim is found in a brothel; or
- A minor victim is medically examined and found with sexually transmitted diseases; or
- The jewellery of a victim is in the custody of the management of the brothel. Nature and type of evidence possible in the given situation.

We have to establish that a person has been detained for

sexual exploitation. To prove this we need:

- Proof of the place being a brothel or a place of commercial sexual exploitation.
- The victim is always accompanied by a person.
- The victim is not allowed to venture out of the premise.
- Statement of the victim.
- Who keeps her valuables?
- If there was consent, it needs to be probed further whether it was under pressure, coercion, force, lure, deceit, etc.
- Intention/knowledge of the accused to be checked by his examination and conduct.
- Medical examination could indicate that the victim is sexually exploited.
- Medical examination report about the age of victim.

In certain brothels the managers keep account of the belongings taken away from the victims. There are documents, which show the transaction and earnings/expenditures in the brothel. Documents also show the debt bondage of the victims.

Such documents need to be thoroughly probed and included as evidence.

*Section 7 of ITPA*: Prostitution in the vicinity of a public place is an offence against the prostitute under Section 7. Land lord of a public place or letting out a place with the knowledge that it will be used for purpose of prostitution is an offence under Section 7. A public place is one that is accessible to the public in general. Nature and type of evidence possible in the given situation we have to establish that a place is a public place and that prostitution is taking place near it.

To prove this we need to establish:

- That it was taking place within a notified area or within two hundred meters from a place of worship/educational institution/hostel/hospital/ nursing home or any such area notified by the Commissioner of Police or the District Magistrate or Sub Divisional Magistrate.

- If a brothel exists within the above area this section will get established.
- If the offence takes place in a hotel, the license is liable to be suspended/ cancelled.
- Liability extends to the keeper of a public place, the tenant, lessee, occupier or manager of the premises and the owner, lesser or landlord or their agents, provided they had the knowledge/ intention.
- The detailed statements of the victims.
- The statement of persons affected/ harmed (other than the victims of commercial sexual exploitation) by the brothel being run in the vicinity. For example, the statements of religious priests, hospital employees, residents in the area etc.

*Section 8 of ITPA:* Seducing or soliciting for the purpose of prostitution from any public place or within the site of or in the hearing of any person in any public place, whether from within a building or house, by means of words, gestures or any exposures is an offence under Section 8. Note: The offender could be a male or female (though S.8 (a) speaks about only a female person, the proviso to the Section 8 does speak about males also). Nature and type of evidence possible in the given situation. We have to establish that seducing or soliciting took place in a public place or near it. To prove this we need to establish:

- That it is a public place and the evidence discussed in the previous Para under S.7 is required in order to establish it.
- That the person was tempting or attracting the attention of any person by words, gestures or willful exposure of one's person or otherwise (otherwise can include telephone sex, soliciting advertisements in yellow journals etc.).
- That the person was soliciting or molesting any person, or loitering or acting in such manner as to cause obstruction or annoyance to residents or passers-by or offends against public decency.
- That the above was done deliberately and knowingly for if a person is made to solicit by force/ threat/ deceit/ lure etc. by another person, the latter is responsible and

not the former.

- That the statement of witnesses as to how it annoyed/ offended them. The witnesses could be residents or passers-by.
- Documents regarding earlier charge sheet/conviction of the person (Subsequent convictions invite graver penalty).

*Section 9 of ITPA:* Seduction of any person when in custody or charge or care of any person in authority is an offence under Section 9. Nature and type of evidence possible in the given situation to establish this we have to prove that the person was in the charge of the accused and that the accused seduced the person. To prove this we need:

- Documents and statements to establish that the victim is in the custody/ charge/ care or under the authority of the offender. This includes registers maintained (more often kept hidden) in the brothel/hotel etc.
- In places where the exploitation is done under the cover of another activity (for prostitution taking place under the cover/board of massage parlour) there may be regular documents to show that the victims are employed payroll, attendance registers, leave registers etc.
- If a trafficked person is confined to a brothel by the brothel keeper to a hotel by the hotel manager. and thereafter seduced/exploited, the brothel keepers or hotel managers, as the case may be, are liable under this section too.
- Medical examination reports of the victims.
- Documents from previous search/charge sheet etc to show that the offender is in command/control/authority over the victim.
- Documents regarding earlier conviction, charge sheet etc.

If a person who is in charge of the victim causes or aids or abets the seduction for prostitution of that person then he is guilty. There is minimum punishment prescribed for the offence and, therefore, can be a deterrent against trafficking, if used against all those who command and control the trafficked persons.

*Section 11 of ITPA:* When an offender is prosecuted and convicted for an offence under this Act and again convicted for the second time within a period of 5 years, the Investigating Officer can file a memo at the time of passing the sentence to the Court requesting the court to notify the address of the convict. (Section 11)

*Section 13 of ITPA:* The special police officers not below the rank of Inspectors appointed by the State Government under this Act are only competent to investigate the offences under this Act falling in their jurisdiction.

*Section 18 of ITPA:* Closure of Brothels The area executive magistrate, on information from the police or otherwise that prostitution is being carried on in a house or brothel within 200 meters of any public place as defined in section 7 (1) of the Act, may issue notice to the owner, lessee or occupier of the place to show cause within 7 days as to why that place shall not be attached for improper use and after making due enquiry and after giving opportunity to be heard, may pass an order: (a) Directing the eviction of the occupier within 7 days from the date of order, and (b) also directing the owner to obtain previous approval of the magistrate if the owner wants to let out the premises within one year from the date of order. This provision can be invoked irrespective of the fact that prosecution is launched or not. In case the prosecution is also launched and the accused is convicted, a memo can be filed in the court itself for eviction of the premises.

A Judicial Magistrate convicting a person u/s 3 or 7 ITPA can order closure of the brothel and eviction of the offenders (without any further notice) Nature and type of evidence possible in the given situation The same evidence outlined u/s 3 of ITPA will establish the ownership of the premise and the fact that it is a brothel. We have then to establish that it is within 200 metres of the public place. To satisfy the Magistrate, following information could be useful:

- Documents and physical measurements to show that the scene of crime is in a public place (refer documents listed u/s 7).

- Bills/ Vouchers/ receipts regarding electricity/ telephone/ water/ hospitality etc to establish linkage of the offender to the place. Also Land deeds/agreements, etc. relating to the ownership/ title of the property.
- Report of police/ NGO etc, regarding abuse of the place, before the DM/SDM so that even before conviction by a judicial court, the eviction can be done.
- Medical examination report of the victim. Earlier reports, if any, of police regarding the exploitation taking place in the same place.

Note:

- Orders passed by the court/ Magistrate is neither appealable nor stayable nor can be set aside by any court Lease/ agreement regarding the house becomes invalid and ceases to be operative on conviction under this section.

*Section 20 of ITPA:* The area executive magistrate, on informatison from the police or otherwise that a prostitute resides in his jurisdiction, may issue notice to the person to appear before him. If, after making due enquiry and after giving opportunity to be heard, he is satisfied that the person is a prostitute he may pass an order asking the person to remove herself from the area of his jurisdiction or to some other place within his jurisdiction. Nature and type of evidence possible in the given situation the evidence required would be broadly in line with section 7, 8 and 9 of ITPA.

**General guidelines for the Police:**

All Police activity from prevention to investigation to trial to conviction must ALWAYS be primarily focused on making the traffickers ineffective. It shall be the bounden duty of Supervisory Police officers to enquire and ensure that there is no involvement of police and other government agencies in the abetment and encouragement of human trafficking.

1. *Proactive Police: Work* Proactive police work is when the police gather information before taking action, with the advantage that you can take the lead, decide who to target, and carefully plan the whole exercise.

Since proactive actions rely on gathering and using information, it involves tracing the trails left by traffickers including:

- Make regular enquiry from *Chawkidar* about missing women and children; mass movement of women and children; women being sold.
- Geographic profiling of city red light areas, brothels, floors and compartments may be done as it assists police during raids.
- Networking of police of various states on the issues of trafficking especially source and destination states.
- Analysis of advertisements in newspapers.
- Using sources - bar owner, NGO, journalists.
- Tracking telephones, mobiles and internet.

Building information involves: Identifying key players Tracking routes and travel arrangements Identifying safe houses and destinations Mobile surveillance Surveillance of premises Undercover work Using cover information Tracing a money trail Get a sense of the scale of business There are more technical forms of information gathering that may be used: Wire tapping telephones Telephone intercepts-mobile and landline Wire tapping a house Tracking devices on cars Recording devices Camcorders When arrests follow a pro-active process there is not much of a need to rely on victim's statement.

2. *Disruptive Police: Work* In this a message goes out to the organizers that trafficking would not be tolerated and will only cause harassment to the suspected trafficker. It is meant to make the trafficker afraid of the consequences. Police uses legal resources to enter a building:

- To ensure there are no minors working there.
- To ensure the compliance of health and safety provisions.
- To ensure the compliance of Licensing laws.
- To enquire into complaints about noise etc.
- To check the violation of land use by-laws on a property, if it is not being used as a residence.

**General Guidelines for Investigating Officers:**

The Investigation Officer should always keep in mind that he is dealing with organized crime. Otherwise, the investigation will be perfunctory.

- He must look at the trafficking routes and halts and source points;
- Locate the traffickers, transporters, conspirators, abettors, financiers, abusers, etc.
- Document through interview, bio-medical tests, psycho-social profiling, the harm done to the victim;
- Investigate into the profit of the exploiters;
- Verify the records maintained in the brothel;
- Follow up of the entries in the registers and clearly bring out the role of each of them. Where a victim comes forward and complains herself or member of the community or NGO provides police with information, then the police officer should first assess the following and then follow up on the information received.
- Listen to the informant/complainant carefully and seek clarification.
- If a criminal case is made out, write the FIR and make necessary entry in the General/Station Diary. If the information points to an emergency the Police Officer should act immediately.
- Send information to senior formations of the department.
- Obtain the services of Special Police Officer, NGOs and lady police. Generally, a woman or girl should be arrested by woman police personnel. If Special Police Officer designated under ITPA is not available, get authorization to arrest and investigate.
- Check the list of willing lawyers at the Police Station.
- Where is the Rescue Home located?
- Are there any witnesses?
- Are the witnesses prepared to testify?
- If the witness is the victim what are her needs?

- There should be adequate number of vehicles so that the rescued person is transported without publicity.

It should be well planned and a range of evidence should be routinely looked for and collected. Police should have a clear idea of how to enter the premises and the number of police officers needed. Summon two independent witnesses, one being women from the locality. Brief them about the raid.

In terms of evidence collection Investigating Police officer should:

- Rescue the victims and arrest everyone involved with management of the brothel/establishment. Only a woman police officer should search a victim/woman. Special care should be taken if the woman is pregnant or has a very small child.
- Look for minor victims in false ceiling, basements, and other hiding places. If victim is below the age of sixteen, the client can be arrested for rape under the Indian Penal Code.
- Allow victims to take her belonging.
- Seize all relevant documents- financial records, travel documentation.
- At the time of raid, if possible take video of the scene of crime. Film/photograph of the raids will also be useful.
- Telephone diaries sometimes certain pages are folded at the corner and they may be notes of numbers and addresses on them.
- Check for fingerprints.
- Always take the rubbish it may include the essential evidence.
- Seize Maps for they may detail the routes taken by traffickers.
- Seize all phones and unload memory from mobile phones.
- Use sniffer dogs to search for minor victims in false ceilings, basements and other places where they are likely to be hidden.
- As and when the rescue is done, please notify the authorities of the concerned Rescue Home regarding the

number of persons going to be lodged so that they could be prepared to receive them and organize themselves.

- Send the victim to the rescue home as soon as possible.

Till such time, Keep men and women in a separate lock up; Do not handcuff her; Allow a relative, if available, to keep a watch on her when she is in the lock up; Provide her necessary privacy to change, use the toilet or for bathing; If possible, provide her privacy when she is sleeping. (NB: This applies to any female who has been arrested) Crime Scene Photography After cursory look of the Scene of Crime, the Investigator should plan and brief the photographer accordingly, and take liberal number of photographs to cover the minutest detail. Video record or photograph the inside and outside of the premises. Take long distance, intermediate distance and close-up photographs of the scene. Measuring tape should be placed by the side of each physical clue while taking close-up photographs. Take a few photographs of the witnesses while recording the scene. The photographer should submit both the negatives and prints and also a note about each photograph, to the investigating officer so that they may be kept in the police station as permanent record.

## Sketching of the Scene

The Investigator should draw a rough sketch of the scene showing the following:

- Size of the area (Length, Breath and Height). Sketch the entry, exit and other routes.
- Position of permanent fixtures, their dimension and distance from each other.
- Position of physical evidences, their measurement and distance from each other.
- Sketch of a room or any closed area may be shown like an un-folded packing box.
- Use proper abbreviations, numbers, and legends in the sketch.
- Distance of an object should be measured from two nearest, permanent, and perpendicular fixtures.

- North direction should always be indicated in the sketch.
- It should also bear the signatures of witnesses.
- Convert the rough sketch into a smooth sketch engaging a professional expert, but the rough sketch should always be retained as permanent record.

## Collection, Handling and Packing of Physical Evidence

Any article found at the scene which has relevance to the crime should be handled, collected, packed and documented properly and carefully.

Adequate care should be taken that their evidentiary value is maintained and not lost due to improper means of transportation, delay, mishandling, poor packing, lack of relevant papers etc.

Chain of custody should always be maintained. Individuality of each item should be maintained by ensuring proper packing and sealing, numbering and specifications, writing forwarding note and other desired information. All information should be entered correctly in a precise and specific manner.

For articles bearing fingerprints the Investigation Officer should take adequate precaution by using gloves for collecting, handling and packing of any article, which bears fingerprints to ensure that the Investigating Officer is not leaving behind his fingerprints on the object. Stained clothes of the victim should be seized and if it corroborates the statement of the victim or implicates the accused it should be sent for necessary examination.

Ascertain the age of the Victim: If age of the victim is a fact-in-issue, all possible evidence such as physical appearance, registration of birth, medical opinion, and ossification test viz. test of bone formation to determine age, school certificate, evidence of neighbours, etc. should be collected. Only "ossification" test is not accepted as conclusive proof of age. Special care should be taken to prove age in border line cases.

Medical Examination:

The Investigating Officer should:

- Depute two lady constables to accompany the victim to the hospital. Medical examination should be done by a lady doctor. If the medical examination is being conducted by a male doctor, then one of the lady constables must be present.

The Investigating Officer should specifically ask for report from the doctor on:--Injuries (type, size, location, cause, relative distances, age of the wounds; typical injuries sustained during struggle cuts, bites, cigarette butt marks, etc.) Injuries should be specially checked at the following places by the doctor:

- Scalp/ Head/Fore Head
- Face/ Neck/ Throat
- Shoulders/ Chest/ Upper arm/ Lower arm/ Back of the shoulder
- Abdomen
- Thigh/ Calf/ Foot
- Genital area
- Back/ Hips Preserve the vaginal swab

Record of any treatment in a hospital, available should be sent to the Doctor to assist him. Dispatch the victim to the protective home after the medical examination. Recording of statement from trafficked victim Interview must be carried out by a female police officer or in the presence of a female NGO worker as mandated under Section 15 (6-A) of ITPA. Chose the most comfortable room and ensure it is private. Does the interview in small parts of about 2 hours, if it takes several days to get the whole story let it be as it is better to have a complete statement?

The I.O. should pay special attention to:

- Full name with alias if any.
- Name of Father and Mother and her full permanent address.
- Caste/ Religion.

- Height, built, complexion, colour of hair and eyes.
- Clothes/ tattoo marks/ ornaments.
- Identification marks.
- Educational qualification and name of school.
- Married/Unmarried and details of children if any.
- Family history especially of brothers, sisters, paternal uncle and aunt; maternal uncle and aunt and their full address, vocation etc.
- Social background/Economic background.
- How, when and by whom was she recruited?
- What she believed she would be doing?
- Was she held anywhere before leaving?
- How did she travel, with whom, who paid for the travel, stay en-route?
- How did she reach the destination, whether moved to other locations with details?
- Any physical or sexual violence inflicted at this point of time.
- How was she initiated?
- How was she controlled? What was the method used by brothel keeper to control her or prevent her escape?
- Her working conditions in detail.
- How many clients did she see per day? Does she have the name and address of regular clients?
- Details of financial transactions. What was the monthly payment made by the brothel keeper/trafficker? Deduction made every month and for what purpose.
- Whether she knows about the organized nature of this crime. How many other girls were there; how many were below 16 years; from which district/state had they come?
- Which govt. agency was paid by the brothel keeper?
- Did she indulge in any substance abuse (drugs; alcohol; cigarettes, etc.) Did she contract any disease and was she treated for it.
- Description of all suspects, their involvement, lifestyle, how they spend money, their property, etc.

When all the information has been obtained, write up a statement and read that back to her for accuracy. Every effort should be made to get her full statement recorded before a Magistrate as quickly as possible. Also, if Test Identification Parade has to be carried out using the victims as witness it should be done at the earliest. Further, every effort should be made to ensure that the same Investigating Officer & other officials stay in contact with the victims throughout her legal case.

## Questioning of Suspects

Detailed Questioning of suspects always helps to establish linkages, and truthfulness of the statements of accused and witnesses. This is very important when we need to prove the organized nature of this offence. The questioning of suspects should include the following:

- Is he known/unknown to the victim/brothel owner/client etc.
- His general place of residence.
- Education/ profession/job.
- Social background/ Economic background.
- Friends/ Profile of friends/ Love affairs.
- Is he married and is his spouse also involved in trafficking?
- Profile/ Profile of the parents, siblings.
- Habits/ Places normally visited.
- Previous criminal record.
- Medico-legal report/ Hospital record (treatment record), STDs.
- Examination of clothes for stains/ Collection of clothes.
- Motive.
- Vehicle used.
- Other accomplices the role and status of trafficked victim.

There is a clear conflict for law enforcers between the fact that many trafficked women will have broken certain laws- in terms of sex work, immigration- but the fact is that they have been victims of human rights abuse, rape, confinement and physical assault. Trafficked women should be always treated as victims and not criminals, and all with respect.

- They may become a witness or provide important information and for this to happen victims must be able to trust the police.
- Victims are fearful of police and traffickers, their families are threatened, and hence may not cooperate with the police.

It is rare of trafficked victims to make a formal statement or complaint against their exploiters; and therefore the need to create 'victimless prosecution'. To protect the human rights of the victims, the following needs to be done:

- Treat with respect and dignity.
- Provide immediate medical or other treatment if needed.
- Do not hold the victim in custody for lengthy periods of time or even in the same or next cells to their exploiters.
- Protect victim from all forms of abuse whilst in custody/ care of public officials.
- Provide victim access to female officials.
- Provide the victim with accurate information about their legal rights.
- Be offered protection and temporary shelter if they are willing to give evidence.
- Be offered the possibility of return reintegration with society through NGOs.
- Provide safe accommodation.
- Provide some living support with assistance from social welfare department.
- Provide protection when victim gives evidence.
- Insist on in camera trial.
- Get victim to and from the court safely unseen by others.
- Use assumed name or alias and to prevent her real name from appearing in the media. Many of the steps will also be applicable to witnesses.

- Rescued children should be produced before the Child Welfare Committee (CWC) constituted under the Juvenile Justice Act.

ITPA is more effective than IPC since burden shifts to accused. Guidelines for Investigating Officer under the ITPA and the Investigating Officer should keep in mind the following guidelines in the investigation of cases under this Act:

(a) *Sympathy towards the victim:* The rescued women should be examined in great detail, with sympathy and not with hostility. We should not look down on her. The grip of the trafficker would be so strong and possibility of their acceptance in society or family being bleak, they tend not to disclose any details. Hence the Investigating Officer should first take all steps in coordination with the Advisory Bodies, voluntary Social Welfare Organizations in the field, the Governmental agencies in charge of correctional and protection homes to give confidence to the women to be able to tell the details of persons who exploited them.

(b) *Procedure of search*: Searches, for rescue of persons from brothels or to detect offences under this Act, can be carried out only by special police officers without warrant, in the presence of two independent witnesses and one among them shall be woman. Any other officer not below the rank of a Sub-inspector can also conduct a search for rescue of persons only under the warrant from a competent magistrate.

(c) *Arrest provisions:* Arrest without warrant may be made by a special police officer or under his direction or subject to his prior approval, a police officer not below the rank of an S.I. may arrest the accused and immediately report to the special police officer.

(d) *Punishment to exploiters:* The law is intended to punish those who exploit the women and trade on them and not the victims. The evidence of victims is therefore extremely important.

(e) *Enquiry about correct identity of the victim:* The names and identity of women is often changed, and hence, the correct identity should be established by gathering information about their native village/town.

(f) *Corroborative evidence:* The persons doing odd jobs in the brothel or place where the women are kept and used as sex workers would be a useful corroboration.

(g) *Working with vulnerable witnesses:* Witnesses who can be blackmailed or threatened with consequences cannot be expected to give evidence unless police officials do everything in their power and resources to protect them from reprisals. Strong links between police and specialist NGOs is the best way of meeting the needs of victims and witnesses. They are able to build trusting relationship; provide practical and emotional support; and ensure that the victim's needs are taken into account in the law enforcement process.

(h) *Documentary evidence:* The chits, papers or bank transactions if any, house owner's title, the rental documents (whether true or false), municipal records, details of previous cases in which the accused may be involved should be collected.

(i) *Means of livelihood:* The means of livelihood of the accused should be thoroughly investigated including the adequacy or otherwise of such means to the style of life being led by him.

(j) *Circumstances of disappearance:* The circumstances under which the girl has disappeared or left her home, workplace, school, etc. should be brought out clearly.

(k) *Medical Examination:* Medical examination of persons found whether women or minors, male or female should be got conducted.

(l) *Penal Code:* Where offences under this Act or the Indian Penal Code are part of Organised Crime,
120 B IPC should be added.

(m) *Care during the trial:* Photographic or video graphic evidence whenever possible should be secured during investigation of the cases. It should be remembered that a sense of shame, unwillingness and even fear very often prevents the witnesses from deposing either during investigation or trial. Necessary precautions to prevent undue publicity with the permission of the concerned court should be taken.

## HUMANE ASPECT OF INVESTIGATION

Every police officer must understand the thinking of the victim of trafficking. It is essential for policemen that they must appear before the victim as a source of hope and help to save them from their present situation, rather than as a person just concerned with dealing with criminal activity. He must be gentle, understanding, helpful and as far as possible, caring. As fellow human being and as a person in authority, the police officer must see that the victim is fully cared and cured of any ailments. Listed below is the usual status and mental condition of such victims:

(a) They don't seek help because of FEAR. Also, they have neither access nor faith in authorities.

(b) They fear revenge if they cooperate with the authorities.

(c) They fear being punished for illegal entry, prostitution, etc.

(d) They are afraid of being exposed and hurt by the media and criminal justice process.

(e) The have no opportunity to seek help as they are kept confined, isolated and is always watched and escorted.

(f) The Traffickers compel them to support the cover story provided by the traffickers.

(g) They blame their fate for the misfortune.

(h) Sometimes they even develop loyalties and positive feeling towards traffickers.

(i) Sometimes, they are reluctant to complain for fear of losing money as the traffickers keep their money for safe custody.

(j) They are generally suffering from poor nutrition, poor health care from before.

(k) They are psychologically upset all the time.

(l) They are often exposed to unsafe, sub-human conditions and undergo personal risk of injury, beating, physical and sexual abuse.

(m) They are continuously exposed to AIDS and Sexually Transmitted Diseases and/or substance abuse in the form of drugs, alcohol, etc.

(n) They are always exposed to unwanted pregnancy, loss of organs and have seldom any access to healthcare.

It is evident that women and children are particularly vulnerable, and need special measures for their protection and well being. Community has a major role to play in the rehabilitation of victims. No long term solution can be found without the cooperation of the community. Much greater gender and child sensitivity towards victims of trafficking needs to be brought about promoted. Rehabilitation In the matter of rehabilitation, rescue and treatment, the welfare departments of the government and recognized non-governmental organizations have an important role to play. The role of the police is complementary to these. However, in the matter of dealing with organized crime against women, particularly, trafficking and serious crimes it is entirely the responsibility of the police.

The Police and prosecution should especially make efforts to send the victims to corrective homes rather than jail. This can be done by taking into consideration the character, state of health and mental condition of the offender and other circumstances, at the time of conviction of female offenders found guilty for the offences under section 7 and 8 of ITPA, and requesting the trial court that instead of sentencing them to imprisonment, to send them to corrective homes. Similarly, the victims of offences under sections 3, 4, 5, 6 and 9 of ITPA may also be sent to protective home or a correctional institution if it is possible to satisfy the magistrate.

## NGOS IN LAW ENFORCEMENT

Non-Governmental organizations have a very important role to play. Police officers, very often, are suspicious of NGOs.

However, it is necessary to change our views and works in tandem with those NGOs who are equally concerned about removing trafficking. Police must maintain list of NGOs with their expertise/specialization, contact telephone, E mail, addresses etc. Section 13(3)(b) of ITPA has provisions for non-official advisory body. NGOs also find a role u/s 17(5) of ITPA for providing intermediate safe custody to victims. They are a valuable source for intelligence on trafficking and they often play a vital role in Rescue as witnesses, as advisors, as partners, as Human Rights guardians. Post rescue role of NGOs lies in carrying out Counselling, giving advice, suggestion and support, and helping the victim overcome the shock, suffering and pain; helping to identify the best interest of the victim; prescribe guidelines and protocols for Police & others.

The role of NGOs in victim support and rehabilitation programs covers identification of suitable programs for the victims; their training to enable them to earn a livelihood; providing them necessary resources to produce goods and then market the products produced by them. All these are of immense help in motivating and uplifting the morale of the victim. Thus, NGOs provide linkage between victim and society and victim and other agencies involved in stopping trafficking. NGOs have also helped in the trial of cases by looking after the child of the victim; acting as language translator; providing assistance to the court - by helping the court with the interpretation of child's perception; getting victim/witness for evidence; providing care and protection to victim/witness.

Research by NGOs in Law Enforcement:

Utilising NGOs for micro research results in proper feedback which, in turn, saves resource and time and ensures the best interest of the victims. NGOs are usually well networked, both nationally and internationally. They can be very useful in developing data base. The data base can be used for (a) Data surveillance; (b) Seminar and workshops; (c) Implementing the findings; (d) Sensitization & orientation of all concerned.

# 11

# Commitment to Fighting Human Trafficking

Abu Dhabi, May 19 (IANS) The United Arab Emirates (UAE) is committed to fighting human trafficking wherever it occurs and would aggressively interdict those involved in it, says the first annual report of the UAE National Committee to Combat Human Trafficking. The report, 'Combating Human Trafficking in the 2007UAE , has been released a year after the committee was formed, and highlights the country's stand on the crime, the efforts to counter it, the obstacles and challenges it has encountered, as well as plans for the future, according to the state-run Emirates News Agency (WAM).

The report, released ahead of the UAE's participation at the UN General Assembly debate on trafficking in New York in June, focuses on the measures taken since Federal Law 51 came into force in this Gulf nation. The 16-article law, effective since November 2006, spells out stiff penalties against traffickers ranging from one year to life imprisonment and fines of 100,000 dirham ($27,225) and one million dirham ($272,250).

"At least 10 human trafficking-related cases were registered by the end of 2007 under the clauses of the new law", the report stated. "Notably, there were also convictions in at least five cases during this period, with the convicted receiving jail terms ranging from three to 10 years for committing, aiding or abetting human trafficking", it added. "The country's resolve to fight human trafficking at home and abroad in collaboration with international partners remains central to our counter-trafficking strategy", the WAM report quoted UAE's Minister of State for Foreign Affairs Anwar Gargash, who is also chair of the UAE National Committee to Combat Human Trafficking, as saying.

He added that General Sheikh Mohammad Bin Zayed Al Nahyan, Crown Prince of Abu Dhabi and Deputy Supreme Commander of the UAE Armed Forces, has cemented this resolve with a generous donation to the UN's Global Initiative to Fight Human Trafficking (UN.GIFT) to establish an international network to fight human trafficking. Gargash said the UAE was not ashamed to admit that the problem of trafficking afflicts this Gulf nation as it does many other countries.

It would be wrong, however, if immediate action was not taken once the crime was recognized, and the UAE was, therefore, pursuing an active and results-oriented strategy that aims to achieve immediate impact, he stated. According to the report, the UAE's commitments under international law include becoming a signatory to three of the UN conventions on human rights the International Convention on the Elimination of all forms of Racial Discrimination; the Convention on the Elimination of all forms of Discrimination against Women (CEDAW); and the Convention on the Rights of the Child.

Stating that the UAE government has a healthy track record of providing assistance and protection to victims of sexual abuse, the report said the government was working with foreign governments and NGOs when cases are brought to its attention. "Victims have been given protection and shelter while their paperwork is processed, and are then repatriated at the government's expense under the 'Crime Victim Assistance Programme'", it stated. It said the Foundation for the Protection of Women and Children, an independent civil society institution established in Dubai in 2007, has assisted 115 women and children after they were designated as victims of a number of crimes including human trafficking, domestic violence, family neglect, employer abuse and other social problems.

"Of these, 28 are suspected victims of trafficking, 24 have been identified as adults and four have been identified as minors less than 18 years of age", the report said. The foundation is currently sheltering 14 suspected trafficking victims from a variety of countries including India, Indonesia, Kazakhstan, Moldova, Uzbekistan, Bangladesh and Nigeria. The UAE has signed agreements with several labour-exporting countries, including India, Pakistan, Nepal, Sri Lanka, Bangladesh, China, Thailand and Philippines, during the last two years to regulate the flow of the labour workforce, the report pointed out.

A large number of the 1.5 million expatriate Indians in this Gulf nation are engaged as contract labour in the booming construction industry and as domestic help. "Further, cooperation with the Philippines and India, for example, has resulted in these two countries announcing their refusal to grant emigration clearance to women below 25 and 30 years of age respectively who wish to work in the region in order to protect younger women from possible abuse."A wage standard has been introduced by some of these countries including Philippines, Indonesia, India and Sri Lanka", it said.

"The new report is aimed at sharing the UAE's efforts with our partners and promoting dialogue, transparency and knowledge exchange in order to learn from the experiences of other nations in combating this crime", the WAM report quoted Gargash as saying. The National Committee to Combat Human Trafficking, established in March 2007, will produce regular reports annually in order to document progress and challenges in fighting human trafficking.

## INDICATORS OF HUMAN TRAFFICKING FOR ASIA

The phenomenon of human trafficking is today one of the major concerns of governments and organisations active in the field of migration, although as recently as ten years ago the term "human trafficking" was rarely referred to in migration policy debates. An example of the growing political priority accorded to combating human trafficking is seen in the organisation of the largest ever European Union (EU) conference on "Preventing and Combating Trafficking in Human Beings" in September 2002 which resulted in the Brussels Declaration, outlining policy recommendations to the EU on trafficking. Similarly in the United States (US), trafficking has become prominent on the political agenda since the creation of the Office to Monitor and Combat Trafficking in Persons in 2001. The annual report produced by this department is now regarded as the most comprehensive anti-trafficking review by any government.

Despite the growing political will to combat human trafficking and the increasing literature on the subject, available information about the magnitude of the problem remains limited, particularly in the area of data collection, and there are relatively few studies based on extensive research. This article examines why producing reliable data on trafficking has proven so difficult and suggests various measures that could be taken to improve such data. It also examines how, in spite of given current data gaps and deficiencies, some disturbing trends and serious implications can still be discerned (particularly in Asia) that must be addressed by more focused and deliberate studies, policies, and government remedies.

One of the reasons why it has been difficult to measure trafficking is because, until fairly recently, there had been little agreement on the definition of trafficking, resulting in it often being treated as a form of illegal migration or smuggling. Today a more detailed, internationally agreed-upon definition on trafficking is available as a result of the signing in December 2000 of the United Nations (UN) Protocol to Prevent, Suppress and Punish Trafficking in Persons. The Protocol against the Smuggling of Migrants (the Palermo Protocol) also helps to draw a distinction between trafficking and smuggling, although commentators have pointed out the continued difficulty of measuring trafficking given the range of actions and outcomes covered by the term. It is still common in many countries to intermingle data relating to trafficking, smuggling and irregular migration.

## OTHER TYPES OF TRAFFICKING

Although the Palermo Protocol demonstrated the need for a clearer and universally accepted definition of trafficking, a great deal remains to be done in order to improve the accuracy of trafficking data. So far few governments have begun to systematically collect data on trafficking and data specific to trafficking tends to be estimates, usually concerning trafficking in women and children for sexual exploitation, rather than other types of trafficking. At the global level the US State Department's estimate in 2003 that 800,000 to 900,000 people are internationally trafficked each year has been released.

In the European region, the European Commission estimates that 120,000 women and children are trafficked into Western Europe annually. Yet, it is unclear from both reports how these estimates are reached. Europol, however, admits that while the overall number of victims trafficked into the EU is still unknown, it is clear is that the number of victims are much higher than official statistics suggest.

At the national level in Europe, a 1998 study of 25 European countries by IOM found that only 12 could produce data on incidents of trafficking in women and seven on cases of trafficking in children. Eleven countries were able to provide data on the number of convictions for trafficking-related offences, with the combined total of convictions since 1996 standing at less than 100. Recent IOM studies in Southeast Asia, South Korea and Russia have produced similar results. A recent study in Central America and the Caribbean concluded "currently, no statistics are available to accurately quantify the magnitude of trafficking in the region or within particular countries".

Only a few countries are able to provide data on trends in trafficking over a number of years, making it difficult to establish the extent to which trafficking may be increasing. Figures from Germany and the Netherlands, two countries that regularly collate data on trafficking, suggest that there has been a substantial increase in the number of victims of trafficking during the last decade. The German Federal Criminal Office reports a 25% increase in the number of trafficking victims identified by police between 1999 and 2001. Most of the recorded victims however, are women because the German definition of trafficking is linked to prostitution. In the Netherlands, the Dutch Foundation Against the Trafficking of Women (STV) reported that the number of victims it assisted rose from 70 in 1992 to 341 in 2000. In both countries, the data refers primarily to cases of trafficking in women for sexual exploitation, but not for trafficking in other sectors.

## TRAFFICKING SEEMS TO BE INCREASING IN EUROPE

It is unclear to what extent the reported increases in European trafficking are due to a genuine rise in cases of trafficking or more due to better police enforcement efforts and improved assistance from NGOs. In the case of Germany, it has been shown that the number of victims identified varies depending on the priority given by police to combat trafficking. Official figures nevertheless, represent just the tip of the iceberg and in the Netherlands, for example, it has been reported that each victim of trafficking knows of at least one other person in a similar situation who has not received assistance from the authorities. The available data however, does give an indication of the most important source countries of trafficking victims into Europe. In Germany, nearly 80 per cent of trafficking cases in 2001 were from Central and Eastern Europe, while in the Netherlands, official statistics show that between 1992 and 2000, 55 per cent of victims also originated from this region.

## IN ASIA

In Asia, as well, there is a general lack of hard data on this topic. However, it is possible to glean some valuable insights from studies on related activities (such as prostitution and sexual exploitation). These studies can frequently provide an indication of the scale of trafficking in the region. Although not comprehensive in scope or coverage, the following estimates do present convincing evidence of the existence of a growing trafficking problem in this part of the world as well:

- A UNICEF survey indicates that between 30 - 40 per cent of all sex workers in the Mekong sub-region are between the ages of 12 and 17;
- In Thailand, it was reported that almost 200,000 foreign children were trafficked into the country in 1996 for the purpose of exploitative child labour, including commercial sexual exploitation (UNICEF, 2001);
- An estimated 13,000 children have been trafficked out of Bangladesh in the last five years, and 300,000 Bangladeshi minors work in red light districts in India;
- Between 5,000 - 7,000 girls are trafficked annually from Nepal to India (UNICEF, 2001);
- And in a 1997 report, the UN Rapporteur on Violence Against Women stated that in some rural villages in China between 30 - 90 per cent of marriages resulted from trafficking, a demand created by the shortage of women available for marriage in some communities.

As can be surmised from the above list of statistics, even with a lack of specifically commissioned research into this area, it is still possible to sketch out roughly the major trafficking patterns and routes prevalent in Asia. Although not precisely or rigorously studied, such overviews can still provide valuable information on the nature of these phenomena in Asia and may prove useful when trying to organize effective cooperation among field practitioners and government officials in prevention programs, victim assistance or prosecution efforts.

## EAST ASIA

Trafficking in China occurs both at internal and international level. In the domestic market, young boys (mostly under seven) are sold for illegal adoption while young girls and women are abducted into prostitution or as brides for bachelors in rural communities where women are in short supply. Between 1996 and1998, 10,503 women and children victims of domestic trafficking were rescued, while 14,709 traffickers were arrested.

As regards to external trafficking from China, Thailand and Cambodia appear to be the favoured countries of destinations within the region, in addition to other destinations including the Hong Kong Special Administrative Region (SAR) of China, Taiwan, Singapore, Malaysia, the Republic of Korea (South Korea), Japan and Australia. Victims usually end up in the sex industry. Furthermore, some of these locations also act as transit stations for eventual transportation to Europe or the United States. Inter-regionally speaking, trafficking victims within East Asia have been reported to originate from Thailand, Myanmar, Mongolia, North Korea, the Lao Peoples Democratic Republic (Laos), Vietnam and also Russia.

Other information related to trafficking within the region also indicates movement from China, South Korea, Thailand and Philippines to Japan, from the Philippines, Thailand and China to South Korea and from South Korea to Japan and the United States. International trafficking routes have also been discerned with victims of trafficking from Colombia and Eastern Europe being found in Japan and well as some victims originating from Russia and Central Asia found in the Republic of Korea.

## SOUTH EAST ASIA

The higher degree of cross border trafficking in Southeast Asia can partly be attributed to the long and porous borders between the countries in this region. Economic disparities between the affluent countries and less affluent countries in South East Asia also create a push-pull factor that spurs trafficking activity. For instance, Thailand's relatively strong economy, in comparison to its neighbours, tends to encourage illegal migration from Cambodia, Laos, and Myanmar. The demand is usually for work in the sex industry, and since 1990 it has been reported that about 80,000 women and children have been trafficked to Thailand for prostitution, predominantly from Myanmar, the Yunnan province of China, and Laos. On the other hand, its central location has made Thailand an ideal regional transit point to more affluent destinations in the region, such as Malaysia, Hong Kong SAR, Taiwan, Japan and Australia.

In Vietnam there is outgoing human traffic to Cambodia, Malaysia, China, Hong Kong SAR, and Taiwan for the purposes of domestic labour, prostitution, and brides, while incoming human trafficking is usually from Cambodia and China, sometimes en route to Australia, Europe and North America. The Philippines and Thailand usually act as sending countries, typically to Japan and Korea, but also to destinations beyond Asia such as countries in Europe, North America, the Middle East, and Africa. It was reported in 1998 that 150,000 women were trafficked to Japan for prostitution. Trafficking from Indonesia is commonly to Malaysia, Singapore, Taiwan, Hong Kong SAR, Brunei, the Gulf States and Australia for both prostitution and domestic labour. An estimated 40 women are sent to Taiwan and Hong Kong SAR every month for these purposes.

## SOUTH ASIA

Many countries in this region act as both source and destination countries, although India is by far the largest destination country, with neighbouring Nepal and Bangladesh being its principal source countries. While a substantial number of women and children are trafficked to work in the sex industry, other victims of trafficking also end up in the domestic, construction, agriculture and garment production industries, or as beggars and hawkers. Bangladeshis and Nepalese migrants use India as a transit country en route to Pakistan or the Middle East, while India itself acts as a country of origin for the thousands of people who migrate to the Middle East and the West. A large percentage of India's trafficking also occurs internally, with victims, usually children, being moved from poorer states to big cities such as Calcutta, Delhi and Mumbai.

Other regional trends include trafficking from Bangladesh, Afghanistan, Iran, and Central Asia to Pakistan. It was reported in 1991, for instance, that about 200,000 young girls and women of Bangladeshi origin between the ages of 12 and 30 were sold in Pakistan. In addition to internal and regional trafficking, many South Asian children have been trafficked beyond the region. There have been reports of Nepalese girls ending up in Hong Kong, and thousands of boys, some as young as five, being trafficked to Dubai, the United Arab Emirates (UAE) and Qatar to work as camel jockeys. Sri Lanka also acts as another primary source country for trafficking to the Gulf region, UAE, Kuwait, Saudi Arabia, Lebanon, and Bahrain for work in exploitative conditions, which also makes them vulnerable to sexual abuse.

## ASIA – DESTINATION AND ORIGIN

One of the most important recent developments in Asia *vis-à-vis* human trafficking is that Asia has emerged as much the origin as the destination of the phenomenon. Even when excluding Japan, the Republic of Korea, Malaysia, Hong Kong SAR and Taiwan are now destinations of trafficked persons. While also being countries of origin, Thailand, India, Pakistan, Turkey and several Gulf States, including United Arab Emirates, are also destination countries in Asia and its neighbouring region.

Most countries are countries of origin, transit, and destination. Major receiving countries in the region are Brunei, Hong Kong SAR, Japan, Malaysia, and Republic of Korea. Hong Kong SAR is also a transit country, whereas Malaysia and South Korea have been reported as source countries as well. Bangladeshi and Nepal are reported to be sending countries. However, this does not mean that in these countries are only either receiving or sending countries. It is quite possible that other related activities have not been widely reported.

## INTERNAL TRAFFICKING

Internal trafficking is widely practiced in South Asian countries, China and in the Mekong region of the Southeast Asia. Indonesia is also frequently mentioned when discussing internal trafficking. In particular, bride trafficking or forced marriage, often involving young women, is said to be widespread in China as well as Nepal and Bangladesh. The United Nations Children's Fund stated in a 2001 report that in recent decades, more than 250,000 women and children have been victims of trafficking within China.

## DISTURBING HEALTH IMPLICATIONS

The health implications of trafficked persons working in the sex industry are alarming. In 1999 UNAIDS and the World Health Organization (WHO) estimated that some 140,000 of the region's children had been orphaned by AIDS. In Thailand, the Ministry of Heath estimates that half a million children may be orphaned by the time they reach adolescence, while a national health survey in Cambodia in 1998 found that 380,000 children under 15 had lost one or both parents.

HIV/AIDS also has a huge economic impact for the families involved as its effects can reduce family income, which may result in children being removed from school and forced into dangerous employment which exposes them to diseases and makes them vulnerable for exploitation. An even more worrying trend spurred by the epidemic is the reported incidents of men who believe that sex with a virgin will protect them from infection or even enhance their virility. This belief has increased the demand for child prostitutes, most of them are not in a position to defend them or insist on the use of condoms.

Although scholars and researchers can infer valuable glimpses into trends and implications of trafficking by scrutinizing data from a wide range of sources (as we have tried to do here in the case of Asia), much of the resulting analyses end up relying on informed judgements and educated guesses. Without focused and dedicated research, it is difficult to generate the hard facts that can force legislators to make often painful choices that can close legal loopholes that traffickers use, or to press politicians and law enforcement officials to vigorously enforce existing anti-trafficking laws. The paucity of solid data on trafficking can be partly attributed to the fact that human trafficking is clandestine in nature. However, experience shows that the police cannot be relied upon to deliver even the trafficking data needed to help fight trafficking related crimes.

Many law enforcement agencies also tend to give a low priority to combating trafficking due to inadequate, unimplemented or the lack of legislation on trafficking, which makes the prosecution of traffickers difficult. Furthermore, trafficking convictions are often based upon victim testimonies, which are difficult to obtain, because trafficking victims are either deported as illegal migrants or often too frightened to testify. As a result enforcement agencies prefer not to prosecute traffickers at all, with the knowledge that much effort only seldom results in a conviction. A 1999 study on human trafficking in the U.K. conducted by Kelly and Regan on behalf of the British government found that the level of priority given by local police forces to combating trafficking has an impact whether or not data is gathered.

The study found that trafficking data is produced only where police forces monitor the local sex industry as part of their mandate to combat vice-related crime. Unfortunately, such monitoring is rare, resulting in the attitude that "a problem unseen does not exist". Another problem is that many governments and, to a lesser extent, NGOs are unfamiliar with trafficking, therefore, where relevant data does exist, it is not properly categorised as trafficking. Despite the lack of data from law enforcement sources, a few new sources of data are emerging as more agencies around the world take action to combat trafficking. The U.S. government reported that in 2001 it supported over 110 anti-trafficking programmes in around 50 countries while in Europe, numerous agencies are implementing programmes to combat trafficking. However, no single agency acts as a focal point for collection and harmonisation of statistics on trafficking either at national or regional level. An exception is a new initiative started in June 2002 to establish for South Eastern Europe, a Regional Clearing Point on National Networks on Victim Protection and Assistance in Belgrade.

Another problem is that existing data is often program-specific. Thus, data is usually based on the various trafficking definitions used by each individual agency and only cover those who have received certain types of assistance (persons participating in voluntary assisted return programs or those accommodated in shelters for victims of trafficking). The resulting situation is that the same individual may appear in data produced by more than one organisation. Additionally, at several levels, there is reluctance on the part of agencies within countries and between countries to share trafficking-related data. For instance, in a recent study of sex trafficking in the Americas, researchers found that the "little information that is being collected is not being meaningfully circulated" and crucial information was not being shared with the appropriate agencies.

Furthermore, valuable information from NGOs does not always reach government actors. In order to combat international trafficking, the sharing of information between countries is essential. At international level however, the sharing of information on trafficking tends to occur on an *ad hoc* basis, especially between countries of origin and destination. Some countries regard data on human trafficking as classified, while others have data protection laws prohibiting the dissemination of personal information. Some ministries simply adopt a policy of restricted distribution, while others are reluctant to release data because their data is so poor. Authorities in destination countries may also be reluctant to share information with source countries, when the authorities and law enforcement agencies in source countries are themselves believed to be implicated in trafficking. Finally, NGOs may be reluctant to share data for other reasons (to protect the confidentiality of the trafficked persons they assist).

In July 2002 the UN Population Division drew attention to the poor quality of international data on migratory movements by organising an inter-agency meeting to discuss ways in which data on international migration could be improved and made more widely available. It was noted at the meeting that data needed to describe international population movements and provide governments with a solid basis for policy formulation and implementation are far from complete, and that systematic co-ordination among those who collect and analyse data on international migration is imperative. Reliable trafficking data can be compiled only when the appropriate capacity to produce it exists. One of the key recommendations that emerged from this meeting is the need for international organisations and governments to provide greater technical and financial assistance to developing countries in order to enable them to collect better migration data.

The need for better use and co-ordination of existing data is particularly applicable in the case of human trafficking data. Although an increasing amount of statistical data on trafficking from a variety of sources is becoming available as the number of counter-trafficking programs increases, a mechanism to co-ordinate and standardise these disparate data collection systems, however, is still lacking. The Regional Clearing Point (RCP) in Belgrade for the Balkans is an example of what can be achieved through better data management. The RCP was established by the Stability Pact for South Eastern European Task Force on Trafficking in Human Beings, in order to ensure standardised regional data collection on the effectiveness and continuity of victim assistance and protection. The project, being implemented by IOM in co-operation with the International Catholic Migration Commission (ICMC) will create a sound mechanism for the collection, consolidation, and analysis of information for the region. This type of project is to be extended to other regions where IOM implements counter-trafficking programs.

Existing sources of information on trafficking should also be fully exploited, including indirect indicators of trafficking. For example, it is well established that victims of trafficking often enter a country legally through the likes of an "entertainer" or "au pair" visa. A more controversial indirect indicator of trafficking is the number of migrant women working in the sex industry of any given country. A recent Europol report on trafficking shows that in Italy, around 6,000-7,000 prostitutes originated from non-EU countries and, in Spain 12,000. As Europol pointed out however, "not all foreign prostitutes are victims of trafficking, but a sizeable proportion is probably exploited to some degree". This kind of statistic may be relevant in discussions concerning the extent of trafficking. Other indicators may include figures on illegal border crossings or statistics of departures of women leaving main countries of origin. Further research is nevertheless necessary to fully examine good practices regarding the collection and analysis of data on trafficking.

The IOM Counter-Trafficking Module (CTM) Database has been developed to facilitate the management of information gathered from all IOM Counter-Trafficking and Return and Reintegration programmes. It aims to strengthen both research capacity and an understanding of the causes, trends, and consequences of trafficking, thus enabling IOM to better target its counter-trafficking policies and programmes. CTM collects first-hand information from IOM field missions working on counter-trafficking. The mission staff carries out in-depth interviews, based on a standardised questionnaire, with all trafficked persons assisted by IOM, which allows IOM to better understand their migration process, from recruitment to destination and assess their needs in terms of health, protection, return and reintegration. The reintegration process of returned victims is monitored, and all information collected is entered into the mission's database and shared between missions directly involved in the assistance of a trafficked person, as well as the central database in Headquarters.

This database was implemented in the Balkan region in 2002 with the intention of expanding it into a global database that gathers information from all IOM's Counter-Trafficking programs. The South Eastern Europe database currently includes information on 826 victims of trafficking, all but one of whom are women and girls. These victims were assisted by IOM during the period May 2001 to December 2002. The database collects data on trafficking victims who were assisted by IOM in Albania, Macedonia, Bosnia, Serbia and Montenegro, Kosovo, Bulgaria, Romania and Moldova. An initial analysis of the data provides some useful findings on the Socio-economic background of the victim, their recruitment and trafficking process, and any exploitation in the country of destination. For instance, over half the victims were aged between 18-24, but a significant minority, about 10 per cent, were children aged between 14- 17.

In recent years, progress has been made in the development of a common understanding of human trafficking and in the establishment of international legal norms regarding trafficking in persons. Much less progress has been made, however, in determining the scale and magnitude of human trafficking and in developing effective ways to collect helpful data. Ultimately, data on trafficking will improve only when greater actions are taken to combat the problem. Unless governments and law enforcement agencies are prepared to combat trafficking with increased vigour and, at the same time, prepared to provide adequate protection to the victims of trafficking, the majority of trafficking cases will continue to go undiscovered. There is also the potential for data to improve when more countries begin to enact and implement the necessary anti-trafficking legislation.

Though this is likely to be a slow process, it is possible that data on trafficking will improve as a result of it. This article has argued that several measures should be taken to address the current data shortage.

These measures include:

- Raising awareness about the need for better data,
- Investing resources in capacity building to enable poorer countries to compile better data, and ensuring that the collection of trafficking data is given sufficient priority,
- Promoting a better use of existing statistics through national and regional for a,

- Encouraging agencies combating trafficking to systematically collect data and develop common data collection systems,
- More comparative research to assess a wider range of sources of data relevant to trafficking and to identify effective data management practices, and
- Finally, properly analyze collected data from such research.

In Asia, as well as in most other parts of the world, the primary source of migration data is governments, whether or not the data are on basic migration such as stocks and flows or on specific kinds of migration such as irregular migration via, for instance, the number of visa overstayers. Other than small-scale surveys and research, there are hardly any mechanisms to systematically collect information on trafficking. Existing data sources on international migration set up by international organizations such as ILO, IPEC or OECD do not usually contain much data specifically on trafficking.

What is needed specifically in Asia is first and foremost establishing a network of governmental officials, researchers, and NGOs who can collect and analyze relevant basic data. It should be noted that in Asia many NGOs gather data on key indicators of trafficking, although those NGOs often do not collect such data in systematic fashion and do not always share the information on a regular basis.

In order for such a network to be set up, initial discussions to reach a set of common definitions must be carried out. Also a framework for information sharing needs to be articulated. In addition, some programs for govern-mental capacity building should be conducted as well.

The government of the Republic of Korea has carried out a survey to examine the government capacity for public awareness campaign under the framework of the Bali Conference on People Smuggling, Trafficking in Persons and Related Transnational Crime, 2002. A similar step can also be taken in order to draw out a basic understanding of data collection practices and capacity among the Asian countries.

Then we can pursue the above-mentioned improvement on trafficking data collection in general.

## TRAFFICKING ROUTES

India is a major country of origin, transit, and destination for trafficking in persons. According to a 2003 United Nations report, India is one of the top nine destination countries for sex trafficking in the world. Because of India's geographical proximity to South Asia and relatively open borders, major trafficking routes have been established between Bangladesh, Nepal, Pakistan and Sri Lanka and different parts of India.

Indian women and children are trafficked to the Gulf States, Australia, Malaysia, Singapore and the United States. Bhutan may also be a destination country for people trafficked from India for use as forced labour.

It is estimated that thousands of people are trafficked into India each year from Bangladesh, Nepal and Pakistan. The primary destination country for Nepalese women and children is India. India is a transit country for traffickers traveling from Bangladesh or Nepal into Pakistan. According to one estimate, 100,000 Nepali girls and 50,000 Bangladeshi girls are trafficked to or through India every year. The girls end up in brothels in India or Pakistan or in Middle Eastern or South Asian countries. Trafficking is also a problem within India. Many women and children are taken from smaller rural regions to major urban centres.

### Factors that Contribute to the Trafficking Infrastructure

Throughout South Asia, poverty, as well as the breakdown of traditional livelihoods, the lack of education and skills for women and children, natural disasters, the breakdown of families from war situations, the low social status of women, and gender-discriminating practices, contributes to the trafficking phenomenon.

Weak legislation and poor enforcement of trafficking laws are also cited as factors contributing to trafficking in the area, and the corruption of local police officials has been cited as another factor influencing trafficking in India. Furthermore, there is a common superstition in the region that a sexual encounter with a virgin girl can rid a man of sexually transmitted disease; this belief fuels the demand for young girls.

Many of the conditions contributing to the high incidence of trafficking in India are rooted in the Indian perception of women and the overall gender inequality that exists in the nation. Many females in India are also subject to domestic and physical violence. As a result of the caste system, which systematically divides society into different socioeconomic groups, women and female children do not enjoy the same social position as men and, in many cases, are severely disadvantaged in Indian society. Nepalese women and girls were trafficked to India even during British rule, but the volume of trafficking shot up in the 1960s.

One explanation offered for this increase is the oil boom in the Middle East. Rich Arabs began to travel to Bombay (now Mumbai) to spend money on the kind of entertainment not available to them in their own countries. They preferred the fair complexions of Nepalese girls to the darker women from southern India, increasing the demand for Nepalese girls. With an average per capita income of US$225, Bangladesh is one of the largest migrant-exporting countries in Asia. Migration takes place to the West, to the Middle East and to Southeast Asia, but most illegal migration flows to India. India shares a 4,222-kilometers border with 28 Bangladeshi districts. Bangladeshi traffickers have built up bases in the border districts of India in West Bengal and Assam, to the north and west.

## FORMS OF TRAFFICKING

Indian women and children are trafficked abroad for forced labour and forced prostitution. Boys as young as 4 and 5 years of age from India are trafficked to the United Arab Emirates to work as camel jockeys and beggars. Even though the Gulf States regulated the use of camel jockeys by imposing age and weight restrictions in 2002, an Australian documentary shot in February 2003 showed that children were still being used as camel jockeys. Sexual and physical abuse of these boys is common and often the boys are not fed adequately in order to keep their weight down. In addition, young people from India are reportedly trafficked and sold into bonded and forced labour in Bhutan. It was reported recently that a total of 22 tribal families from India's Gumla district in Jharkhand were trafficked 6 years ago to Phuentsholing in Bhutan and forced to work breaking rocks for the roads. Some of the families were recently rescued with the help of the Indian Army.

Women and children are also trafficked to India for prostitution and forced labour. According to one report, every day 50 Bangladeshi girls are lured across the Indian border and sold. Bangladeshi girls who are trafficked to India by organized networks usually end up in brothels in Kolkata or Mumbai. According to another report, 400,000 Bangladeshi women are engaged in forced prostitution in India and 300,000 Bangladeshi boys have been trafficked to India. An estimated 200,000 Nepalese women and girls work in Indian brothels, in cities such as Mumbai, Pune, New Delhi and Kolkata. According to one estimate, 20 percent (40,000) of trafficked Nepalese women working in the Indian sex trade are younger than 16 years of age. In addition, thousands of Nepalese children are trafficked to India each year to work in carpet factories in Bhadoi (Mirjapur), in the circus and in the domestic service industry. Boys also work on potato farms and road construction projects or they are forced to beg.

Within India, women and children are trafficked for forced labour, forced prostitution and forced marriage. Illegal trafficking in human organs also takes place, as does illicit adoption of infants and children. A March 2004 report, which was based on surveys of villages in the districts of Araria, Katihar, Kishanganj and Purnia, points out that a large number of girls have vanished from the villages under the pretext of marriage, love affairs or job promises. The report suggests that a large number actually end up in the sex trade throughout India. A researcher with the National Human Rights

Commission conducting research on child trafficking in India stated in January 2004 that on average 30,133 children disappear every year. Twenty-seven percent of the missing children are never found.

Girls are trafficked within the country for forced marriage. Girls from West Bengal (particularly Murshidabad and Chaubis Pargana) have been sold in Haryana for marriage. One 16-year-old girl was tricked into boarding a train and was taken from Murshidabad to Delhi, where an agent sold her to a 40-year-old man for marriage. When the girl refused to marry the man, he and his family beat her. After the girl was confined in the man's house for 4 days, police, who had been tipped off by neighbours, rescued her. Child sex tourism has only been recognized relatively recently in India. Until the arrest of a 76-year-old man of unknown origin in April 1991, there was very little awareness of organized sexual abuse and exploitation of children in the country. India is estimated to have between 300,000 and 500,000 child victims of commercial sexual exploitation.

It is believed that foreign sex tourists may be switching to India because of its lax laws, its cheap and abundant supply of young girls working in the commercial sex industry, and a perceived lower prevalence of HIV/AIDS. In spite of the abundance of vulnerable children, there is no real consensus on the prevalence of child sex tourism in India, though the problem does indeed exist.

In southern India, two popular destinations emerging for pedophile activity are Kovalam in Kerala and Mammallpuram in Tamil Nadu. Goa is a popular destination for pedophiles looking for sex with boys. There has been a reported increase in sex tourism from the Gulf States to India in the past three decades. Young men from the Gulf States have come to India for sexual relations with Indian women. New Zealand men in India and have been charged with child sexual abuse.

One report asserts that destinations of child sex tourists are changing. As protection and prevention efforts are strengthened in one state, child sex tourists choose another state as their destination. This phenomenon can be witnessed as such tourists forgo the traditional destinations of Goa and Kovalam in Kerala and choose instead the now-popular destinations of Varkala, Cochin, and Kumily in Kerala and of other coastal villages in Karnataka.

The United States has investigated reports that Indian nationals were victims of trafficking to Iraq and were mistreated while working there as contractors in U.S. military camps. Indian press reports said that Indian nationals in Jordan and Kuwait were recruited for jobs in U.S. military camps in Iraq as cooks, butchers, laundry workers and handymen. Some of the Indians charge that they signed up through Indian employment agencies to work in Kuwait but ended up in Iraq working for low pay and were refused permission to leave the country.

Four Indians claim that they escaped from a U.S. military camp in Mosul after enduring a 9-month ordeal. One man told India's Indo-Asian News Service that, during the holy fasting month of Ramadan, he was forced to cook pork, a practice forbidden under Islamic law.

India has one of the world's largest underground markets in human organs. Though commercial trading in organs was banned in 1994, it is believed that regulation has merely pushed the trade underground to a market controlled by organized crime gangs. "Veritable organ bazaars" operate out of private clinics, especially in cities such as Bombay and Madras.

According to one 2002 report, 2,000 Indians sell their kidneys every year, mostly to affluent Westerners, who fly to India for the surgery.

In a Chennai (Madras) slum in South India, one U.S. anthropologist met five local women, each of whom had sold a kidney for US$1,200 (in 1999). They were mostly low-paid domestic servants whose husbands were in trouble or in debt. They had sold their kidneys after some sort of financial crisis, and they claimed that they would do it again if they could. Babies are also sold for illegal adoption within India, usually for Rs 40,000 to Rs. 60,000.

## Government Responses

The Indian constitution explicitly prohibits "traffic in human beings". The offense is also punishable under the Penal Code and the Immoral Traffic (Prevention) Act. India's Penal Code prohibits kidnapping or abducting any woman with the intent of compelling her into "illicit intercourse" or with the knowledge that she is likely to be so compelled, forced, or seduced. The code also prohibits kidnapping or otherwise inducing a woman to marry any person against her will. The offense is punishable by a fine and up to 10 years of imprisonment. However, the prohibition does not apply to cases in which a woman is accustomed to offering herself promiscuously for money to customers and is encouraged or assisted by another in following that profession.

Kidnapping or abducting a person with intent of subjecting such a person to "grievous hurt, slavery or to the unnatural lust of any person" is punishable by imprisonment for up to 10 years and a fine. The code prohibits procurement of a girl under the age of 18 to engage by force or seduction in illicit intercourse. Punishment is imprisonment for up to 10 years and a fine. "Importing a girl from a foreign country" is also prohibited. The prohibition applies to anyone who imports from any country outside India any girl under the age of 21 with the intent of forcing her into illicit intercourse or with the knowledge that she is likely to be so forced or seduced. Punishment is imprisonment for up to 10 years and a fine.

Anyone who sells, lets to hire, or disposes of a person under the age of 18 in any other way for the purposes of prostitution is subject to punishment for up to 10 years and a fine. Anyone who buys, hires, or obtains possession in any other way of a person under the age of 18 for the purpose of prostitution or "illicit intercourse" or who knows that such a person can be employed for such purposes commits an offense punishable by imprisonment for up to 10 years and a fine. Prostitution-related activities are prohibited under the Immoral Traffic (Prevention) Act. Keeping a brothel or allowing premises to be used as a brothel is an offense punishable by imprisonment for 1 to 3 years and a fine. Living on the earnings of prostitution is punishable by imprisonment for up to 2 years and a fine. Procuring, inducing or taking a woman or a girl for the purpose of prostitution is punishable by imprisonment for 3 to 7 years and a fine. If such an offense is committed against the will of any person, the punishment is increased to imprisonment for 14 years.

Detaining a woman or a girl in premises where prostitution is carried out is an offense. Punishment is imprisonment from 7 years to life. Carrying out prostitution in a public place is punishable by imprisonment for up to 3 months. Carrying out prostitution in a public place with a sex worker who is 18 years old or younger is punishable by imprisonment from 7 years to life. Seducing or soliciting for purposes of prostitution is punishable by imprisonment for up to 6 months and a fine. The act, therefore, "does not aim at abolition of prostitutes and prostitution as such", nor does it aim to make prostitution a criminal offense per se or to punish a woman in prostitution. Rather, its purpose is "to inhibit or abolish commercialized vice", which the act defines as trafficking in women and girls "for the purpose of prostitution as an organized means of living".

For a conviction under the Penal Code, which prohibits sexual offenses against women and children, corroborative evidence is required. If the only direct evidence of the accused having imported a girl into the country is the testimony of the girl herself and if it is not possible to obtain sufficient corroborative evidence, courts hold that such testimony should be treated with caution and should not be "safely regarded as a basis for conviction in the absence of independent evidence". Courts also have held that, if it is found that the girl in question has been definitely lying on important points in her story, it is unsafe to rely on other parts of her evidence to convict any person of illicit intercourse under article 366A unless that evidence is corroborated in material point.

The Immoral Traffic (Prevention) Act provides that the government may, at its discretion, establish "protective homes" and "corrective institutions". A "protective home" is defined by the act as "an institution, by whatever name called,... in which women and girls, who are in need of care and protection, may be kept under this Act, but does not include (i) a shelter where females under trial may be kept in pursuance of this Act, or (ii) a corrective institution." The courts have held that anyone concerned with running a protective home must discharge his or her duties with the aims and objects of the act and "without offending human rights and dignity". The Bonded Labour System (Abolition) Act of 1976 prohibits forced or bonded labour. The National Human Rights Commission of India monitors the implementation of the 1976 act.

The constitution prohibits all forms of forced labour, and it provides that no child under the age of 14 will be employed to work in any factory or mine or be engaged in any other hazardous employment. In addition, India's Penal Code punishes those who compel a person to labour against his or her will by imprisonment for up to 1 year, a fine, or both. India banned the commercial trading in human organs with the 1994 Transplantation of Human Organs Act. Removing human organs without authority is an offense punishable by imprisonment for up to 5 years and a fine. Commercial dealing in human organs is an offense punishable by imprisonment from 2 to 7 years and a fine.

Additional proposals to strengthen anti-trafficking laws include a fine of 200,000 rupees or US$2,600, and compensation for victims. The government of India has also established a special court to hear all cases involving the trafficking in women. The government has created a central advisory committee on child prostitution and a second committee to suggest rescue and rehabilitation approaches for sexually exploited children. The National Commission for Women has also established expert committees to address these problems. In a fall 2004 policy draft, the government recommended reviewing the licensing mechanism of massage and beauty parlors and bars in India. The draft report adds that a licensing authority should conduct regular inspections of such establishments, passing on any relevant information to the proper authorities.

In April 2003, Delhi police uncovered an organized racket involving illicit trafficking in babies from a nursing home in Uttam Nagar. A buyer would go to the hospital and get herself admitted; there hospital records would be manipulated and a fake birth certificate issued. The doctors had been running the racket for 2 years and did not know the exact number of children that had been sold. In June 2003, 13 people in Hyderabad in southern India who were believed to be members of a gang responsible for selling more than 50 kidneys for transplants were arrested. The gang supposedly facilitated the organ transplants by pretending that donors and recipients were blood relatives. Police were also investigating the role of several doctors in the smuggling ring in Hyderabad. In October 2003, Daler Menhdi, a top pop rock star in India, surrendered to police in the state of Punjab to face charges of trafficking in persons. He was charged with 31 counts of immigration law violations.

According to police, the multimillionaire rock star used his concert tour visits to Western cities as a cover for his trafficking racket. In January 2004, three people were arrested in Mumbai for involvement in illegal organ trafficking. The suspects paid as many as 20 people for their kidneys and prepared fake documents, which indicated that the donor and recipients were related, for clearance with the health department. In February 2004, the Mumbai city crime branch arrested two more people in connection with the racket. In late March 2004, police in Mumbai raided 64 dance bars and arrested 572 people, including bar girls and customers. This was the second such raid of bars in Mumbai in less than a month. Three bar owners were charged under the Prevention of Immoral Trafficking Act. Thirty-two bar managers, 261 bar girls, 50 other employees, and 229 customers were arrested. In that same month, the chief executive officer of a private news channel and his associate were arrested on charges of trafficking in persons.

The two men took people abroad on the pretext of providing them employment. The arrests were made after one of the victims, who had been taken to Israel, made a complaint. When the victims arrived in Israel, the accused traffickers allegedly took their passports and return tickets and returned to India. In September 2004, police in Delhi uncovered a ring responsible for trafficking in 50 kidneys. Three people were arrested for suspected involvement in the ring. The kidneys were removed at four top hospitals in Delhi and one hospital in the western state of Gujarat.

## Nongovernmental and International Organization Responses

NATSEC (National Action against Trafficking and Sexual Exploitation of Children) is a network in Maharashtra state comprising 300 organizations representing 32 districts. NATSEC has organized a program to raise social awareness against trafficking and sexual exploitation of children in 22 districts in Maharashtra state with support from the United Nations Development Fund for Women. Sampada Grameen Mahila Sanstha works to prevent the spread of HIV/AIDS among truck drivers and women in prostitution through promotion of condom use and counseling services. The organization operates in the Sangli District of Maharashtra. ATSEC (Action against Trafficking and Sexual Exploitation of Children) has chapters in New Delhi and West Bengal.

Bhoomika Vihar surveyed girls in 58 villages in four districts—Araria, Katihar, Kishanganj and Purnia—in Bihar's Kosi region. On the basis of the survey findings, a report titled "Bojh" (Burden) was released in March 2004 by Patna State Women Development Corporation. Save our Sisters (SOS) is a movement that was launched by Save the Children India to combat trafficking and sexual exploitation at the national and regional levels. SOS's four main objectives are advocacy, prevention, legislation and rehabilitation.

The Indian Committee of Youth Organizations is a national youth coordinating network of 348 organizations across India. It aims to strengthen nongovernmental organization activities aimed at preventing sexual abuse and exploitation of children and at providing improved services for victims. Terre des Hommes runs projects to combat child trafficking in the state of West Bengal.

The Human Welfare Association was recently granted the first project in Uttar Pradesh to sensitize the public and the government to the problem of child trafficking and formulate a strategy to combat child it.

Manav Seva Sansthan organized a 2-day South Asian regional conference in March 2004 in association with Japan Foundation Asia Center. The main aim of the conference was to work on the basis of the South Asian Association for Regional Cooperation (SAARC) forum to combat cross-border trafficking jointly. Sanlaap supports child protection programs for children of women in prostitution in red-light areas of Kolkata, provides psychosocial counseling to child victims of prostitution, and runs shelters for rescued and at-risk women and children. Prerana works for the rights, protection, welfare and development of the victims of commercial sexual exploitation and trafficking. It provides a wide spectrum of services to victims of trafficking and prostitution, including those with HIV/AIDS.

Women residents of the largest slums in Delhi, Yamuna Pushta, have come together to put an end to trafficking of women and children in their neighbourhood. The women started the group after children started disappearing from their neighbourhood. The group gathers local intelligence, keeps an eye on suspects in the neighbourhood, and even accompanies police on raids. The women operate from a small makeshift office with a thatched roof and claim to have rescued 25 girls between early 2003 and early 2004. The Asian Development Bank (ADB) undertook regional technical assistance in July 2001 in Bangladesh, India, and Nepal. ADB wanted to increase its understanding of how its existing country programs and regional policy could be used to support and strengthen anti trafficking initiatives in the region and to improve capacity-building and other efforts by stakeholders to develop effective anti trafficking programmes.

## Multilateral Initiatives

In November 2001, the Bangladeshi government and UNICEF co-hosted a 3-day South Asia Consultation for the Second World Congress against Commercial Sexual Exploitation of Children. One hundred and fifty participants from seven member countries of the South Asian Association for Regional Corporation (SAARC) attended, including high-level government delegates, children and representatives of NGOs and media and international organizations. The SAARC forum, founded in 1985, aims to promote cultural ties and economic and social development among its member states (Bangladesh, Bhutan, India, Maldives, Nepal, Pakistan and Sri Lanka).

In January 2002, the Bangladeshi government signed the SAARC Convention on Prevention and Combating Trafficking in Women and Children for Prostitution. Resolutions were adopted to step up cooperation among law enforcement authorities to fight trafficking in women and children, terrorism and drug trafficking. In January 2004, leaders from SAARC member states met in Islamabad for the first summit in 2 years. In October 2003, Indian President A. B. J. Kalam arrived in Dubai, United Arab Emirates, to talk with officials about Dubai's large Indian migrant population. During the biennial meeting of the Border Security Force (BSF) and the Bangladesh Rifles (BDR) in April 2003, India proposed joint patrolling of the common border between India and Bangladesh.

In November 2003, the BDR rejected the BSF's draft proposal on the modalities of that agreement. The Australian Human Rights and Equal Opportunity Commission facilitated the 23–24 October 2003 Stop the Traffic 2 Conference with the National Human Rights Commission of India and the Human Rights Commission of Malaysia. The conference focused on women trafficked to Australia for prostitution and other women experiencing abuse within the sex industry. On the 55th Human Rights Day (10 December 2003), the foreign affairs parliamentary secretary of Australia announced initiatives to promote and protect human rights in the Asia–Pacific region and recipients of the 2003-04 Human Rights Small Grants Scheme were also announced.

Under this scheme, judges, lawyers, police, community leaders, and other citizens in Bangladesh, India, Laos, and Sri Lanka are to receive Australian support for human rights training activities. The governments of Nepal and India announced in late December 2003 that their human rights commissions would sign an agreement to control cross-border trafficking. In March 2004, the Australian government announced funding of $A 200,000 to help India, Nepal, and Sri Lanka stamp out forced prostitution. The money is to be used for raising awareness of trafficking in persons, for improving regional police and judicial understanding of trafficking, and for assisting officers in those countries in prosecuting incidences of trafficking.

In June 2004, it was announced that India would be one of eight countries to receive US$50 million from the US government to help fight human trafficking. The other recipients were Brazil, Cambodia, Indonesia, Mexico, Moldova, Sierra Leone and Tanzania. In September 2004, the United Nations Children's Fund (UNICEF) sponsored a 3-day meeting of South Asian government officials, representatives from United Nations agencies and representatives of nongovernmental organizations. The meeting took place in Colombo, Sri Lanka. Government officials signed a five-point joint statement, agreeing that children in South Asia deserve better protection from traffickers and sexual abusers. Participating countries were Afghanistan, Bangladesh, Bhutan, India, Maldives, Nepal, Pakistan, and Sri Lanka.

## GROWING CRIMINAL MARKET IN THE U.S.

Human trafficking has become a lucrative criminal market in the United States. The commodities involved in this illicit trade are men, women and children. Traffickers transport undocumented migrants into the U.S. for work in licit, semi-illicit and illicit industries.

The traffickers' foremost goal is to maximize profits – often resulting in physical and mental exploitation of the victims. The sale and distribution of trafficked humans in the U.S. is a global, regional and national phenomenon. Women and children are trafficked short distances within the U.S. (small towns to bigger cities), as well as coming from as far away as China, Ukraine and Thailand. The International Organization for Migration (IOM) estimates that of the100 million migrants worldwide, about 4 million are undocumented, migrants who have been smuggled or trafficked.

The U.S. Department of State has estimated that at any given time, there are hundreds of thousands of people in the pipeline, being warehoused by traffickers, waiting for new routes to open up or documents to become available and their primary target is the United States. Human trafficking shares certain dynamics with alien smuggling, but is different in having the additional elements of coercion and/or exploitation. Alien smuggling produces short-term profits. Trafficking, on the other hand, includes long-term exploitation to continue to produce profits. The criminality associated with trafficking usually continues after the migrants reach the U.S. There are degrees of voluntariness associated with human trafficking. It can be completely voluntary where the migrant freely chooses to work overseas. Or, it can be completely involuntary, where migrants are kidnapped, abducted, confined and subjected to other human rights abuses. Examples include women who agree to come to the U.S. as waitresses or dancers, but then are forced into prostitution or domestic servitude.

Also included are children who are abducted from abroad to work in child pornography and prostitution rings and migrant workers who are forced to work in indentured servitude in order to pay off their trafficking fees. Clandestine migration operates in very much the same manner as legal migration, except that U.S. borders are illegally avoided or migrants are trafficked using forged or altered documentation. In the typical case, the migrant signs a contract and makes a down payment to the trafficker. Often these contracts contain the stipulation that smugglers can hold their clients hostage if they or their families cannot pay the entire smuggling fee. This makes migrants highly vulnerable to abuse and exploitation, and many migrants are held in slave-like conditions until they are able to pay off their fees.

Female migrants are especially vulnerable to sexual exploitation during their overseas travel or while being housed in "safe houses" and they may be forced to work in the sex industry until their debts are paid off. Prices are largely based on market principles, depending on the local demand, the distances involved and the mode of transport. The emergence of international smuggling organizations has helped to substantially drive up the traffickers' fees. INS reports indicate that fees can range from a few hundred dollars for Central Americans to up to $50,000 for Chinese. According to an IOM report, almost all migrants attempting to gain entry into the U.S. employ the assistance of smugglers or traffickers. A bi-national study of migration between the U.S. and Mexico found that 70 percent of the Mexicans who entered the U.S. illegally entered with the help of traffickers.

The actors driving this criminal market vary, depending on the region of the U.S. and the nationality of the migrants. Traffickers may be individual entrepreneurs, small "mom and pop" operations, or sophisticated, organized rings. There is little consensus among those who have studied the problem as to the proportions of each of those types; nor with respect to their level of organization and sophistication. Irrespective of type, human trafficking is typically intermixed with other illicit activities, including fraud, extortion, racketeering, money laundering, bribery of public officials, drug use, document forgery and gambling (Richard, 1999). In some cases, traffickers have emerged specifically to meet the migration demand and in other cases, there are established international criminal syndicates who have incorporated the trading of humans into their existing spheres of criminal activity. For example, Chinese triads and gangs that have been traditionally involved in prostitution in the U.S., are now recruiting and smuggling both sex and non- sex workers from overseas.

A review of cases since 1990 found that traffickers in the U.S. tended to be smaller crime groups and trafficking rings, gangs, loosely organized criminal networks, entrepreneurs and corrupt individuals who were victimizing their own nationals. The individual actors within trafficking networks include enforcers, who are also usually also "illegals" and are hired to work on ships to maintain order and distribute food and water; transporters (guides and crew members); recruiters; document forgers; brokers; brothel owners; debt collectors; and employment agencies. Obviously, when there are different groups and individuals focusing on different aspects of the trafficking process, this makes law enforcement's task even more difficult.

There are little empirical data to support the belief that there are well organized, transnational criminal enterprises, controlling the trafficking process from beginning to end. Chin's data challenge the notion that traditional Chinese organized crime groups are heavily involved in Chinese trafficking. While individual Chinese triad and gang members may be involved, Chin believes that this activity is mostly entrepreneurial. "In short, the human trade is in many ways like any other legitimate international trade, except that it is illegal. Like any trade, it needs organization and planning, but it does not appear to be linked with traditional `organized crime groups'". Thus, there is an important distinction to be made between professionalization and tight organization traffickers in the U.S. can be highly professional, but loosely organized. Globally, the main smuggling pipelines stretch from Asia, across Europe, through Central America and the Caribbean to the United States.

The largest influx of humans trafficked to the U.S. are coming from the less developed regions of the world. The most popular transit route for Chinese, South Americans and South Asians is through Central America and Mexico. Panama is a also a major transit point for migrants coming from Colombia, Ecuador, Peru, Cuba, India and the People's Republic of China. In addition, South Africa has also become a major transit point into the United States. And traffickers are increasingly utilizing the U.S. Canadian border as a corridor into the U.S. The

Southwest border continues to serve as the biggest point of illegal entry into the U.S., largely because traffickers are able to get aliens across without documents. The major points of entry into the United States are located in southern and central Texas, Southern California, Tucson, Arizona and areas of New Mexico. While the Southwest border is often used as the main portal into the United States, traffickers are increasingly moving migrants into the U.S. through New York, Chicago and San Francisco. Other newly emerging ports of entry include Atlanta, Houston, Orlando and Washington D.C.

In addition, the U.S. has seen a re-emergence of Chinese boat smugglers using both the East and West coasts. Traffickers share a common goal of circumventing national regulations and evading law enforcement. There is increasing evidence of producers in the U.S. trafficking industry forming collaborative networks and alliances in order to increase their operational efficiency and profit potential. In order to maximize profits, different ethnic groups have recognized the need to collaborate, to provide safe houses, local contracts and documentation. There have been specific cases of Italian organized crime groups in New York and New Jersey collaborating with Russian crime groups to supply women in nightclubs and peep shows. In addition, smugglers from Mexico are being subcontracted by Chinese groups to smuggle Chinese migrants over the U.S. Mexican border. Smugglers are using "legitimate businesses" such as bus transportation companies and employment agencies as covers for their activities.

Diplomatic security agents have identified dance and modeling agencies in the U.S. that serve as fronts for trafficking operations for larger Russian crime syndicates. Many producers within this market have established a "chain" of operations involving a number of individuals and various means of travel to pass migrants through a network of safe houses and transit points. Larger operations have developed elaborate networks that include document venders, travel agencies, guides, transportation and local area border smugglers. There is a relatively high degree of collusion among government officials in both source and transit countries that are facilitating these clandestine operations. Indeed, there has been evidence of cooperation (involving corruption and/or intimidation of public officials and partnerships with illcit business) or at least acquiescence occurring at every level. INS reports that international traffickers have reportedly corrupted foreign senior-level officials as well as officials in key positions, such as immigration officials at airports, consular workers, embassies abroad, members of law enforcement and officers at border checkpoints in both source and transit countries.

Corrupt public officials are accepting bribes in exchange for passports, visas, citizenship and safe transit across borders. "Indeed, in this area of criminal activity, as in others, corruption provides the lubricant which allows criminal organizations to operate with maximum effectiveness and minimum interference". Many migrants fall victim to inhumane treatment and conditions, suffering immensely at the hands of their traffickers. Some traffickers have thrown migrants overboard in an effort to stifle complaints and maintain order. Violence, intimidation and brutality are especially common with trafficking victims in the sex industry. Chinese gangs and their enforcers are notorious for being especially brutal with migrants who cannot come up with the money for payment. Their tactics include ransom, extortion, repeated rapes, cutting off fingers and sexual assault.

Chinese gangs employed as debt collectors, for example, commonly resort to mental and physical forms of coercion in order to extract payment, subjecting their human cargo to torture, persecution and revenge. Many migrants in "safe houses" are subjected to horrible treatment including death threats, beatings and rapes in front of others, or while on the phone with their families. Some police raids have discovered sickly and beaten captives shackled to prevent them from escaping. In the economy of human trafficking, demand is high. The risk of punishment and capture are low. Like most other criminal markets, it is largely driven by demand from migrants seeking work in the U.S., to (legitimate and illegitimate) U.S. employers who rely on undocumented labour, to the clientele of the sex industry. The global integration of technology and values, and the increase in world-wide opportunities for mobility and in resources, are factors that have helped to create this global demand.

More and more people want to migrate, but cannot do this legally; most often, migration barriers cannot be crossed without help from traffickers. Another aspect critical to understanding the role of demand in this market is the willingness of many U.S. employers to hire undocumented workers. For example, the illegal job market is flourishing in Florida and the INS estimates that about 350,000 illegal immigrants are currently living there. Some farms have earned the nickname, "sweatshops in the sun" as farmers and other business owners prefer illegal workers who don't complain and are willing to work for low wages. This is exacerbated by the fact that often migrants will accept the jobs that no one else will. In response to the need, some trafficking organizations have even begun to provide transportation directly to the work sites.

The absence of laws against trafficking in some countries makes the trafficking in humans difficult to control. In particular, it allows the activity to flourish in many source countries. Trafficking cases are often difficult to prosecute in the U.S., because the trafficking victims are the only witnesses to the crime and are unwilling to come forward. In addition, if convicted, traffickers rarely spend much time in U.S. prisons. Because of a law enforcement tendency to view trafficking as a "victimless" crime, adequate resources are generally not devoted to investigating trafficking cases. The U.S. Congress passed the Illegal Immigration Reform and Immigration Responsibility Act of 1996. This law significantly expanded potential sentences for individuals convicted of alien trafficking, and doubled the maximum penalty for alien smuggling to 10 years. In addition, prosecutors can now seek the death penalty for smugglers who cause deaths.

The goal of the anti-trafficking strategy of the U.S. Immigration and Naturalization Service is to deter and disrupt alien smuggling at all levels of operation, including overseas, at the border and in the interior of the United States, as well as to dismantle trafficking operations. In accomplishing this goal, the INS has utilized a number of investigative techniques. These techniques include the application of expanded asset forfeiture laws; the use of wire intercepts; the establishment of an undercover proprietary business; and the use of the Racketeer Influenced and Corrupt Organizations Act (RICO), which now designates alien smuggling and immigration-related visa fraud as RICO predicate offenses.

# 12

# Transnational Organized Crime

## MILLIONS TRAPPED IN FOREIGN LANDS

Anita Sharma Bhattarai, a Nepali woman, had faced a difficult life: Her husband mistreated her and the children and when she separated from him, selling produce was one of the few ways she could support herself. These burdens, however, seem light compared to what she experienced next. At age 27, on a bus ride to work, a man gave her medicine to cure a headache. Anita immediately fell unconscious. The man, a slave trader, sold her to a brothel in India, an unfamiliar land where she knew neither the people nor the language. Anita's Nepali owner, her "Madame" told her that she had spent a lot of money to purchase her. In order to, Anita had to pay off as debt the amount that the Madame paid. But Anita was never told the amount. To make money to pay off her debt, Anita was forced to prostitute herself.

When she insisted that she wanted to leave, Anita was beaten repeatedly, sometimes with iron rods. A large metal gate kept her locked inside the brothel. Unfortunately, Anita's case is not unique. The State Department reports that, "over the past year, at least 700,000 and possibly as many as four million men women and children worldwide were bought, sold, transported and held against their will in slave-like conditions"· Various means are used to trap victims: violence or threat of violence, abuse of authority or dominant position, destruction of travel and identification documents, debt-bondage or deception are used to trap victims. The victims are mostly women and girls from developing countries, but can sometimes be men and boys, as well. They are enslaved for purposes of prostitution, domestic servitude, street begging, camel jockeying, sweatshop labour, construction work, pornography, forced marriage, false adoption and other criminal activities.

As defined by the United Nations Protocol to Prevent, Suppress and Punish Trafficking in Persons Especially Women and Children, trafficking in persons is the "recruitment, transportation, transfer, harbouring or receipt of persons, by means of the threat or use of force or other forms of coercion, of abduction, of fraud, of deception, of the abuse of power or of a position of vulnerability or of the giving or receiving of payments or benefits to achieve the consent of a person having control over another person, for the purpose of exploitation". Although trafficking in and of itself is not a form of slavery, it is a vehicle for leading unwilling victims into slavery. By illegally transporting victims to foreign lands, traffickers make them especially vulnerable to enslavers' demands.

Across borders, victims are unfamiliar with the surroundings and culture and may not speak the language. They are without their support network of friends and family and may either lack immigration documents or have fraudulent papers provided by the traffickers. Once the victims arrive at their destinations, traffickers sell them to captors, who often force the victims to work in slave-like conditions until they have paid off debts. The amount of the debt is usually the cost of travel and/or the purchase price that the captors paid to buy the victims. However, victims may never be able to pay off the debts because captors determine the wages, charge high interst rates, control the bookkeeping, and claim additional expenses. Furthermore, when victims are close to paying off the debts, captors often resell them, beginning another debt-bondage process.

Trafficking is a not a new problem. In 1904, the first Convention on Trafficking was held in Paris when European leaders became concerned about the trafficking of European and Asian women· During World War II, the Nazis trafficked gypsies, Jews, homosexuals and resistors to labour camps, and the Japanese trafficked Asian women for sexual slavery in military camps.

Today, trafficking is a multi-billion dollar, international industry. Trafficking generates $6 billion per year by selling women for the purposes of commercial sex alone· As Gary A. Haugen, the president of International Justice Mission, said, traffickers "operate without fear of effective criminal sanction...

A vast and brutal industry is able to operate only because it is tolerated by the civil authorities of the country". Trafficking has many victim as many as four million are trapped in foreign lands and forced to work under the threat of violence. But the scope of trafficking continues to escalate: Poverty, wars, demand for female flesh in the sex industry, and harmful views of women help to create new victims each year. Madeline Albright, former Secretary of State, reports that the fastest growing criminal enterprise in the world is human trafficking.

Although many people do not know much about contemporary slavery, trafficking is a global and transnational problem, with a significant presence in nearly all parts of the world, even in the United States. It is difficult to monitor because traffickers use different countries as sources, transits, and destinations.

A person can become a victim due to many factors:

*Globalisation:* The emphasis on a global economy has encouraged political elites in many countries to focus on the requirements of global financial institutions instead of on the needs of peasants. As Kevin Bales writes, "the forced shift from subsistence to cash-crop agriculture, the loss of common land, and government policies that suppress farm income in favor of cheap food for the cities have all helped bankrupt millions of peasants and drive them from their land - sometimes into slavery"·

At the same time, globalization continues to exacerbate the widening gap between the world's rich and poor. Images of industrial abundance projected around the globe tempt the world's poorer citizens to travel abroad in search of promising job opportunities. Traffickers can easily trick their victims into believing that legitimate, paying jobs await them in foreign lands.

*Demand*: Hundreds of thousands, possibly millions, of women and children have been trafficked from their homes for the purposes of pornography, prostitution, exotic dancing, and sex tourism. Many sex tourism companies have sprung up with customers willing to pay thousands of dollars to go to southeast Asia and Latin America to prey upon vulnerable girls, some as young as eight. According to World Vision, 45% of Cambodian travels agents have seen tour guides lead foreign visitors to child prostitutes· Many global, internet based companies prosper because they have found that there are many people who will pay about $30 a month to see child pornography. Before officials conducted searches, Landslide Productions Inc. of Fort Worth, Texas made $1.4 million from selling child pornography to 250,000 subscribers.

*Economic Collapse*: The economic and political turmoil from the collapse of the Soviet Union combined with a reduction in the opportunities for legal immigration to the West have made sex trafficking a major problem. Once well guarded borders are more open, and young women, who dream of better lives in the West, have turned for opportunities to the sex trafficking network· In Southeast Asia, the economic crisis of 1997 has thrown many into desperate situations. In Thailand, a 10% decrease in school enrollment at primary school level suggests that more children than ever are turning to the sex market instead of attending school·

*Law Enforcement*: Trafficking is profitable because there is low risk — traffickers have little fear that governments will fine or imprison them, and they are confident that their victims will get little or no help from the local law enforcement. In Japan, the largest Asian market for sex, with some 150,000 non-Japanese women, the police are reported to sell back the women to traffickers if they attempt to escape· In Greece, law enforcement imprisons, deports, and prohibits victims from re-entry into the country. In Macedonia, police are reluctant to raid brothels because of fear of ruining the uneasy peace between the Slavs and the Albanian minority. When the police decide to raid, brothel owners are usually informed by corrupt policemen beforehand so they can hide themselves and their prostitutes though secret exits· Even when the local law enforcement is supportive of victims, victims may not know that they can turn to the police for help. They may believe the captors' lies that seeking help will only bring more trouble.

*Wars and Oppression*: Many around the globe are desperate to flee persecution, yet persecutors at home may try to prevent escape, and neighbouring countries may not want the refugees. The UN High Commissioner for Refugees (UNHCR) reports that, "human trafficking is the only excape route for many genuine refugees who flee persecution in Europe". The UNHCR also reports that although Europe treats Afghans and Iraqis as illegal migrants, these people are Europe's most smuggled and trafficked nationalities. In the Balkans, threats of civil war breaking out between the Slavs and Albanians in Macedonia have decreased tourism, and the economy is growing worse. Meanwhile, selling women's bodies for cheap sex remains a steady, lucrative business for the captors and pimps.

*Fear of Disease*: Traffickers capture young girls in order to feed the demand for sex with virgins. Fearing HIV/AIDS, predators want sex with younger girls who may have had fewer sexual encounters. About 30 percent of females who are trafficked for prostitution are under age 18· Furthermore, in many Central Asian countries, it is commonly believed that HIV/AIDS can be cured by having sex with virgins.

*Profit*: Hard numbers on how much traffickers make are hard to come by. However, it is known that trafficking is the third largest source of profit for crime organizations, just behind the sale of guns and drugs.

The resellability and reusability of humans and the low risk associated with the sale of humans make trafficking extremely profitable. Not only do traffickers make money through trafficking fees, but they can also gain economically through the labour of the victims. As Amy O'Neill Richards of the CIA reports, "Whereas alien smuggling usually involves short-term monetary profit, trafficking usually involves long-term exploitation for economic gain... In some cases, the traffickers may profit even further by using the trafficked persons as 'manpower' for other criminal purposes, such as selling drugs".

*Social Dysfunction*: In many developing countries, lack of money is not the only problem. People may also face sexism, oppressive caste systems, domestic abuse, and lack of opportunities. Kamala, an 18 year-old Nepali woman, is a survivor of sex trafficking who is now at a shelter for former victims. When asked to draw, she drew a picture of a girl locked in a box. Her drawing reinforces the fact that oppressive social structures in Nepal are a major reason why women are vulnerable to trafficking. She explained that her drawing is a message about society and family: "A ten-year-old child is shown in this picture; she is required to marry a man of 35 to 40.

The square around the figure symbolically represents the nation of Nepal, the people of the village and their customs and traditions.

The girl is always restricted and kept inside, deprived of everything". Downtrodden by oppressive village social structures, women such as Kamala and Anita are easy prey for traffickers. Thinking that anything is better than life at home, many are all too ready to believe the traffickers' false promises.

The world's population is now 6 billion, and it continues to increase rapidly. Most of the increase occurs in the poorest countries· Poverty combined with over-population means there is an abundance of potential slaves. Traffickers find that recruiting victims is cheaper and easier than ever before.

Various methods include but are not limited to the following:

*Deception:* Various sources, ranging from false advertising to trusted acquaintances, promise legitimate, well-paying jobs to lure the victims. Seba, a newly freed slave trafficked from Mali to Paris, told her story to an investigator: "I was raised by my grandmother in Mali and when I was still a little girl a woman my family knew came and asked her if she could take me to Paris to care for her children. She told my grandmother that she would put me in school and that I would learn French. But when I came to Paris, I was not sent to school, I had to work every day. In their house I did all the work; I cleaned the house, cooked the meals, cared for the children, and washed and fed the baby. Everyday I started work before 7 A.M. and finished about 11 P.M. I never had a day off".

*Kidnapping:* In the last decade, the Chinese police discovered several human smuggling rings that have abducted thousands of women and girls between 13 to 24 years-old and forced them into slavery. Mostly members of the Tai or Akha tribes in southern China, the women and girls have been trafficked through the Burmese mountains and forced into prostitution in Thailand. Mae Sai, a victim rescued by the Thai police and the Chinese Embassy in Bangkok, was sold for 10,000 baht (U.S. $400). On one afternoon, two people in the village offered to take her on a ride in their car and to a picnic. Mai Sai accepted their offer because she had never ridden in a car before, and revolutions in the area have interrupted her schooling and left her ignorant of the ways of the world. Only when it was too late, Mae Sai realized that she had been sold to the Vieng Thon Hotel, which services Malaysian men with girls under age 15.

*Sale:* According to Anti-Slavery International, 19,000 young boys have been sold by their desperate families to camel jockey in the United Arab Emirates. Although it is illegal to use child jockeys in the Gulf States, the practice is widespread because children are light on camels' backs. Sadam, a scrawny 6-year-old Pakistani boy, was sold by his father to a wealthy sheik in the United Arab Emirates. Trafficking agents obtained false immigration documents, and the sheik taught him how to handle the camels. Sadam has won many times, but he was not fed properly so that his weight stays low.

*Flight:* Fleeing from the brutal Burmese military regime, thousands of ethnic minorities in Burma become trafficking victims in order to avoid persecution. In Thailand alone, there are as many as 40,000 Burmese women who have been trafficked for sex· One Burmese woman in Bangladesh told an investigator, "We have come all the way here, not just because we were trying to escape poverty and find a way to earn a better living like the Bangladeshis, but because it was our only option to save our lives"·

Victims of sex trafficking are mostly women and children from developing countries. Trafficking in females younger than 18 years old mostly for prostitution accounts for about 30 percent of total trafficking.

## LIFE AS A TRAFFICKING VICTIM

To keep the victims isolated and unable to seek help, traffickers often move them to unfamiliar locations, such as to other countries or to other locations far away from home. Without contact with friends and family, the victims lack support systems and have no-one to turn to for help, even the police. In many cases, victims have fraudulent immigration documents provided by the traffickers or no documentation at all. Without proper documentation, they may fear that the law enforcement will only deport or jail them instead of help.

Traffickers often choose to move the victims to another country also because the language barrier will help to isolate them. Furthermore, traffickers often allow the victims no contact except with other victims, the captors and the clients. Sometimes, victims are mingled with women who have chosen to become prostitutes in order to make it seem that they have freely chosen to be prostitutes. But otherwise, victims are kept from talking to strangers and from making relationships. Victims may be frequently moved in order to prevent establishment of firmer links in the area.

To render new recruits into submission, captors' rape, beat, and humiliates the victims until they no longer have the will to resist. MSNBC reported that one woman was forced to clean a dirty toilet with her tongue while her captor laughed.

Debt bondage is frequently used to keep victims from freedom. For example, traffickers offer women in Thailand immigration to Japan, and then tell the women that they must repay the costs that have incurred through months or years of unpaid labour as prostitutes. Captors usually lie to the victims about the costs, telling them the costs are exponentially greater than the costs that have actually incurred. The victims may never get out of debt bondage because the debt bondage places the women under highly-controlled circumstances and keeps the women from changing their decisions.

Threats are the main way captors discourage their slaves from attempt to escape. As warnings, those who try to escape and get caught are killed cruelly in front of the other prostitutes. Sometimes, traffickers are on good terms with the slaves' families, and use threats against family members to keep the victims from attempting to escape. In Velesta, Macedonia, victims are kept in the locked back rooms of "kafane", or café-bars that are also brothels. When clients come, the victims are paraded in skimpy lingerie so that the clients can choose whoever pleases them. Ms. Magazine reports that in the Falkland district of Calcutta, minors from Nepal and Bangladesh are kept in cages, and men go up and down the street to pick those they want. About sex slaves in Bangkok, Ms. states, "some are in brothels sealed up so tight, they never have fresh air."

Most victims are forced to have sex with several people per day. Sex is often unprotected and they are vulnerable to sexually transmitted diseases and to unwanted pregnancy. When victims become pregnant, the captors may force abortions by using a bamboo whisk or other methods. If the victims get STD's, the brothel expels them. If they refuse to meet the quota on clients, their captors severely beat them. Those who attempt to escape also get beaten. Vulnerable to the whims of the clients, victims also get beaten or bitten by the clients. Many victims refer to clients who only have sex as "good clients" because of the high frequency at which clients physically hurt them. Unless the client orders food, victims are fed the same low-nutrition food every day. One woman who was trafficked for sex in Macedonia reported that she was only given macaroni.

Frequently, owners have "favorites", whom they force fewer clients upon and shower with gifts. These "favorites" are usually the owners' lovers. In order to survive and become the "favorite", slaves often inform on each other when anyone plots to escape. Once the victims arrive at the destination, their passports or travel documents are taken from them or burned.

Often they do not know what country they are in or the language of the country. Even if they escape, without a passport they find themselves in trouble with the authorities and are even returned to the pimp or madam. When governments discover international victims of sex trafficking, they often punish them for entering the country without papers.

In Japan, the police are reported to sell back the women to traffickers if they attempt to escape. In Greece, law enforcement imprisons, deports, and prohibits victims from re-entry into the country. In Macedonia, police are reluctant to raid brothels because of fear of ruining the uneasy peace between the Slavs and the Albanian minority. Even when the police decide to raid, brothel owners are usually informed by corrupt policemen beforehand. Before victims can be rescued, pimps hide themselves and their prostitutes through secret exits.

Many other countries also lack laws to keep traffickers in prison. In 1996, the Indian government rounded up Nepali women and girls who were captives in Indian brothels. These women had HIV and they were not welcome in India. Two plane loads of women and girls were sent back to Nepal. The Nepali government would not let them land and sent them back. This action mobilized NGOs, which eventually arranged for the women and girls' return.

Once victims become too old, do not make enough money or get diseases, brothels expel them. Victims are usually without any money and means to make money. Many women have neither family nor country to which to return. Even if they have places to go back to, families consider them objects of shame and often do not take them back. Their untreated illness often cannot be reversed. Feeling ashamed, the few who return to their village will not talk about their experiences. Younger girls see women returning from the big city and may imagine they have experienced a better life, one for which to strive. Sometimes, recruiting others is the only way a victim can escape slavery. A victim may return to her hometown and tell the younger girls promises of well-paid work.

## THE INDIAN PERSPECTIVE

Criminal gangs have been operating in India since ancient times. There is no firm data to indicate the number of organized criminal gangs operating in the country, their membership, their modus operandi and the areas of their operations. Thousands of organized criminal gangs operate in the countryside. Their structure and leadership patterns may not strictly fall in the classical Italian Mafia module. They may sometimes be operating in loose structures, but the depredations of such criminal gangs are too well known to be recounted. However, the purpose of organized crime in India, as elsewhere in the world, is monetary gain and this is what makes it a formidable force in today's socio-political set up. In India, organized crime is at its worst in Mumbai, the commercial capital of the country. The first well-known organized gang to emerge in recent times was that of Varadharajan Mudaliar in the early sixties. His illegal activities included illicit liquor, gold smuggling, gambling, and extortion and contract murders.

Three other gangs emerged shortly thereafter, namely, Haji Mastan (gold smuggling), Yusuf Patel (gold smuggling) and Karim Lala (drug smuggling). During the emergency in 1975, when there was a crackdown on the Indian Mafia, new gangs emerged. Dawood Ibrahim, the most successful, came in conflict with the Pathan gangs of Alamzeb and Amirzada which led to bitter internecine gang warfare. The Pathan gangs were liquidated to leave the field free for Dawood Ibrahim. In 1985, there was increased police pressure which made Dawood Ibrahim flee the country. In March 1993, Dawood Ibrahim was behind the serial bomb blasts in Mumbai in which 257 persons died and 713 were maimed. Public and private property worth several million rupees was destroyed. Investigation revealed the transnational character of the conspiracy, the objective of which was to cripple the economy, create communal divide and spread terror in the commercial capital of India. Dawood Ibrahim, Tiger Memon and Mohammed Dosa are presently reported to be operating from Dubai.

Their field of activity primarily extends to extorting money from builders and film producers, mediating in monetary disputes, and undertaking contract killings. The other major gangs of Mumbai indulging in organized crime are those of Chhota Rajan (Drug Trafficking and Contract Killings), Arun Gawli (Contract Killings and Protection Money), Late Amar Naik (Protection Money) and Chotta Shakeel. Organized crime exists in other cities too, though not to the same extent as in Mumbai. There are several gangs operating in Delhi from neighbouring State of Uttar Pradesh indulging in kidnapping for ransom. Om Prakash Srivastava, alias Babloo Gang of Uttar Pradesh, has been responsible for organizing kidnappings in Delhi and Mumbai in which ransom amounts were paid in foreign countries through *Hawala*. Land Mafia has political connections and indulges in land grabbing, intimidation, forcible vacation, etc. Of late, the gang lords of Mumbai have started using Delhi as a place for hiding and transit. Chhota Rajan group is strengthening its base in Delhi. Ahmedabad city has been a hotbed of liquor Mafia because of a prohibition policy (banning of liquor).

The Mafia became synonymous with the name of Latif, who started in the mid-seventies as a small time bootlegger and grew up to set up a 200 strong gang after eliminating rivals with intimidation, extortion, kidnappings and murders. He won municipal elections from five different constituencies with strong political patronage. He was killed by the police in an encounter in 1997. A boom in construction activities in Bangalore city has provided a fertile breeding ground for the underworld. Builders are used for laundering black money. Forcible vacation of old disputed buildings is a popular side business for the underworld. The local gangsters in the State of Karnataka have connections with the underworld of Mumbai. One of the Mumbai gang operations here is the Chhota Rajan gang. Brief profiles of three major transnational organized criminal groups are as follows:

*A. Dawood Ibrahim Gang:* Dawood Ibrahim group is the most dreaded mafia gang with countrywide network and foreign connections.

He has stationed himself in Dubai since 1985 and has indulged in drug and arms trafficking, smuggling, extortion and contract killings. His brother Anees Ibrahim looks after smuggling, drugs and contract killings, Noora looks after film financing and extortion; and Iqbal is in charge of the legitimate business which includes stock broking in Hong Kong. Anees is in legitimate business too, managing the Mohd. Anees Trading Company in Dubai. His business interests in India are shopping centres, hotels, airlines and travel agencies in Mumbai with an annual turnover of about Rs.20000 million. Extradition of offenders from Dubai has not been possible since there is no extradition treaty with Dubai. Moreover, some of these offenders have strong social links with politicians and other top personalities in Dubai.

*B. Chotta Rajan Gang:* Chotta Rajan was a member of the Dawood gang but parted company after the 1993 serial bomb blasts in Mumbai. He raised his own gang in 1994-95 which is reported to have a membership of several hundred persons today. Chotta Rajan himself is in a foreign country to avoid elimination by the Dawood gang. His gang indulges in drug trafficking and contract killings.

In collaboration with another local gang, he organized the killing of a trusted leader of the Dawood Ibrahim gang, Mr. Sunil Samant, in Dubai in 1995.

*C. Babloo Shrivastava Gang:* Om Prakash Shrivastava in Babloo Shrivastava is facing 41 cases of murder, kidnappings for ransom, etc. He was arrested in Singapore in April 1995 on the basis of a Red Corner Notice issued by INTERPOL and extradited to India in August 1995. He has since been in jail but his gang continued to indulge in organized kidnappings and killings. The ransom amount is received by them in foreign countries through *Hawala* (alternative non-banking remittance channel). The power of this gang has dwindled after his arrest.

## HUMAN (WOMEN AND CHILDREN) TRAFFICKINGS

Emigration of human beings from one country to another for trade, commerce, religious and other purposes is as old as human civilization itself. However, the word 'traffic in human beings' implies illegal movement of people from one country to another in violation of existing national laws and procedures. The countries of the West have become highly vulnerable on this count as they are attracting hoards of illegal emigrants mainly because of their relative economic prosperity. Illiterate, innocent and gullible persons from under developed and developing countries, in their urge to earn more money from overseas employment, fall easy prey to unscrupulous and unauthorised agents. Such activities in India have turned into a lucrative business as the agents induce/ make the immigrants' part with large sums of monies towards their commission/service charges, expenses on journeys as well as for arranging passports, visas and statutory clearance. Often the travel documents are not valid and sometimes they are simply dumped into foreign lands without giving them promised employment. India has also been significantly affected by such immigrants. India is found to be both the country of origin and destination for trafficking in women.

According to intelligence reports, about 1200 thousand emigrants from Bangladesh have settled in the border States of West Bengal and Assam after independence. The problem, however, has spread as far wide as Mumbai, Rajasthan and Delhi, which have an estimated 300 thousand emigrants from

Bangladesh. Similarly, a large number of Indians are working abroad, particularly in the Gulf region. A number of young girls from southern India have been sent to the Gulf countries.

There have also been reports that India has served as a transit point for trafficking of young virgins from Nepal, Myanmar and Bangladesh to the Middle East, mostly Dubai. An estimated 5,000 to 7,000 Nepali girls are annually sold into brothels in India for prostitution. According to a press report, 9 Nepalese girls aged between 14 and 25 years, were rescued at Nepal-India border point at Kakarbhitta in Eastern Nepal in September, 2000.

The rescued girls said that they were lured by the agents on the pretext of getting them married or obtaining jobs for them in India. According to another press report, the Nepal police arrested one Dhan Bahadur Gurung in November, 2000 on charges of selling more than 300 women and girls. He is accused of luring them into prostitution by falsely promising marriage and jobs in the circuses in India. In early 2001, an emigration racket, in which a nexus of policemen deployed at the Hyderabad airport and travel agents facilitated more than 3,000 people sneaking out on fake papers, came to light when nearly 40 women mostly illiterate were being sent to the Gulf countries from Hyderabad airport on fake papers. Paedophiles now have a titillating new tool—the Internet.

It allows them to access pornographic photographs of children, enter their homes, and 'groom' them for rape. The first case of paedophilia appears to have come to light in India in April, 1991 when the police raided the house of Father Freddy Peat, who had been running an orphanage in Goa, and recovered drugs and 2,305 photographs of children forced into sexual acts. Peat was arrested and later sentenced for life. It is believed that copies of a large number of pictures seized from Peat in 1991 have made their way onto the Web.

On December 16, 2000, a Swiss couple William and Loshier Marty, who were part of an international paedophile racket with operations in the West, Thailand, Sri Lanka and India, were arrested at a resort in Madh Island, Mumbai with two minor girls. According to the police sources, photos of the couple's victims some as young as seven—were supplied to paedophiles rings and were also posted on the Web. The internet has facilitated the organisation of paedophiles, who can now easily down load pictures, forward them to friends, enter chat rooms and pick out targets and eventually lure them into a meeting. Another site came into the focus of CBI's Cyber Crime Investigation Cell during routine surfing. The site sold itself as a platform for those who would like to buy or sell sex slaves. In business since 1998, it offered members a sickening variety of slaves: virgin, black, teen, and pregnant and more. A membership fee could be waived if a person tortured a slave and sent in photographs. The CBI set up a decoy customer and were promptly offered a teenage girl.

The site's pimp was learnt to be operating from cybercafés in Delhi. At the last minute, however, he backed out of the deal and remained untraceable. India's first case of child porn on the Net came to notice last year. The site in question had a deceptively innocent homepage. But persist with the links and the site brought out 27 files with titles such as "Little bitches on the beach" and "All in the family". By paying a little more one could watch the "VIP series" and customized videos. Most of the girls featured were under 10 and South Asian. Investigation reveals that the site was created in Lima, Peru. But its domain server was being provided by Arvind Shyam Jagdam from Hyderabad. Jagdam was arrested in September, 2000. Information was sought from Peru police but the response is still awaited. An interesting fact revealed during investigation was that the naked children shown on the site were missing from their homes. Child-porn sites showcase India as a paedophile's paradise.

However, most Indians still discount child porn on the net as a western perversion. Paedophilia and more so its prevalence online is still not a priority crime for the police in India. The Indian mind set is such that few are willing to accept that their children can be at such risk. India has sufficient legislation to deal effectively with the problem of Suppression of Immoral Traffic as well as illegal emigration out of India. The Suppression of Immoral Traffic in Women's and Girls Act,

1956 to deal with these offenses, was re-enacted under the name of Immoral Traffic (Prevention) Act, 1986 to rectify some lacunae in the earlier Act. The National Commission for Women reviews laws, conducts inquiries for redressal of complaints, undertakes promotional research for policies, advises the Government and ensures custodial justice for women. The Commission enjoys the powers of a Civil Court by virtue of Section 10(4) of National Commission for Women Act, 1992. It has formed an Expert Committee and has formulated a 10-year National Plan of Action (1997-2006) to coordinate with the 9th and 10th Indian Five Year Plans. The law relating to emigration of citizens of India was consolidated and amended by enacting the Emigration Act, 1983 which repealed the earlier Act of 1922.

In order to protect and aid, with advice, all intending emigrants, a provision was made for the appointment of a Protector-General of Emigrants and Protector of Emigrants by the Central Government. The Act prohibits a recruiting agent to commence or carry on the business of recruitment except under, and in accordance with, a certificate issued on that behalf by the Prosecutor- General of Emigrants or any other officer notified as registering authority under the Act. It further prohibited an employer to recruit any citizen of India for employment in any country or place outside India except through a recruiting agent competent under the Act to make such recruitment or in accordance with a valid permit issued on this behalf under the Act. The Act provides for a punishment of imprisonment for a term which may be extended to two years and with a fine which may extend to two thousand rupees for contravening the above provisions or collecting, from an emigrant, any charges in excess of the limits prescribed under the Act or cheating any emigrants, etc. All offenses under the Emigration Act, 1983 are cognizable.

The use of traditional investigative methods to combat transnational organized crime has proved to be both very difficult and ineffective. This demands that law enforcement agencies utilise special investigative tools such as controlled delivery, undercover operations and electronic surveillance (wiretapping, communications interception etc.) to effectively fight transnational organized crime. However, the use of these tools are often surrounded with controversy because there is always public fear that they might infringe on human rights to privacy or are likely to be misused by the government to oppress citizens. Controlled delivery techniques have proven an important enforcement tool in identifying the principles involved in drug trafficking and other major smuggling offences. It is particularly important in countering the criminal activities of drug traffickers who, by the use of couriers, creation of false documents and other deceptive practices, carefully disassociate themselves and try to be remote from the drug trafficking operations.

## TRAFFICKING IN THE ASIA-PACIFIC REGION

The definition of the term "trafficking" is a difficult question in itself and has been the focus of discussion for a considerable time. It's most recent definition can be found in the Protocol to Prevent, Suppress and Punish Trafficking in Persons, Especially Women and Children, supplementing the United Nations Convention against Transnational Organized Crime. In any attempt to deal with the problem of trafficking in human beings, due consideration should be given to this definition, for this Protocol contains various provisions to cope with this crime, such as the criminalization of the acts of trafficking and the protection of victims of trafficking. On the other hand, one can adopt another kind of definition of the term trafficking depending on the aspect of the problem one is dealing with, since strict adherence to the Protocol's definition may be very difficult due to the lack of statistics or studies following this definition.

Nevertheless, in this presentation which tries to draw a rough picture of the actual situation of trafficking in persons in the Asia-Pacific area, the following two factors pose practical difficulties rather than the question of the definition itself: firstly, as in illicit drug trafficking, it is difficult to grasp the true gravity of trafficking activities since this is a clandestine crime involving organized criminal groups, and, in addition, most victims are kept under the control of the persons exploiting them; secondly, unlike drug offences, many countries do not specifically criminalize the act of trafficking per se, and even if they do so, the definitions of trafficking in their laws are not identical. Because of this lack of a specific offence, many countries do not have any statistics on trafficking offences. Moreover, statistics on immigration laws do not distinguish trafficking from smuggling in many countries, which reflects the difficulties in defining the term "trafficking" as well as the difficulties in distinguishing them in practice.

For the above-mentioned reasons, it is extremely difficult, if not impossible, to focus precisely on the issue of trafficking in this presentation. Therefore, in the following presentation, the term "trafficking" is used in a rather broad sense, referring to the illegal crossing of borders in general as the case may be, thus including the notion of smuggling, and in some cases, including trafficking within borders. The sources of this presentation include, information obtained from the visiting experts and participants of the 122nd International Training Course of UNAFEI, held for eight weeks from 2 September 2002 to 25 October 2002 on the theme of "The effective administration of criminal justice to tackle trafficking in human beings and smuggling of migrants". The participants on this course included 24 practitioners and experts from 11 countries in the Asia and Pacific region. In addition, the Australian Institute of Criminology has offered very useful information on the trafficking problem in Australia.

In spite of the fact that trafficking in human beings, especially women and children is a global issue, there are no accurate statistics on how and to what extent these crimes are actually committed. However, there are several dismaying estimates based on various researches:

- UNICEF reports that, in the last 30 years, trafficking in women and children for sexual exploitation alone has victimized more than 30 million people in Asia;
- The International Organization for Migration (IOM)

estimates that 200,000 to 250,000 women and children are trafficked every year in Asia;

- The US Department of State suggests that 150,000 South Asians are trafficked every year;
- An expert from IMO attending the above-mentioned International Training Course at UNAFEI said that it is estimated that nearly one-third of the global trafficking trade in women and children are trafficked from South-East Asia. He also stated that about 50,000 women and children were trafficked annually to the United States from other countries, approximately 60% of which originate from South Asia.

These figures eloquently show that the Asian region is one of the regions most seriously affected by trafficking in human beings, especially women and children.

## MEKONG SUB-REGION

The Mekong sub-region basically consists of developing countries. However, Thailand, which is also the traffic hub of this region, is developing rapidly, surrounded by countries and areas following it. Thus the status of Thailand is peculiar in this sub-region, making this country an origin, transit and destination state all at the same time. As an origin country, Thai women and children are trafficked to almost all regions in the world, such as Japan, the United States and Western Europe. An ILO report estimates that 100,000 to 200,000 Thai women are in brothels and nightclubs in other countries. In Asia, Japan is one of the main countries of their destination.

On the other hand, the ILO report also estimates that 200,000 to 300,000 women are trafficked for prostitution into Thailand from neighbouring areas, such as Cambodia, Laos, Viet nam, Myanmar and southern China. Some of the trafficked victims are further trafficked to other countries. Thus Thai has also become a destination and transit country. Trafficking in children is also of concern in this sub-region. According to other ILO research, it is estimated that 80,000 women and children were trafficked into the commercial sex industry in Thailand, of whom 30 % were under 18 years.

Children are being trafficked into Thailand for other purposes, such as for work in construction, fisheries or domestic service. One of the major concerns is that children trafficked into Thailand end up working as child beggars. Research on trafficking in this sub-region is numerous and many domestic and international initiatives have been conducted.

## SOUTH EAST ASIA AND AUSTRALIA

In South East Asia outside the Mekong sub-region, it is the Philippines which suffers most from trafficking in women and children although other countries such as Indonesia and Malaysia also suffer from this problem. The Philippines is the second largest exporter of labour in the world. The participant from the Philippines, in the above mentioned UNAFEI Course, reported that ILO estimated that there were about 1,776,000 Filipino workers of irregular status abroad which includes trafficked victims. The Commission on Filipinos Overseas, a Filipino organization, reported that, in the year 2000, 1.84 million Filipinos were working throughout the world irregularly, while the total number of Filipinos overseas is 7.38 million.

Filipino women are trafficked for prostitution purposes worldwide. The Philippines participant also explained that 959 cases were recorded for human trafficking from 1992 to March 2001 in that country, and 53% of these cases were ones where victims were trafficked to Asia-Pacific region, 25% to the Middle East and 19% to Europe. 51% of victims were neither known nor related to the recruiters. This figure is only the number of the cases reported to the authorities, and no accurate estimate is available which reflects the true magnitude of trafficking in women and children in this country. As for Australia, the number of trafficking incidents is considered to be low, due to its geographical location and its immigration policies. Australia does not appear in the Trafficking in Persons Report 2002, prepared by U.S. Department of State which lists countries "of origin, transit or destination for a significant number of victims", significant number meaning there is "credible reporting that the country was a country of origin, transit or destination for a number of victims on the order of one hundred or more".

Nor is New Zealand listed in this Report. However, this does not mean that there are no trafficking cases in Australia. According to the Australian Institute of Criminology, 13 cases have been referred to the Australian Federal Police so far since the creation of Division 270 of the Commonwealth Criminal Code in 1999, which covers sexual servitude, slavery and deceptive recruitment. Australia is very active in the fight against trafficking and it co-chaired with Indonesia the Bali Conference on People Smuggling, Trafficking in Persons and Related Transnational Crime, held 26-28 February 2002.

## North East Asia

In North East Asia, Japan dominates the sub-region as a major destination country. Many people visit Japan for the purpose of earning money, including those who come on their own free will, from a'l over the world, two-thirds of which are from China, Korea, Thailand and the Philippines. In addition to these four countries, people from the Latin American countries have been increasing recently. According to the statistics of the Japanese immigration authorities, the number of foreigners deported in 2001 and who had engaged in illegal labour in Japan amounted to 33,508, of which 14,195 (42.4%) were women. Of these women 39.8% worked as hostesses in bars or cabarets, 15.5% worked in factories, 10.9% worked as waitresses in restaurants or cafes, and 8.2% engaged in other service sectors.

As for the age distribution of these women, the most numerous were those 30 to under 35, amounting to 3,417 (24.1%), next comes the age group of 25 to under 30 which is 3,044 (21.4%), followed by 35 to under 40 accounting for 2,518 (17.7%), 40 to under 45 accounting for 1,517 (17.7%), 20 to under 25 numbering 1,445 (10.7%). Women under 20 years of age consisted of 1.7% (239) of the total number. Naturally, these figures are for those who have been actually processed by the immigration authorities, indicating that there are significantly more people working within Japan irregularly.

The Immigration bureau of the Ministry of Justice estimates that 232,000 foreigners were staying illegally in Japan in 2001. And although there are no statistics on how many of these persons were "trafficked" into Japan, it can be estimated that a considerable portions of them are placed under sexual exploitation or other harsh working conditions.

## SOUTH ASIA

In South Asia, Bangladesh and Nepal are the main countries of origin for human trafficking. There is an estimate by the Global Alliance against Trafficking in Women (GAATW) and ESCAP that 300,000 Bangladeshi women have been trafficked to India and 200,000 to Pakistan, and over 200,000 Nepalese sex workers are reported to work in India, one fifth of whom are supposedly under the age of 16 years. At the Nepal-UNAFEI Joint Seminar held in Kathmandu, it was pointed out that four to five thousand women were taken to India for sexual exploitation every year. In Nepal, it is found that many children were also trafficked internally to Kathmandu for sexual and other types of exploitation.

For example, it is estimated by UNICEF that between 5,000 and 7,000 Nepalese girls are trafficked every year across the border to India. In India, trafficked children have been working in construction, brick kilns, tea plantations and manufacturing, in addition to the sex industry. India and Pakistan are countries of destination or transit to other countries such as the Gulf States or South East Asia. South Asian countries are trying to cope with the problem of trafficking internationally in the framework of the South Asian Association for Regional Cooperation (SAARC), which adopted the Convention Against the Trafficking of Women at its 11th Summit in Kathmandu in 2002.

## VICTIM PROTECTIONS

Human trafficking has become a fast-growing global criminal activity, and it affects just about every country in the world. Each year, at least four million people are trafficked worldwide, with an annual profit of up to seven billion dollars for the trafficking network. Trafficking victims often believe they are accepting jobs in the labour, domestic service, restaurant, and factory sectors, 3 and are taken across borders sometimes through coercive methods where they often end up in exploitative situations. However, not all those who leave their home countries are necessarily trafficking victims. Trafficking and migration are not the same.

It is difficult to get an accurate accounting of the numbers of people actually involved because of the complexity of the reality of trafficking which would inevitably lead to different interpretations, analyses, and definitions. This has led to a plethora of confusion and responses within such bodies as the United Nations, other international, government and non-governmental organizations. The numbers quoted also vary in amount, and they are usually based on the estimations of illegal or irregular migrants or on numbers of prostitutes. While there is a link between trafficking and migration, there are some distinctions, as highlighted by the United Nations' definition of trafficking. The biggest distinction is that in initially agreeing to migrate, the person has made an autonomous decision to seek employment and/or a new life elsewhere, and this is not necessarily done via coercion or deception. It is only when a person migrates, and upon reaching their destination is then subjected to coercion, violence or threat of violence under exploitative circumstances, that the distinction from migration to trafficking becomes clearly evident.

This will address the rise of human trafficking, the motivations and incentives that drive people to leave their homelands, and why they pay exorbitant fees in exchange for an often hazardous and sometimes fatal, journey, without fully understanding or realizing the implications to them and their families. Much of the flow of human trafficking may be historically rooted in changes that occurred in the post-colonial era. The development of industrialization brought drastic changes to the lives of many peoples, and caused the formation of a new class of wage-earning industrial workers. Agrarian societies underwent a transformation from an economic base of agriculture and "cottage industry" to market production and wage labour. These changes affected cultural traditions and gender relations, sometimes to the detriment of the women. In the last three decades, industrialized countries shifted their production facilities to less developed places.

In the past, undeveloped countries were exploited for their natural resources and indigenous labour. The ability for large corporations to transfer production to low-wage areas promoted the establishment of "duty-free zones" across Asia, Africa, and South and Central America. While both men and women flocked to these factories, women composed the majority of the low-wage workers, and were subjected to increased wage exploitation as a result. Factory work is not a secure means of employment for these women. The destruction of subsistence economies, which often follows the inception of new forms of industrialization, eliminates the basis for alternative strategies and increases dependency on factory work". With the advent of "duty-free zones", peripheral countries originally producing goods for internal consumption now produced goods for the "world market". This affects the livelihood of a large portion of the labour force and benefits the transnational corporations by maintaining an overall low investment rate due to relaxed tariff laws, the inability of workers to unionize, and the resulting low wages of a predominantly female force. Global integration of production has not decreased the inequalities between men and women.

Quite the opposite has happened; the most visible examples include the wage-gap and gender-based allocation of work. Caste and ethnic differences also contribute to the glaring inequalities; for example, management has the tendency to use certain rules allegedly to "protect" women from night shift work, heavy lifting or working in mines, emphasizing the biological rather than the socio- economic and cultural factors of gender discrimination. This prevents women from gaining the technical experience that would enable them to earn higher wages and reproduces the notion that women's work is less valuable than men's. The transition from a rural to urban setting has had its effect on families and the local economy, due to the dislocation of the family because of "out-migration". For example, whereas rural girls and women worked on farms with little or no supervision, once they entered factory life, they discovered that time was measured in profits, savings and waste. Many found the rigidly structured style of the shop to be repressive and alienating as well as dangerous because the factory operators blatantly ignored health and safety laws. Family dynamics were also disturbed, in particular when daughters earning low wages in factories refuse to turn over their wages to their parents.

While paternalism may persist, the role of the "company patriarch" as a general "parent" figure is not the paternalism of old. The new corporate paternalism neglects to fulfill the physical and spiritual needs of the worker and does not provide for basic housing and welfare necessities. Today's corporations and their subsidiaries display "temporary" paternalism. Once the multinational corporation exhausts the utility of a particular area, due to "seasonal or cyclical downturns in production", whole families may lose their jobs and homes. This pattern of corporate behavior disregards the overall consequences to the family structure and the local economy. While industrialization negatively affected formerly agrarian societies, this alone did not cause the rise in human trafficking. The continuing subordination of women in many societies exacerbates economic, educational and work disparities. Since many societies view daughters as economic burdens, very poor and sometimes desperate parents will sell their daughters to traffickers. Dislocations stemming from war, internal strife or famine, also add to the migration pattern.

The high demand for women and children for the sex industry, as cheap labour, and as domestic workers are other factors driving the continued trafficking of individuals. The large tax-free profits, combined with the marketability of women for sex, provide financial incentives to traffickers, limited employment and educational opportunities, and a variety of restrictive cultural norms force many people to engage in emotionally and physically degrading forms of labour. Men and women seek better economic opportunities overseas as sweatshop labourers, nannies, dancers, hostesses and sex workers, with many of these migrants ending up victims of "illegal and unscrupulous trafficking networks".

While the increase in globalization has forced men and women to seek opportunities elsewhere, women and children have been more severely impacted because of the dramatic decrease in government food subsidies and the increase in prices. For example, the First Asian Human Rights Workshop documented that the conditions imposed by the World Bank on Sri Lanka contributed to the total governmental expenditure for food dropping from 16.6% in 1977, to just 1.50% in 1992.

As a result, food prices rose by 400% for rice, 293% for sugar, 823% for milk powder and 828% for flour. Privatization, displacement of people, sometimes whole villages, from sustainable lands now used for high rises or resort hotels, and a widening gap between rich and poor, exacerbate the problems of some less-wealthy countries. With the decrease in quality of life and the failure of locally operated garment factories to pay even subsistence wages, women and men are forced to out-migrate in order to find work in India, the Middle East, Western Europe or North America. Little or no job skills prime the atmosphere for exploitation at the hands of unscrupulous traffickers. Globalization created a network of inter-dependency of the world's people at an unprecedented scale. Economies, cultures, technology and governance are affected by globalization. Events occurring across oceans affect people in ways undreamed of, and not always to their benefit. For example, when the Thai baht collapsed, throwing countless people out of work in Thailand and all over Southeast Asia, social investments in South America slowed down considerably while prices of imported medicines to Africa rose dramatically.

As a result, the push to open up borders for liberalized and privatized market expansion of capital and information has outpaced the capabilities of governance in some areas, creating a widening gap between those who would benefit fully and those who would not. The rights of those on the margins are neglected while the players of profit markets often lose a sense of respect for justice and human rights. The desire for largely agrarian countries such as those within Southeast Asia, to push their economies towards market-based economies, has resulted in the alienation and dislocation of a large part of their populations. In order to attract foreign investors and foreign capital, countries like Thailand have developed policy geared towards that end. However, what is created is a society overly concerned with money and material wealth. This has widened the gap between rich and poor Thai citizens. Women are generally the ones affected the most profoundly in transition economies.

Policies implemented by organizations such as the World Bank contribute to the exploitative conditions that tend to increase poverty rather than alleviate it, particularly in rural areas. They are especially vulnerable because they are often without the necessary education and do not have access to the land or capital that would enable them to take advantage of any current economic boom. While women withstand the worst of marginalization, men also are victims of trafficking networks. In countries such as Nigeria, poor and middle-class men and women have been severely affected by political and economic upheavals. Just ten years ago, for example, a teacher in Nigeria could afford a car in one year's time; now that teacher would consider him fortunate if they could afford a bicycle. Corruption, theft, and bribery are rampant and have become an accepted part of daily life.

On August 19, 1997, eighteen individuals pled guilty to recruiting and smuggling approximately sixty Mexican nationals into the United States to exploit them for profit. Seventeen of the eighteen were sentenced to terms ranging from eleven months to fourteen years. The remaining defendant was sentenced to five years probation. The Mexican nationals were both deaf and mute, and were lured to the United States with promises of good jobs. They were forced to work under conditions of servitude by peddling key chain trinkets on the streets and subways of New York City. Just a few years earlier, in El Monte, California, eight Thai nationals pled guilty to acts of conspiracy, involuntary servitude and harboring illegal aliens. Upon arrival into the United States, the Thai labourers were transported to a "work compound" where they were confined, some chained to tables, and forced to work up to twenty hours at a time.

The traffickers enticed would-be immigrants to the United States with promises of good jobs, high wages, and a better life. High profile trafficking cases revealed a lack of anti-trafficking laws, prompting national and international governmental and non-governmental organizations to call for broad legislative expansion. Slavery was considered a thing of the past, and the few reports that trickled in from aid workers or human rights activists were regarded as isolated cases having nothing to do with "over here". The indictments, trials, and convictions of defendants in the "Deaf Mexican case" and the "El Monte case". forced state and federal law enforcement and prosecutors to realize that such crimes did indeed exist at the very door of the United States. Beginning in 1999, prompted by these two cases, Democratic Senator Paul Wellstone, Democratic Representatives Louise McIntosh Slaughter and Sam Gejdenson and Republican Representative Christopher Smith, introduced several anti-trafficking bills in both the Senate and the House. These combined efforts merged to form the Victims of Trafficking and Violence Protection Act of 2000 (hereinafter VTVPA), signed into law by President Clinton on October 28, 2000. Prosecutors had several options with which to approach and prosecute these cases.

For example, by focusing on the employment relationship, various possible criminal violations stemming from coverage could be prosecuted under the Involuntary Servitude and Labour statutes which would cover all facets of the abuse. As more trafficking cases came to light, law enforcement and prosecutors realized these cases did not always entail forced sweatshop or restaurant labour. Many of the trafficking cases also involved the forced prostitution of women and to some extent, children. The Victims of Trafficking and Violence Protection Act of 2000, defines "severe forms of trafficking in persons" as: sex trafficking in which a commercial sex act is induced by force, fraud or coercion or in which the person induced to perform such act has not attained 18 years of age; or, (b) the recruitment, harboring, transportation, provision, or obtaining of a person for labour or services, through the use of force, fraud or coercion for the purpose of subjection to involuntary servitude, peonage, debt bondage or slavery.

Trafficking in persons is international organized crime's third largest profit source, after drugs and arms smuggling. It is estimated that at least 700,000 people a year, are trafficked internationally as well as within borders. The majority of trafficked persons are women and children. Of the 700,000, approximately 50,000 are trafficked into the United States each year. Former United States Attorney General Janet Reno recognized the pattern of widespread exploitation of documented and undocumented immigrant workers in the United States, and approved the formation of what is now called the Trafficking in Persons and Worker Exploitation Task Force (hereinafter TPWETF). This inter-agency task force is jointly chaired by the Assistant Attorney General for Civil Rights at the Department of Justice and the Solicitor of Labour at the Department of Labour. TPWETF contributing agencies include the Federal Bureau of Investigation (F.B.I.), Immigration and Naturalization Services (I.N.S.), the Executive Office for United States Attorneys (EOUSA), the Criminal Division and the Office for Victims of Crime, and the Violence Against Women Office.

All of the above are within the Department of Justice and the Department of Labour. The TPWETF also works closely with the national Departments of State and Agriculture, the Equal Employment Opportunity Commission, and individual state offices of the Attorney General. The TPWETF created a toll-free complaint line to better identify and address the needs of the victims. Once a report of a potential Involuntary Servitude violation is brought to the attention of the Criminal Section of the Civil Rights Division in the Department of Justice, it can be referred to the Department of Labour's Wage and Hour Division, the F.B.I.

Hate Crimes unit, the I.N.S., the local District Attorney's office or any number of points of contact that are within the fifteen regional task forces also set up by the TPWETF. Many community-based nonprofit organizations working primarily with documented and undocumented immigrant, migrant and indigent workers, are also utilized as points of contact and partners to assist trafficking victims.

The Criminal Section of the Civil Rights Division has primary responsibility for enforcing the involuntary servitude and peonage statutes and is an active and leading member of the TPWETF. The Criminal Section conducts general investigations and grand jury investigations and prosecutes cases, working closely with the F.B.I., the I.N.S., the ninety-four United States Attorneys' Offices and Victim/Witness Coordinators from the above agencies, as well as the EOUSA. Through the experiences of investigating and prosecuting trafficking cases, the Criminal Section also assists the Administration in formulating policy to combat trafficking of humans and worker exploitation. It has also created an outreach program to "educate victims of trafficking about their rights; create dialogue and build trust with community and non- governmental organizations... [and] provide education and training assistance to law enforcement officers, prosecutors, and victim/witness staff". The Victims of Trafficking and Violence Protection Act of 2000 serves to not only combat trafficking in persons, but also to ensure a just and effective punishment of traffickers.

The Act outlines definitions of trafficking as well as legal alternatives and options that protect the victims of sex trafficking and prosecutes the perpetrators. The Act determines the degree of trafficking and the appropriate punishment based on factors including coercion, involuntary servitude, debt bondage and forced prostitution. As required by the Act, the Department of State instituted an annual country report of human rights practices in countries receiving economic and security assistance, in order to determine the extent that individual governments combat severe forms of trafficking within and without their borders. The annual country report reviews the efforts of these countries in actively prosecuting traffickers under the various statutes and legislation available within their court systems, and in providing direct services to those victimized by traffickers. The United States may withhold non- humanitarian aid from countries that fail to prevent and prosecute trafficking.

While the assessment of anti-trafficking efforts is subjective, the Act raises some important issues that should be used to determine a country's ability to combat human trafficking. The assessment must address the following:

- Whether governments authorities in that country participate in, facilitate, or condone such trafficking.
- Which government authorities in that country are involved in activities to combat such trafficking?
- What steps the government of that country has taken to prohibit government officials from participating in, facilitating, or condoning such trafficking, including the investigation, prosecution and conviction of such officials.
- What steps the government of that country has taken to prohibit other individuals from participating in such trafficking....
- What steps the government of that country has taken to assist victims of such trafficking....
- Whether the government of that country is cooperating with governments of other countries to extradite traffickers when requested or to the extent that such cooperation would be inconsistent with the laws of such country or with extradition treaties to which such country is a party, whether the government of that country is taking all appropriate measures to modify or replace such laws and treaties so as to permit such cooperation.
- Whether the government of that country is assisting in international investigations of transnational trafficking networks and in other cooperative efforts to combat severe forms of trafficking in persons.

The Act, in striving to achieve its goals of combating and preventing global trafficking, lists some economic alternatives as a means of prevention and deterrence. For example, micro-credit lending programs, training in business development skills and programs to promote women's participation in economic decision-making, assist in providing modes for women to generate sustainable income. This enables women to remain within their communities rather than be forced to seek employment in their countries' urban areas or beyond their borders. Other programs, such as keeping children, particularly girls, in grammar and secondary schools, increase their chances of escaping the poverty that can make many easy targets for traffickers who fill them with exaggerated or false promises of a better life elsewhere.

Public awareness campaigns detailing the dangers of trafficking, development of educational curricula and grants to non- governmental organizations are crucial solutions to the sex trafficking problem and will accelerate and advance the political, economic, social and educational roles and capacities of women in their respective countries.

Among the most important aspects of the Act are the provisions for victims' protection and assistance. The Act states that "[t]he Secretary of State and the Administrator of the United States Agency for International Development, in consultation with appropriate nongovernmental organizations, shall establish and carry out programs and initiatives in foreign countries to assist in the safe integration, reintegration, or resettlement, as appropriate, of victims of trafficking". Under the proposed assistance, victims of trafficking are eligible for the same Federal or State benefits and services available to refugees under section 207 of the Immigration and Naturalization Act as stated in the VTVPA.

However, the victim becomes eligible for such benefits on the condition that he or she has not only been willing to assist in the investigation and prosecution of the perpetrator or trafficker in every reasonable way, but has also made a bona fide application for a visa under section 101(a)(15)(T) of the Immigration and Nationality Act, and has been in the United States continuously from the day of his or her arrival. Grants are allocated to non-profit, non-governmental victims' services organisations, and victim service programs for victims of trafficking, among others.

The Act goes on to discuss minimum standards that other countries should follow in their attempts to eradicate the trafficking of persons. For example, carrying out programs and initiatives to "assist in safe integration" or resettlement are among some of the standards discussed in the Act. The Department of State's Trafficking in Persons Report, released on July 12, 2001, further expands this notion. The compilation of the report will establish each country's "actions, or in some cases, inaction to combat" the problem of trafficking. The reports from each country will also determine the degree of assistance that the U.S. will give to those countries that meet the minimum standards set forth in the Act, as well as any actions to be taken against those governments who fail to meet those standards.

The trafficking of persons has continued throughout the world, for centuries. The increase in technological advances enables traffickers to expand their networks and to more easily move desperate people who want to get out of unstable and unsatisfactory situations within their home countries. Internal strife, like civil war and economic meltdowns resulting from globalization, contribute and facilitate the luring of susceptible men or women from mainly Asian, African, Latin American and Eastern European countries to Western European and North American countries with promises of a better life and better wages. While women make up a large proportion of trafficking victims, children also are victims. For example, in Sudan, India, Pakistan, and other African and Asian countries, children are often used as servants, carpet makers and concubines.

Children from Benin and Togo are sold to wealthier citizens of Nigeria and Gabon, to name a few countries, for domestic, agricultural and sexual servitude. In the Dominican Republic, bonded labourers slave away in the cane fields, in Thailand, young girls are not only sold as prostitutes within Thailand, but also as slave chattels in Mauritania. Some trafficking victims, in the United States, are domestic workers brought over from their country of origin by non-U.S. employees of the World Bank, the International Monetary Fund (I.M.F.), or foreign diplomats living in the United States. The Washington D.C. based nonprofit organization, Campaign for Migrant Domestic Workers Rights, seeks to assist those who have been physically or emotionally abused by their employers. In some cases, the victims are not paid the promised wages stated in their contracts, but instead have to work long and punishing hours with very little food or rest. Other trafficking victims become sweatshop garment workers, or are brought to the United States to work in restaurants. Sometimes, the victims migrate knowing they will be engaging in sex work. However, once they arrive at their destination, they are coerced into debt bondage, forcing them to work and service clients in dangerous and harsh conditions. Wherever these victims land and whatever work they are involved in, their commonality is their trafficked status.

Once the trafficker has successfully lured his or her victim to the destination country, he or she may demand repayment of "expenses" incurred. Traffickers often deceive their victims into believing that they are responsible for the costs associated with their transportation, food and lodging. To prevent the victims from escaping and reneging on their "debt", traffickers may use violence, force, or the threat of violence and force. The workers are often foreign nationals, poor, disenfranchised within their own home countries, and often have little or no foreign- language skills. This makes them more vulnerable in the hands of traffickers who try to control them through isolation, denial of medical care, placing security guards in front of their places of "employment", withholding wages, or invoking their fear of arrest or deportation.

There are many non-profit organizations, geared to helping trafficking victims, seek to assist them in any way they can. These organizations may be state-funded or privately-funded through foundations such as the Ford Foundation. Cooperation between federal and state governmental agencies and the non profit groups that trafficking victim's turn to is vital to the well-being of the victims. Without such cooperation, the already limited resources of each would be further stretched to the detriment of those victims. Victims of trafficking are often dependent on agencies that seek to help them repatriate to their home countries and reintegrate into their society. For example, the International Office of Migration [hereinafter I.O.M.] seeks to primarily assist women and children victims of trafficking that are stranded in the destination country and wish to return home but have no means of doing so. Since I.O.M. has extensive operational experience in helping trafficked women and children, they may receive funding to establish a "mechanism for rapid, case-by-case assistance to trafficked migrant women and children stranded outside their country of origin, who require immediate protection and return suppor". Another agency helping trafficked persons is the Coalition Against Slavery and Trafficking (hereinafter C.A.S.T.). C.A.S.T. is a Los Angeles-based nonprofit, providing direct service to victims of trafficking, involuntary servitude, or forced labour.

They work closely with the Office of Victims of Crime as well as the Department of Justice's Civil Rights Division. A well known case that C.A.S.T. handled involved a Thai boy nicknamed "Got". Suspicious U.S. Customs agents stopped an Asian couple before they entered Los Angeles. Upon questioning the adult male accompanying Got, agents discovered that the man and woman were not Got's parents. The man was a sex trafficker and the woman was his female trafficking victim. Unfortunately, both the trafficker and his female victim were simply deported; however, Got was removed from the couple and placed into protective custody, then C.A.S.T. took custody of the young boy. Further investigation by the I.N.S. revealed that traffickers had used Got twice before as a decoy. Using Got enabled the trafficker to enter a destination country with a female trafficking victim easily since they appeared to be a family traveling. It came to light that Got's mother, back in Thailand, was also a trafficking victim. She married one of her clients (Got's father) who later died of AIDS. C.A.S.T. placed Got in the home of a Thai social worker, while a long legal battle ensued between the boy's mother and his grandparents in Thailand.

Got's case represents only one example of C.A.S.T.'s efforts to protect victims of trafficking by providing food, shelter, counseling, and medical care to trafficking victims. Other organizations that do not provide direct services to trafficked victims serve an important role in providing other vital services. For example, Captive Daughters is a nonprofit organization based in Los Angeles dedicated to combating the trafficking of women and children, with a special emphasis on girls. While the organization is small, it disseminates information through its web-site, and establishes ties with organizations in the United States and abroad. Through a joint effort with the Philippines-based organization GABRIELA and the New York- based organization Equality Now, Captive Daughters successfully focused media attention and social pressure on operators and organizers of sex tours. Euphemistically called "gentlemen's holidays", these sex tours are vacation packages sold to men traveling from the United States to the Philippines for purposes of sexual exploitation.

An important role for each of these groups is providing victims with information they need to escape, survive or avoid being trafficked. Disseminating information, as well as providing education is critical to combating the lure of the trafficker. By keeping connected and involved in politics and with those in policy making positions, more widespread attention can be brought on the plight of current and potential trafficking victims. This can lead to passage of new legislation, such as the VTVPA, and create more protections and services for victims, as well as establish stricter guidelines in bringing traffickers to justice. The dedication of U.S. Representatives such as Senator Paul Wellstone and Representative Chris Smith, among others, helps bring into focus the seriousness of an issue that does not promise to disappear soon. By enacting legislation such as the Victims of Trafficking and Violence Act of 2000, and releasing reports such as the Trafficking in Persons Report, prosecutors have the necessary ammunition with which to go after perpetrators. The efforts of these individuals and agencies can also encourage other governments to participate in the global stamping out of human trafficking.

Human trafficking is a transnational crime with transnational implications. It must be recognized as a serious offense, with any moral or racial condemnation set aside, for any progress to be made in bringing the perpetrators to justice. Although the trafficked victim's pain and oppression is a personal one, the perpetrators themselves are often members of transnational criminal syndicates. As such, one would hope that the crime of trafficking will someday be addressed in a coordinated international effort. Until then, nations must be urged to enact stringent laws and provide funds and prosecutorial resources to combat traffickers locally. As shown in the case of the United States, a uniform anti- trafficking law can give prosecutors and judge's stronger ammunition with which to convict traffickers.

Although the profits from human trafficking are enormous and the traffickers have great resources at their disposal, human rights activists must persevere in their efforts to assist law enforcement and prosecutors. Some countries have implemented various stringent laws to combat this problem, while other countries still have much to do in terms of combating official corruption before effective laws can be successfully implemented. Though many anti-capitalist activists and environmentalists point to globalization as the primary culprit in promoting inequities that lead to trafficking in human beings, it is not quite as simple as that. The legacy of historical colonization, policies of governments, racial, economic, and social class divisions as well as gender inequities, continued unrest in certain regions of the world, the general scarcities in even the basics of food, water, and healthcare, create a desire for a better life and the willingness to take the risk to ensure that such a life can be attained.

# Bibliography


Amnesty International (2006), Returning *"Irregular" Migrants: The Human Rights Perspective,* Brussels, Amnesty International.

Anti-Slavery International (2005), *Protocol for Identi-fication and Assistance of Trafficked Persons and Training Kit,* London, Anti-Slavery International.

Antonopoulos, Georgios A.; Winterdyk, John A., Techniques of Neutralizing the Trafficking of Women. In *European Journal of Crime Criminal Law and Criminal Justice,* Vol.13, no. 2, 2005, 136-147.

Asia ACTs Against Child Trafficking (2007), *Defending the Dignity and Human Rights of Trafficked Children,* Quezon City, Asia ACTs Against Child Trafficking.

Asia ACTs Against Child Trafficking (2007), *Protecting the Rights and Dignity of the Trafficked Child in South East Asia,* Quezon City, Asia ACTs Against Child Trafficking.

Asia ACTs Against Child Trafficking; UNICEF Philippines (2006), *Stop Child Trafficking: A Handbook for Community Educators,* Quezon City, Asia ACTs Against Child Trafficking.

Askola, Heli (2007), *Legal Responses to Trafficking in Women for Sexual Exploitation in the European Union,* Oxford, Hart Publishing.

Beddoe, Christine; ECPAT UK (2006), *The End of the Line for Child Exploitation: Safeguarding the Most Vulnerable Children,* London, ECPAT UK.

Beeks, Karen; Amir, Delila (2006), *Trafficking and the Global Sex Industry,* Lanham, Lexington Books.

Belser, Patrick (2005), *Forced Labour and Human Traffic-king: Estimating the Profits* , Geneva, International Labour Organization (ILO).

Bureau for Europe Policy Unit (2005), *Combating Human Trafficking: An Overview of UNHCR Activities in Europe*, Geneva, United Nations High Commissioner for Refugees (UNHCR).

Carling, Jørgen (2006), *Migration Human Smuggling and Trafficking from Nigeria to Europe*, Geneva, International Organization for Migration (IOM).

Carling, Jorgen; International Organization for Migration (IOM) (2006), *Migration, Human Smuggling and Trafficking from Nigeria to Europe*, Oslo, International Organization for Migration (IOM).

Cashmore, Judy; Trimboli, Lily (2005), *An Evaluation of the NSW Child Sexual Assault Specialist Jurisdiction Pilot*, Sydney, NSW Bureau of Crime Statistics and Research.

Council of Europe. Directorate General of Human Rights (2006), *You Are Not For Sale*, Strasbourg, Council of Europe.

Dottridge, Mike; Terre des Hommes (Tdh) Foundation; United Nations Children's Fund (UNICEF). Regional Office for CEE/CIS (2006), *Action to Prevent Child Trafficking in South Eastern Europe: A Preliminary Assessment*, Geneva, United Nations Children's Fund (UNICEF).

Dottridge, Mike; United Nations Children's Fund (UNICEF) (2006), *Reference Guide on Protecting the Rights of Child Victims of Trafficking in Europe*, Geneva, United Nations Children's Fund (UNICEF).

International Centre for Migration Policy Development (ICMPD) (2006), *Anti-Trafficking Training Material for Judges and Prosecutors: Handbook*, Vienna, International Centre for Migration Policy Development (ICMPD).

International Labour Organization (ILO) (2006), *The End of Child Labour: Within Reach*, Geneva, International Labour Organization (ILO).

International Organization for Migration (IOM) (2007),

*ASEAN and Trafficking in Persons*, Geneva, International Organization for Migration (IOM).

Lehti, Martti; Aromaa, Kauko, Trafficking for Sexual Exploitation. In *Crime and Justice: A Review of Research*, Vol. 34, 2006, 133-227.

Naim, Moises (2006), *Illicit: How Smugglers, Traffickers and Copycats are Hijacking the Global Economy*, New York, Anchor Books.

O'Connor Vivienne; Rausch, Colette; Albrecht, Hans Joerg; Klemencic, Goran (2007), *Model Codes for Post Conflict Criminal Justice*, Washington D.C., United States Institute of Peace Studies.

O'Connor, Monica; Healy, Grainne (2006), *The Links between Prostitution and Sex Trafficking: A Briefing Hand-book*, North Amherst, Coalition Against Trafficking in Women (CATW).

United Nations Children's Fund (UNICEF) Innocenti Research Centre (2007), *Law Reform and Implementation of the Convention on the Rights of the Child*, Florence, United Nations Children's Fund (UNICEF) Innocenti Research Centre.

United Nations Children's Fund (UNICEF) Innocenti Research Centre (2006), *The General Measures of the Convention on the Rights of the Child. The process in Europe and Central Asia*, Florence, United Nations Children's Fund (UNICEF) Innocenti Research Centre.

United Nations Department for Peacekeeping Operations (UNDPKO) (2007), *Standardized Generic Training Modules for United Nations Peacekeeping (SGTM 17)*, United Nations Department for Peacekeeping Operations (UNDPKO).

United Nations Population Fund (UNFPA) (2006), *State of World Population 2006: A Passage to Hope: Women and International Migration*, New York, United Nations Population Fund (UNFPA).

United States Agency for International Development (USAID) (2006), *Trafficking in Perons: USAID's Response*, United States Agency for International Development (USAID).

United States Department of State (2007), *Victims of Trafficking and Violence Protection Act 2000: Trafficking in Persons Report*, Washington, United States Department of State.

Velkoska, Violeta (2007), *Criminal Justice Response to Organized Crime*, Skopje, Coalition All for Fair Trials.

Wijers, M.; Haveman, R. (2006), *Guidelines for Traffic-king in Human Being for Criminal Justice Chain in Ukraine*, Geneva, International Organization Migration (IOM).

Yordanova, Maria; Markov, Dimitar (2007), *Reinforcing Criminal Justice in Border Districts*, Sofia, Center for the Study of Democracy.

# Index

## A



## C



## D



## E



## F



## G



## H

## S



## T



## V